A Hippo Love Story

With love from

Karen Paolilla & all the Turgwe Hippos

Zimbabwe 2017

& xx

A HIPPO LOVE STORY

Karen Paolillo

PENGUIN BOOKS

Published by Penguin Books
an imprint of Penguin Random House South Africa (Pty) Ltd
Reg. No. 1953/000441/07
The Estuaries No. 4, Oxbow Crescent, Century Avenue, Century City, 7441
PO Box 1144, Cape Town, 8000, South Africa
www.penguinbooks.co.za

Penguin
Random House
South Africa

First published 2014
Reprinted 2014 (twice), 2015 (twice) and 2017

10 9 8 7 6

Publication © Penguin Random House 2014
Text © Karen Paolillo 2014

Text design and typesetting: Triexie Smit
Cover design: mr design
Cover photograph: Trevor Carnaby
Photographs © as per individual credits
Bob's Family Tree reproduced courtesy of Jan Rees

Set in 11 pt on 14 pt Sabon LT Std

Printed by **novus print**, a Novus Holdings company

MIX
Paper from
responsible sources
FSC
www.fsc.org   FSC® C022948

Penguin Random House is committed to a sustainable future
for our business, our readers and our planet. This book is made
from Forest Stewardship Council ® certified paper.

ISBN 978-0-1435-3905-6 (print)
ISBN 978-0-1435-3153-1 (ePub)

In memory of Bob and Blackface, and for Cheeky, Tembia and all the Turgwe hippos. May your laughing calls echo forever, the sun always shine on your backs and the River waters embrace you.

Contents

Prologue

He should not have been there. In the heart of a drought Bob should not have been lying in such a place, even in the shade. But he was.

Three tons of solid bull hippo. Admittedly his eyes appeared closed, but that did not still the loud beating of my heart. My legs began to tremble, the shaking dropping into my shins as though my muscles had a life of their own and making it impossible to run, even if I thought I could. I knew I could never outrun a hippo; at full speed they can clock up around 35 kilometres an hour.

Bob was asleep but I was in a very bad place – much too close to one of Africa's most notorious animals, one that supposedly kills more humans than any other animal. Being so close, I could see his gigantic frame shudder with each breath. His immense bulk of muscle, with a lot of very dangerous teeth within those massive jaws, underscored his fierce reputation.

He was even larger than I had imagined.

Bob was more than two-and-a-half metres long, and about as tall as I am. At 1.63 metres my petite size six English frame must have looked somewhat ridiculous, standing motionlessly beside this enormous bull. His huge weight centred on that large head. Those solid muscular shoulders and that great jaw holding 36 teeth could easily snap me in half.

Directly in front of me was the hippo trail that I had been following. It should not have been used by a hippo during the hottest time of the day, not when there was a tiny pool left in the Turgwe River where the hippos, including Bob, should have been wallowing.

It was December 1991, the year of the worst drought in living memory in this south-eastern part of Zimbabwe. The pool in which Bob's family of hippos lived remained, but the immense dehydrating heat was rapidly destroying their last habitat.

Bob slept under the shade of a large Natal mahogany tree. According to all those books I had studied in order to get my Zimbabwean professional safari guide's licence, no hippo should have been lying out in this heat at midday, shade or no shade.

I cursed myself for walking into such an awkward position. Nothing like this had cropped up when I was studying. A British girl who had dared to enter a man's world, to become a professional safari guide, I had thought that this could be a stepping stone towards my childhood dream of working with wild animals. An idea the child had nurtured while growing up in the English countryside.

I had passed that exam, the first woman to do so. I then had to find a job in the safari world; one that would allow me to take tourists into the bush to view wild animals. Yet this situation I now found myself in was not something I had encountered before.

Coming around the bend in the river walking on the hippo trail, I had nearly walked smack bang into Bob. If I tried to retrace my steps, this would mean having to turn my back on him, not a wise move. There was not one other tree apart from the one he lay beneath and the hippo trail passed within feet of him. To my immediate right, thick thorny acacia scrub blocked any exit in that direction.

I could just make out another game trail winding its way up the bank, perhaps 15 metres ahead of Bob. The actual riverbank was about 12 metres high, made up of loose sand – all right for a cloven-hoofed animal, but very slippery. I hoped that this would prove to my advantage if Bob chose to charge after me. With no alternative, I went for it.

I crept as quietly as I could past the sleeping giant. Then, with an agility I did not know I possessed, I went up that vertical bank faster than even a goat could have done as the adrenalin pumping through my veins kicked in. I was completely winded once I got to the top of the bank. But nothing had happened.

There had been no sound of large feet in hot pursuit, not even a hippo grunt or snort. All remained still as only the bush can be during the heat of a summer's day, not a bird call or an insect's buzz: absolute silence.

I tried to steady my hands, which now joined my legs in shaking. I shook as though I were lost in the Arctic snows without adequate clothing. Everything trembled; the after-effect, I supposed, of that adrenalin rush. I wondered just how many people had walked within a few feet of such a huge animal and survived.

I managed to hold up my binoculars to peer down the bank at Bob, amazed that he had not heard or smelt me. Hippos' hearing and sense of smell are acute, which makes up for their not particularly good eyesight. To my astonishment, through the binoculars I watched him open one eye, and then close it again. I had the strong impression that he was winking at me. Perhaps he had sensed my presence all along and was playing dead, a behaviour practiced by quite a few species, but surely not a hippo?

My year of living in the Zimbabwean bush had certainly sped by.

ONE

Setting up camp and meeting the hippos

Arriving in the Lowveld on my birthday, 7 October, in 1990 had felt like an auspicious beginning. October is not one of the most popular months in the Lowveld; in fact, it is known colloquially as the 'suicide month'. The heat is all encompassing, wrapping you in a miasma of air that sucks out the last of your energy. Putting your hand out of an open vehicle window is like holding it next to a fire. Wild animals lack spirit; being short of food and conserving any energy they have left after the months of extreme heat. The land is dry, for not a drop of rain has fallen for several months; both animals and people wait impatiently for the first rains. It is a time of short tempers and sweat-soaked bodies. The Africans call it 'the weeks of the sun biting'.

My husband, Jean-Roger, was born in the French Alps, and his metabolism and needs still centred on cold weather. He had worked for his doctorate in geology in a cool climate. On this first eight-hour drive to a new job and lifestyle, his Latin temper slipped on quite a few occasions. At times the perspiration dripping from his back and face made him look as though several bottles of water had been emptied all over him.

We were traveling with four cats and one golden cocker spaniel, Sammy. All our animals found the heat exhausting. Several times on the journey we had to pull over to the side of the road so that I could give them water, while keeping them secure inside their traveling boxes. Sammy sat on the seat without even his customary tail-wagging, just the odd half-hearted swipe every so often. I tipped some water onto the animals' ears to cool them down and then we continued.

We met the turn-off to the private ranches by driving onto a dirt track. For the next 50 kilometres it just seemed to go on and on.

Bumping along the corrugated surface was nobody's idea of fun. The four-by-four Toyota Cruiser had to negotiate dry riverbeds and often-rocky surfaces. We crossed a causeway known as the Turgwe Drift, where a much-shrunken river flowed under a man-made construction of cement plastered onto rocks that was also extremely uneven.

We then turned off onto a small track bearing to the right, thankful to leave that uncomfortable road. This new dirt track wound its way through a forest of mopane trees. There were no vehicle tracks, thus eliminating the ruts and corrugation of the previous road. For nine kilometres we meandered through the forest. Wild animals seemed to be everywhere. We passed five different species of antelope in just over one kilometre.

The first antelope happened to be my favourite, the kudu: a bull, with his horns twisting into elegant points, and his harem of hornless females with their exquisite large ears and liquid brown eyes apparently curious at our passage. We saw herds of impala, as many as 40 in one family gathering with one ram leading them, his herd of females won from lesser rams. That ram's horns were probably bigger and heavier than those of the rams he had beaten. His prize, a bunch of dainty females, closed around him, ready for instant flight.

A pair of klipspringers jumped from rock to rock on an outcrop known as a koppie. The 'klippies' mate for life and can outdo even a goat in their agility on such surfaces. Their hooves are poised on tiptoe as they stand like statues on a jutting rock.

A duiker crossed the road ahead of us, his zigzagging run making him easy to identify. Duikers are the one antelope that can survive even in urban areas, escaping persecution from human and dog. They have this ability to turn by winding in and out of the bushes, which gives them that extra edge, allowing them to live near human habitation.

The fifth antelope was the largest of all in Zimbabwe: an eland bull, which, even in the extreme heat, had energy left to trot through the bush, his head carried high.

As we drove nearer to the river, the leaves took on a green hue as they absorbed not only river water but also the underground water seeping into the sandy soil. It was a pleasant change after the dryness and the seemingly dead landscape of the drive down, where only leafless trees and lacklustre clumps of grass bordered that corrugated route.

We turned onto an even smaller dirt track and there, amid a cluster of white syringa, nestled the mining camp, our new home. Just one small off- white caravan stood under the trees. Next to to the caravan was a large green plastic water tank. A small strip of lawn had been planted and surrounded the caravan, which had been positioned to look down upon the Turgwe River. The view was of nothing but bush-land, with not a constructed intrusion in sight.

After parking the vehicle in the shade for the animals we walked down to view the camp – just as in the interview when Jean's new boss, Vince, had driven us down. We found ourselves drawn to the river's edge. Perched about 20 metres above the river we stood holding hands, gazing out at nothing but the space of nature. Across from us a large, tree-covered hill resembled the body of a woman, her knees bent and her tummy quite pregnant. Her knees were raised, ready to give birth.

My skin shivered with a cold sensation as though I had been here many times before. This atmosphere calmed me and gave a feeling of such peace that it pervaded my senses. It was as if I were inside a church, nature's church.

Near the caravan was an outside shower with grass mats screening it from either side, but giving an open view to the picturesque scene. An upturned bucket with a shower rose attached allowed one to bathe *al fresco*. On the other side of the shower, some distance away, was a long-drop toilet. This consisted of a deep hole that had been dug into the soil with mopane poles supporting the foundations and a bricked, box-shaped toilet with a proper toilet seat at sitting level. It was certainly a loo with a view!

Away from the main camp, about 90 metres downstream, were the prefab buildings that mining companies use for their labourers. The company, Rio Tinto, employed 20 temporary local workers as well as its own permanent employee, a general supervisor. Lawrence had heard our arriving and, walking over to shake our hands, welcomed us to our new home. Jean-Roger would now be the geologist in charge as they explored the area in search of gold.

Lawrence was short, solidly proportioned and, like most African people who work on the land, had not a bit of fat upon his body. His muscles would have put most athletes to shame. The people who don't live in suburban areas have much better physiques from their natural lifestyle than those who follow rigid diets and so-called healthy living.

Africans living in the bush and on communal lands can out-walk any urbanite, their lean frames evidence of a life of walking since they could first toddle behind their mothers, often for kilometres. Their fitness despite their often poor diets is truly unbelievable.

Lawrence told us that drinking water had to be collected from the nearest neighbours, a property called Humani Ranch, owned by the Whittall families. They were 18 kilometres from us, with the next neighbours being almost 50 kilometres away. This magic spot was now ours to enjoy.

The company had given Jean a small allocation to buy any items we needed. Among others we chose a large sheet of canvas, as we had decided we wanted to live outside. It would be attached to the caravan, making a kind of enlarged tent but leaving the front open to the elements and the incredible view. We did not want to sleep within the confines of the caravan; instead, it could be used for cooking and storage and for our animals' safety. Lions and leopards will eat domestic animals given half a chance, as will raptors, and the larger owls go after cats and small dogs, so the animals needed a secure home.

We bought a mattress and some hardboard so that Jean could make a bed base, as well as a set of wicker chairs purchased at the side of the road driving down. The locals weave these chairs from reeds growing along the river edges. I added cushions in bright ethnic colours, as well as a small wire garden table with four matching chairs to make up the rest of our furniture.

A very important purchase was an enamel bath and, to finish it all off, we had an old bookshelf and a couple of earthen flower pots. We had managed to pack all this into the Cruiser, with some items spilling over into the trailer.

The canvas needed one final touch: a roof of tin sheets to keep the coming rains from soaking us.

In the caravan were a small gas cooker and gas fridge, crockery and cupboard space more than sufficient for our needs. We only had to bring linen for our bed. Jean bought a huge roll of chicken wire and set to work immediately, attaching this to the back of the caravan and encompassing an open window. This would allow the cats to have a run outside at night while being protected from attack by predators. Sammy could sleep in the caravan and the cats could also sleep in the sun during the daylight hours when we were away from camp.

Smudge, Elsa, Fol-de-Dol and Moustique could have some space to enjoy and the caravan would be their security.

The cats' lives had been eventful, with two going with me to Holland from Africa when I had first left Zimbabwe to live with Jean-Roger and later marry him in his home town of Chambéry in the picturesque French Alps. Moustique and Fol-de-Dol had joined us in Holland. I had volunteered at an animal sanctuary in a small town near where we lived in the north of the country, and one day they came back home with me.

All four cats had accompanied us to Gabon in West Africa, Jean-Roger's next posting. The cats, in a roundabout way, had been responsible for Jean-Roger's life taking a complete about-turn, culminating in him now living in a remote bush camp in Zimbabwe.

After seven months of living in the jungle of Gamba in Gabon, an evacuation from a volatile situation saw our lives taking a totally different path. Initially, violence had erupted in the two major cities, Libreville and Port Gentil. The powers-that-be at Shell made a corporate decision to evacuate all employees in those cities back to Europe. We lived in a small ex-pat community in the jungle, the only access being by boat or plane, so for a while the upheavals in the country didn't affect us. Eventually, though, the problems filtered into Gamba and the management decided on a new course of action. Women and children would be evacuated, but not pets. Then, if the situation combusted, the men would leave within a 24-hour period, but there would be no room for domestic animals.

Some of the ex-pats had their pets put to sleep. There was not a hope in hell I would follow that route. So we stuck to our guns: no cats, no Karen. In the end, the two of us and our four cats left Gamba, supposedly for Jean to report to The Hague. He could be in quite a lot of trouble because of our refusal to leave the cats.

We arrived in The Hague after an evacuation through Congo-Brazzaville and into Switzerland with the cats on our laps in cardboard boxes for most of the journey and then, believe it or not, strapped with seat belts into first class on the Swissair flight from Geneva to Amsterdam. This was thanks to Jean working his magic on a very pretty air hostess, so the cats had priority treatment. When we arrived in The Hague Jean was not disciplined by the company. Instead, we were put up in a nice hotel with a view of the beach and a veranda for the cats. Here we lived for the next four weeks while Shell worked out a new plan.

Jean was told that he would be returning to Gamba, but that his wife would have to remain in his home country. The post had been given bachelor status until the situation stabilized. This was not what we wanted and so we decided that I would return to Zimbabwe to my mother's and Jean would go back to Gamba and work his notice. We had planned a year previously to take a holiday in Zimbabwe with Jean's closest French friend, Dominique, and his partner, Anne, so it seemed a good enough place to base ourselves and then make new plans after the holiday. Shell's management had told Jean that only the company's employees could return, but we both knew the truth. I had rocked a few boats in Gabon, writing in the Shell local newsletter explaining why one should not buy orphaned wild animals, ivory or snake skins. The mothers of these animals had been killed in order for them to become orphans in the first place.

Once I discovered when having a lively argument, all in French, that my command of the language was actually pretty good. I had caught the woman on her doorstep buying bloodied ivory from a local poacher. I hadn't realised that I could understand and speak French as well as I did that day! Shell's policies prohibited employees or contractors from buying ivory, but that did not stop some people from smuggling it to their country of origin.

Our cats accompanied me back to Zimbabwe, while Jean-Roger returned to Gabon. We had not planned to stay in Zimbabwe, it had been just a stop-off point, but fate moved in when, while we were touring the country with our friends, my mother met a chap looking for a geologist in gold exploration. Mainly out of curiosity we went along for an interview. As Vince, the manager of the exploration company, turned out to be a fun guy, we drove down to the Lowveld to take a look. A total life change for Jean-Roger was not at all something he had envisioned in his career.

I had given my dog, Sammy, to a lovely family when I had joined Jean in Holland. On our return, we found that this family was emigrating to Australia and did not want to take him, so he came back home with us. This new life in the bush would be exciting for us all.

We had the camp up and I had dinner prepared before dark. Later, as I lay in the new bed under the canvas with the full moon emitting that special glow that you seem to notice more in wild places, I felt wide awake, just buzzing with energy. I could look out from our bed straight over to the pregnant lady hill, and by looking up I could watch the stars. Jean had, as always, fallen asleep as soon as his head touched the pillow, but I lay there surrounded in that beautiful blanket of space and revelled in the spectacular African night sky.

Safari clients of mine were often fascinated by the African night. I knew that in European countries, or in any industrialized country, it was hard, especially within cities, to be aware of the night sky. False light obliterates the stars and streetlights remove the darkness. Here we were in a totally unpolluted part of Zimbabwe; the air was clean and it was as if a paintbrush had painted the millions of stars onto that nearly jet-black background. I felt as if I could reach up and grab a star, they shone so brightly and so large. Then, out of that darkened night and very close to camp, came the first wild animal call. A laughing bellow that reverberated in the night, over and over again. It was the voice of a hippo, one that I intended to find in the morning. I could hardly contain my impatience for the dawn.

At first light we were awake, with Jean having his day cut out for him organizing labourers and learning the daily routine from Lawrence. Once I was sure the cats were fine and could not escape and that Sammy had been fed alongside them, I left them all at camp with Patrick, a solemn-faced man who Lawrence had suggested could work for us as a domestic. His main responsibilities would be to look after the camp when neither of us was there and take care of the animals. He seemed to get along with Sammy and definitely preferred the work in camp to his previous field labour in the bush. He had domestic experience and seemed perfect, so I asked him to let Jean know I had gone off to check out the river's surroundings. With excitement bubbling inside me, I left camp.

I came across the fresh tracks of a family of warthogs and many of antelope, mainly kudu and impala, and then the unmistakable pad of a large leopard, his tracks overlapping the warthogs' spoor, made some time just after dawn.

When working in the safari business I had been taught by a brilliant tracker called Tendai how to read the 'bush newspaper', as he called the stories of the natural world's inhabitants. The paths in the bush are a veritable lesson in what animals have been up to. You can measure tracks with a stick, which will give you an idea of the size of the animal. By knowing your tracks, you can know what animal might be tucked up in dark, thick bush, so as not to find yourself surprising a sleeping rhino, and a snake's trail can give you an idea of the species and the size.

The animals' tracks led me down into the riverbed. At first sight the river was not particularly big, but it was very scenic. Bush islands separated the two main channels, while rocky outcrops were scattered across the riverbed.

As it was October and the height of the dry season there was not a lot of water, so it was easy to cross over to the other side of the river-bank using the rocks as bridges in the deeper parts. Yet I knew that during the rains all of this would be submerged and the river would become impressive in depth and width.

The game trails, made mainly by buck or bush pigs, meandered through some of the thicker riverine undergrowth. I checked the sandy soil for larger mammal spoor. It was not too long before I came across tracks made by hippos – at least five animals. I knew I should use caution; their reputation as the biggest killers of human beings resonated in my head.

Just as these thoughts flitted through my mind, a snort to my immediate left got my full attention. I took a step back, but when it wasn't followed by any other sounds I cautiously moved forward, peering into the thick tangle of riverine vegetation. There I spotted a glimmer of water as sunlight caught its surface. The loud laugh of a hippo was immediately followed by another call and then one more, really close by. Such an impressive sound: one hippo's voice bellowing out and then the rest of the hippos vocalizing back. Really wonderful.

Everyone has their favourite African animal call that they relate to as the voice of Africa. For me it has always been the hippo. My first bond in life had been as a child with my pony, a Welsh mountain pony called Kuchek. My passion as a young child for anything horse somehow made the hippo my number one animal in Africa. After all, they are known as river horses. Their dung scent is practically iden-tical to the strong odour of horses' and, as both are herbivores, they enjoy similar grasses. The hippo's snort is much like that of a horse, just louder.

Horses and hippos are magnificent animals and can run faster than a person. Both are also potentially dangerous if one underestimates their power. Yet the hippo is a kind of prisoner of his environment. Hippos need water to live in and, although they leave rivers and dams at night to graze, they have to return to their water haven. In the early hours of the morning they re-enter the water to spend most of the daylight hours sleeping, in order to digest the grass eaten the night before.

There is a wonderful story that originated among the San people, the first human inhabitants of southern Africa. They say that when God created the animals, the Hippo saw his reflection in the water and was not pleased.

'Oh, God,' said the Hippo, 'may I ask you to let me live in the water so that I can hide this large, fat body away from all the other animals who are thin and beautiful? The water can hide my shame.'

God replied, 'No, Hippo, for if you live in the water with that huge mouth and so many teeth you will eat all the fish. I cannot allow this.'

'God, I promise you that if you let me stay in the water I will prove I do not eat fish. Every night when I go out to eat grass I will shake my tail on to a bush or boulder and make you see I tell the truth,' said the Hippo.

God was puzzled, asking the Hippo for a demonstration. So the Hippo backed into a bush and, as he swished his tail from side to side his dung was spread all over the bush.

God was amused, but he said, 'How does this show me you are not eating fish?'

The Hippo turned to God. 'Well, do you see any fish bones in my dung?'

Of course God could not, and from that day on the Hippo was allowed to live in the rivers as long as for evermore he scattered his dung on leaving the water, to prove to God that no fish had been eaten.

TWO

Lion man George Adamson and romantic fate

Throughout Africa, nature's most treasured gift is water. Wherever there is water, apart from in private wildlife areas and national parks or on government land, there are people. Hippos are losing their homes daily. Once humans take over an area, the wildlife must either adapt or depart, and there are only so many water sources that a hippo can move to before he is harassed by man.

A loud snort and the sudden appearance of a giant head rising up out of the water some six metres from where I stood brought me back to the moment. It had to be the bull, as his head was so much larger than any of the others that now were bobbing to the surface. His muscular neck and broad head proclaimed his masculinity. I moved into an opening, which was a bit foolhardy for the bull immediately turned towards me. Hippos' eyesight is poor, but the wind had changed and my scent must have carried to him.

He lunged forward, coming at me in full charge.

In a situation like that your legs can start running before you even realise what you are doing. I had passed a large tree as I had walked into the thicket, so I ran in that direction. I got up that tree just in time, as the bull had left the water and I could hear him coming – he wasn't that far behind. My legs were scratched and blood seeped from the wounds, but it could have been far worse, for this hippo was really angry.

He snorted and stomped around at the base of the tree. Then, as quickly as he had left the water, he turned and went back to his haven, his head held high in a somewhat puffed-up posture that seemed to enlarge his already massive bulk. At the base of the tree he had been opening and closing his mouth in short jerky movements and I guessed he must weigh around three tons – one huge bull hippo.

Once I felt sufficiently recovered, I chose a name for the bull. He would be Bob, after Robert Mugabe, the president of Zimbabwe. Bob was surely a dominant animal in his stance and build and, although Zimbabwe's president is short in stature, he had proven to be a strong leader and his personality demanded respect.

I had never seen hippos act in such a determinedly aggressive manner towards a human. I had worked in national parks as a safari guide and the hippos had kept relatively quiet, never leaving their water home to charge at a person. There had to be more to Bob's anger than met the eye. He certainly didn't seem to like people too much – but why?

Bob could still smell me, as his eyes wore a tight expression and his posture remained full of anger. While guiding, I had learnt that most animals, even the big guys, do not want to pick a fight; they just want to live out their lives and be left in peace. Usually an incident or several incidents in an animal's life would make it dangerous in its attitude towards people. Generally within national parks larger mammals like elephant, hippo and buffalo would be relatively relaxed around vehicles and even people on foot, as long as you did not get into their immediate space. The big mammals all have a reputation that is justified if you put yourself in a position where the animal has no other means of defence but attack. All of them could kill you, but none of them particularly wants to.

Elephants and hippos have a supremacy that commands respect, a hippo because of his rotund weight and those formidable canine teeth. These lower canines can be as much as 90 centimetres long in a large animal. The ivory can cut a crocodile in half and a croc's skin is pretty leathery, so imagine what damage a hippo could do to our fragile bodies. The elephant's powerful build and dexterity with its trunk can turn it into a very aggressive animal if you push the wrong buttons. All animals have a circle of space around them that should never be entered, as they might respond in fight mode. An angry elephant is just as dangerous as an angry hippo or, for that matter, any animal pushed past its tolerance level.

Here was a bull hippo that had only taken seconds to become uptight and leave his haven to try to dispose of my annoying presence. I wondered why.

After taking some precautions to ensure that Bob would not realise

I was about to leave the tree, I slowly climbed down and slunk away. I was not sure my heart could withstand a repeat performance.

My dented pride was somewhat restored on the walk home as I came across two dainty bushbucks, a mother and her young son, whose tiny horn buds had begun to break through the skin. At least they were not afraid and just moved quietly into another thicket, watching me inquisitively as I walked past. I was thrilled with this new life. I knew the animal species, their tracks, and the vegetation. Everything here was familiar, unlike West Africa, from where we had just returned.

Gabon, with its humidity and equatorial forests, had a particular beauty, but Southern Africa was where I had begun my quest for a life with wild animals. I had trained as a safari guide right here in the Lowveld, so it felt like coming home.

For the next two months the time rushed by. I turned our camp into what I felt was a pretty sight. I collected bird feathers that I found on my walks, put them into plastic sleeves and attached them to the outside caravan walls, hiding the paintwork. I often found porcupine quills on my walks and used these as further wall decorations. Porcupines are nocturnal and often shed a quill or two when wandering along their usual routes. I would always know when one was around, as their scat red- or orange-coloured dung clustered in long slivers – would be left on the game trails. Porcupines eat the bark of the bird plum tree and it turns their dung this particular shade of red/orange.

There was always so much to do and see. I managed to identify many birds, butterflies, spiders and bugs that I had not come across before. Each night we read, using the light of the gas lamp while sitting under the canvas listening to the nocturnal animal calls. Our bathroom was open plan with grass mats around the back and the sides of the bath, but with the front left open so that we could lie in the bath and look down into the river.

Jean-Roger had installed piping for a shower and bath, with the water fed from the river tank. Once the rains came the bath water would turn a dirty-looking brown that was so dark you could hardly see your own limbs when submerged. Brown with the silt washed into the river, it might put a visitor off having a bath, but as we didn't intend to have visitors this was not really of any concern. I would cook our meals on the gas cooker in the caravan and we ate either at the little wire table or upon our laps. We would be in bed by ten at the latest and up with the dawn.

The hippos called quite a lot during the daylight hours and often at night as they left the river, returning in the early hours of the morning. I learnt that each had his or her own voice. Bob's was the deepest and very easy to recognise.

On my walks I had come across the tracks of a small herd of elephant and every now and then the massive paw print of a lion, but it was the hippos that fascinated me. Especially Bob. I have always been attracted to independent individuals, be they animal or human, and Bob stood out. He had such presence. Bob didn't intimidate me; I was curious about his attitude. He was a handsome hippo and I wanted to get to know him better, but how do you go about getting a large, angry, wild mammal to accept your presence?

I would learn his ways, find out his favoured habitats and follow him from pool to pool. I had discovered that there was another family of hippos with a bull and females less than a kilometre from our camp. This bull I named Happy, as he had a much quieter character than Bob. Although he would not let me get too close to his family, he had a much more relaxed, even temperament. As the days passed, I was spending on average about five to six hours each day in the riverbed, moving between the two families.

Jean-Roger was fully occupied exploring other parts of the bush with his men and I had a lot of time to really get to know the hippos. I began by naming them and looking for differences in their appearances, which I managed with the use of binoculars. The closest I could get to Happy's pod was about 30 metres; with Bob I was much more cautious, not wanting to spend most of my day up a tree!

Bob's family of seven had one female whom I named Blackface, for obvious reasons. She could be even more aggressive than Bob. At that time I wasn't aware she was pregnant, which would obviously have given that extra edge to her attitude, but she never lost her aggression. Just like Bob, she would charge out of the water without even a mock charge or snort. One minute she would be watching me, the next an immensely powerful and really angry hippo would be rushing straight at me, often on just that first whiff of scent. Surely two rogue hippos in one family group was way above the normal statistics? I wondered why two adult animals would be so unhappy with a human's presence.

I had learnt after that first encounter with Bob to make sure the wind was always in my favour, but sometimes the wind changed direction rapidly and that was all it would take to provoke a charge. If Blackface was behind the family group in the water she was not at all assertive, but if she was in the foreground, it was another story altogether. Then a charge was a given. I made it a habit to make sure whenever I came close to Bob's pool that I knew exactly where the nearest climbable tree was. With an adrenalin rush you can probably climb most things, but I needed to know I could get myself out of danger if one or other of the hippos was in a particularly aggressive mood.

Jean-Roger was not really aware of my daily adventures as he was far too busy with his own. The previous day he had been extremely fortunate, but then his luck was something that had amazed me from our first date.

On our first encounter he had just climbed Mount Kilimanjaro in Tanzania and I had been visiting George Adamson, my childhood hero, up in Kora in Kenya. Jean-Roger and I met on the coast in a charming place called Malindi.

I had been to meet George, a man whose life had been made famous by his late wife Joy, who had written *Born Free*, the story of how the Adamsons had hand-reared a lion cub and then released it back into the wild. Joy's book about Elsa became famous. *Born Free* had been my African animal bible when I was a child and the movie was one of my favourites.

Jean-Roger had moved on to Malindi for a bit of a break after climbing the mountain and my mother and I had chosen Malindi for a similar reason. As the eight-hour trip up to George had been an arduous drive through dry, barren land in intense heat, it seemed appropriate to end at the Indian Ocean.

I had gone to Kenya to follow my dream, not to look for romance. George had invited me and at last I had met this legendary hero and seen how he rehabilitated lions. My mother had been sceptical about the whole adventure, for George was no longer a young man, having turned 81 that year. His lion at that time, Lucifer, had been released back into the wild, but George was battling with the Kenyan authorities. They were trying to stop him releasing lions into their natural habitat and were putting up all kinds of barriers. The truth of the matter was that George was a thorn in some powerful government officials' side. He knew about all the illicit hunting going on in the

Kora area. He had watched his elephants and rhinos being poached to oblivion. This poaching had been funded by people high up in the Kenyan government. His fame had made it difficult to evict him, but even so these same men were trying to stop him in other ways.

George turned out to be all I had hoped for, a gentleman and a 'bush man' all rolled up into one. He offered me a position as his assistant at Kora as the woman he had at that moment was leaving to live with her boyfriend, Tony Fitzjohn, George's assistant for the past 16 years who was moving to Tanzania. George warned me that he could not give me any guarantees that the Kenyans would allow me a residence permit. I would have to follow the example of so many of his previous assistants and leave the country regularly, returning a few days later with a new immigration stamp.

It was all a somewhat loose arrangement, but he was the answer to everything I had searched for up till then. He lived in the bush and helped animals, specifically lions, and it was a project from his heart, with no form of financial gain or scientific acclaim. He simply believed that a captive lion should be free, and had proved with over 33 lions born into captivity that their natural instincts could return and that he could teach them to live as wild and free as a lion should.

I had been working as a safari guide in Zimbabwe, but it hadn't panned out as I had hoped. It was a way of being in the African bush, but if you were good at your job you spent more time concentrating on the tourists and their needs than on enjoying the bush and the animals yourself.

I have what in England is called the 'gift of the gab', meaning the ability to talk to absolute strangers or anyone else, for that matter, which I inherited from my mother, but my heart was not in the safari world. Also, it seemed to create so many egotistical people, all proclaiming to know more than you about something and all of them so competitive. Surely the animal world didn't need that kind of attitude? George and I had been corresponding for nearly a year when he invited me to visit his bush camp. My mother went along as she was paying for both the flights and the hire of the Suzuki jeep that I drove up to Kora.

She was not prepared, though, for his offer of employment to her daughter. To appease her fears as well as give her a much-needed break, we flew to the coast and Malindi. I figured that the sea and the tranquil environment would give me a quiet place to make up my mind. It would be a serious gamble to quit Zimbabwe and move to Kenya without any kind of guarantee of even being allowed to remain in the country – but then, most of my life had been like that.

On our third day at Malindi, when I still didn't know what I was going to do, a local found us on the beach and managed to sell us a trip on a glass-bottomed boat. We would view the many colourful fish of the Indian Ocean and I would try snorkelling. We had made friends with a wonderful Australian couple, so Jenny and Paul decided to join us.

As we stood on the small jetty waiting for the boatman to arrive, a strikingly attractive man began walking towards our boat. Jenny gave me a nudge in the ribcage. We had spent a lot of time discussing guys and she knew I liked tall, dark men. This guy looked Spanish and had the most beautiful face, nearly too beautiful for a man. He was wearing short white shorts, which showed off his muscular legs to their best advantage. His hair was black and, as he came closer, I saw he had large, gentle brown eyes with lashes like a woman's.

Who was to know that this chance meeting would totally reshape my life?

Jean-Roger, as I was to find out, was French with Italian ancestry, born in Chambéry in the French Alps. His profession as a geologist and his hobby of flying gave him the independent outlook that I value most in people. His African adventure had taken him to Tanzania and he had climbed that most spectacular of mountains, Mount Kilimanjaro. He, too, had decided afterwards to take a break by the ocean, and here serendipity played its part, for, like me, he chose Malindi.

When two people meet for the first time and connect it is an awesome experience. Our connection was, as they say, electric. Every whistle and bell rang when I looked into those eyes. That strong jaw and his large forehead gave me a touch of understanding that this man would be highly intelligent but probably stubborn. His humour, though, was what won me over on that very first day.

I made a total fool of myself by trying to snorkel and making a dismal failure of it. At that stage I was a heavy smoker and panicked as the water came into the mask, spluttering and floundering like a beached fish in a most unfeminine way. Even my blonde hair stuck out in a parody of poodle perfection as I had only recently had it permed. To say I was not a pretty sight was an understatement, and yet he was still interested and, using his Gallic charm, offered to help me with the snorkel mask, though I'm sure he knew that as far as snorkelling went I was a pretty hopeless case.

The five of us ended up having Italian ice cream at a beach hotel. Here he hired a small windsurfing board. I went down to the sea, supposedly searching for shells but obviously hoping he might meet me there. As I sat by the sea's edge, my bikini bottom started to fill up with sand, with the tide washing it into my pants. Just as I was about to empty it, hoping nobody would see, I found Jean-Roger offering me his hand and asking me to accompany him back to the others. How does one stand up gracefully when one's knickers are filled with half the Indian Ocean? Well, somehow I walked up that beach next to this gorgeous man and my bikini bottom didn't fall down. I must have looked a peculiar sight – once again. Yet he was still with me that evening, joining us for supper at the hotel.

Needless to say, against the wishes of my mother but with a gentle push from Jenny, Jean-Roger and I became an item by the next evening. It was an attraction that was far too powerful to resist. I think being in a foreign country probably gives you more confidence in some situations. Whatever it was, I had made the right move, as I am now married to the man.

Jean-Roger and I do seem to attract adventures, but at that moment he was not too impressed with what had happened to him earlier that morning.

He had been leading his men in single file through the bush in the north of the area. They were looking for the right place to take soil samples. His intuition, but more probably his amazing luck, made him stop abruptly. A specific rock had caught his eye. Only at that moment did he realise that immediately to his right, in a short scrubby tree not more than one foot from him, was a black mamba. It was not a particularly large one and no more than 60 centimetres in length, but as the mamba's venom can kill you in about three hours if you cannot get medical help it certainly drew his attention.

Jean, like me, enjoys snakes and we keep a record of all the snakes around camp and in the bush that either of us comes across. We do not kill them and, if possible, Jean will capture a snake if it moves too close to where we camp, releasing it further away. A mamba, though, is a different story. They can be cheeky if upset and can come at you if you are too close. This snake was angry and had already spread his small hood. If Jean had kept walking, it could easily have struck at him. The snake's mouth was agape, showing why it is so named. The black interior of its mouth and its coffin-shaped head give it the most sinister appearance.

The snake was far too close. Jean had no option but to remain motionless and hope for the best. His legendary luck held out, but most amazing was what happened next. The snake slithered down the bush and then used Jean's lower right leg to manoeuvre itself to another bush; first sliding over his ankle, then moving a bit up his shin and down his leg to the bush.

Once the snake was at distance where it could not strike at Jean, his adrenalin kicked in. He told me that he gave the most impressive shriek, leaping high in the air, a perfect impersonation of Tarzan. His employees all followed suit, leaping about like crazy. Had it not have been so serious it would have been hilarious, but then, that's Africa. One can normally find the humour in even the most bizarre events.

Jean and I complement each other in many ways. We each need our own personal space. We are happiest in nature, in wide-open areas without a sign of human habitation, and we enjoy our own company. Neither of us is a social creature. We are both stubborn and independent and have a rebellious side. He, though, is more negative than I am. I wake up on most days with a happy heart and look at life optimistically. However, I am a worrier.

Jean never wanted to take away my love of the bush and the animals; he knew this was my main passion as I had been living a wild life when we got together. I had given it up for him and moved from Africa to Holland, one of the most densely populated countries in Europe. I had turned down George's offer and my dream of living in the bush with wild animals, but I had known exactly what I was doing. I had not realised, though, how hard it would be to adjust to being back in Europe. Love, as they rightly say, is blind.

Fortunately Jean-Roger's boss Joop at Shell had realised how homesick I was for Africa and offered Jean a post in Gabon. We would move to Gamba, a coastal location surrounded by jungle and only accessible by plane or boat.

However, in the end Africa's unpredictability forced us to change direction again and end up back in Zimbabwe.

THREE

Birth of a baby hippo

In some ways my life had now come full circle. When I met Jean-Roger I had given up Africa. Now, here I was, once more living in Africa and in a position to learn more about wild animals. We were living with them and I did not have to work as a safari guide.

At the interview, Vince had told us a lot about this new area and the people from whom the camp was leased. Most of the land here belonged to second-generation white Zimbabweans, farming as their fathers had done, with cattle being the main source of income. The indigenous animals found themselves competing with cattle for grazing and some of the wild animals preyed on the cattle, so these same men killed them. This seemed to be the sad story of most of colonial Africa. As time passed, the increasing pressure of people's co-existence with the environment and the many droughts that occurred in the Lowveld made people think of alternatives to cattle ranching. The descendants of the initial pioneers now looked at ways of utilizing wildlife as a business concern.

This area in which we now lived in had 21 private companies, including two government properties, with the hectarage of each property ranging from as 'little' as 7 000 to as much as 60 000. Recently, they had amalgamated their properties into one large area where the wildlife could roam freely and were in the process of removing the cattle. This would be especially beneficial to elephants, which need more space than most wild animals. This area would cover 3 400 square kilometres of mainly natural bushveld.

They intended to erect a boundary fence on the outer limits of the land, fencing in approximately 340 000 hectares. It would be known as a wildlife conservancy and would become the largest conservancy in Africa. The fence would be constructed to keep the wildlife inside, so the animals would not move into adjacent communities where they might cause problems in highly populated places. The conservancy would operate like a national park, but because it would be privately owned the individual owners could run businesses dealing in wildlife.

This huge area had unique and varied ecosystems, making it possible to replenish the land with all the original animal species. The owners intended to buy elephant, buffalo, even lion, from overstocked national parks and bring them back to the areas these animals had previously inhabited. Some wild animals could still be found here, but the intention was to build up their populations.

Our neighbours, the Whittalls, at that stage our landlords, ran cattle, crops and wildlife on their property, Humani. Roger Whittall, one brother, had been the first person to introduce white rhinos to the area. He had also been the first to pioneer sport hunting safaris and later photographic safaris. From the day he took over from his father, he had plans to conserve the wildlife, at first through hunting, which goes with the Southern African mentality. I disagree with sport hunting, but it is standard practice in Zimbabwe. Roger's argument was that he would prefer to make money from his wildlife from trophy-hunting individuals and then allow the various species to co-exist with his cattle, as the wildlife would then be worth something financially to him.

My view is that once you put a monetary value on an animal's head you open a Pandora's box. Human nature is often greedy. An animal is a sentient being and, surely, by putting a financial value on it you are doing what we no longer do to human beings. We stopped selling slaves over a hundred years ago, so why put a price on a wild animal? The purpose of the new conservancy, which they called the Savé Valley Conservancy, was to create an area for the protection of endangered animals such as rhino, both black and white, and painted wild dogs, and to describe it as a sanctuary. However, it would be run as a business proposition with each property still individually owned. Some would use sport hunting, others photographic or eco safaris to make their money.

We had met no other Europeans since our arrival, having been too involved in setting up our camp. As Christmas approached, we realised we should introduce ourselves to the neighbours, who, after all, owned the land on which our camp stood.

We felt it was the right time to go and meet the Whittalls, but Vince had warned us that as pioneer stock they were very suspicious of anyone doing anything on their land. I had some sympathy with this attitude. I knew in my heart that Jean would never want to find any gold or heavy minerals in such a pristine place. He had had great difficulty accepting the damage that Shell had allowed to happen in the hitherto untouched jungles of Gamba. Jean had told me that this job was just a stopgap to have some fun in the bush before he looked for work in the oil industry, which was his chosen profession. As no oil had been found in Zimbabwe, it would mean another move for us.

On that particular morning we came across Roger Whittall driving on the main corrugated road. He drew up next to us and, without a formal greeting and before we could say hello, asked, 'What are you doing on my land? I had information you had arrived, but I would have thought you would have introduced yourselves, as you are on my land. So have you found any gold?'

Roger Whittall was an angry man. His tight eyes and gruff manner were something we had not expected.

Jean-Roger has a certain type of humour and, thinking he could use it at that moment, he replied with a glib, 'Why? Are you fishing?'

Wrong move!

Roger glared at Jean and moved as if to drive away, so I jumped out of the passenger seat, going quickly to his open window and, using every bit of feminine guile I could muster, said, 'Mr Whittall, I actually know you. I am sure you do not remember, but we have met on several occasions. I used to work a few years back for Graham Ford, Ndanga Ranch Safaris, about 80 kilometres from here. I ran his photographic set-up. It is so wonderful to be back in the Lowveld. My husband is a Frenchman. This is his first time in Zimbabwe. I promise that we have no intention of doing anything damaging to your land. I am opposed to dirty miners as much as you are. We are just here to enjoy the bush, not exploit it.'

I gave him one of my sweetest smiles.

Little did I know then that Roger was to become a prominent person in our lives and would be instrumental in saving Jean-Roger's life.

I had heard from Jean's employees that his staff called Roger 'Boss Shumba', meaning lion. It is common for African people who work alongside whites on farms and in the bush to give them a name other than their own. I was already known as Madam Mvou, 'Madam Hippo'. Although my body frame didn't fit that picture, the labourers knew I spent each day with the hippos. Jean-Roger was 'Miri Piri', meaning chilli pepper, as he has a bad Latin temper that can erupt in seconds.

We were to find out that Roger, like the two of us, did not have much patience and expected people to act immediately. We are all born under the sign of Libra and like our lives to be balanced, but unfortunately it never works out that way. The difference with Roger is that he is very much a 'boss man' and likes to be in control. If he gives an order he will lose his temper quicker than a rattlesnake's strike and he really is known to roar when having one of his tantrums.

Later, as we got to know him, I would find that when he was in a good mood his smile could make you forgive him anything. His face lit up into a kind of teddy-bearishly angelic expression, making you forget his bite.

He is about 1.7 metres tall and was at that time probably in his late forties. I noticed that he had the customary pot belly that many of the men in Zimbabwe cultivate once married. If you question them about their physique they appear proud of their huge bellies, patting that expanse of blubber and exclaiming how it cost them a lot of money in beer. As a wife I would never enjoy a man with a belly, but I suppose not all women are so particular.

Jean was the largest man I had ever dated, as I tend to be attracted to typical dark, handsome types with lean bodies. Jean is 1.85 metres tall, but has a larger frame that could easily gain a lot of weight. As his partner I try to keep him fit and aware that healthy bodies are far cooler and turn me on much more. I hope he will stay fit until old age.

Roger had not fallen for my attempt at appeasement. He just gave me a long, hard look and drove off without another word. How rude! I had thought Zimbabweans were supposed to have had good educations, and with that came the customary good manners. Mind you, Jean had definitely rubbed him up the wrong way!

We returned to our camp, as one Whittall a day was enough.

We had spent two months without any contact with people other than Jean's staff, who kept very much to themselves. In Africa there is a kind of old-fashioned class situation where employees are exactly that. The workers do their work and then go home. Socializing with them is not something that most people do. We both had to learn how to live in Africa and respect the cultures. I had had a lot more practice than Jean; there is a system and it is always best not to rock it too hard.

I went back that afternoon to visit Bob's family, deciding that hippos offered a far nicer way to spend the day than meeting people who were not very friendly. I reckoned even Bob and Blackface were preferable to Roger Whittall's attitude.

Blackface was not with Bob and the others, which seemed a bit unusual. I left Bob and his family, continuing downstream to a smaller pool where I had found Bob on his own in the past. As I reached the pool, a movement near some reeds on the opposite bank caught my attention. Sure enough, it was Blackface, who, having an entirely black face compared with the brown or grey of all the others, stood out even when alone. Much to my astonishment she was not by herself. Tucked up beside her was a tiny baby hippo. Blackface had had a calf!

This was the first new baby hippo since our arrival. It was late November and the rains were on their way. Surely this minute little hippo would never withstand a river in flood? It was the first time in my life that I had seen a newborn hippo. I was amazed at how small they were. Blackface probably weighed in at about 1.5 tons, probably about the size of a dairy bull. This calf could not have been more than 15 kilograms, say similar in size to a cocker spaniel. Against its mother, it looked about a quarter of the length of her head.

Where they were tucked up the pool was shallow enough for the calf to be standing, albeit very shakily, in the water. It nosed its mother's flank, looking for the milk bar. Blackface, fortunately, was unaware of my presence, as for once the wind was in my favour. I had enough riverine scrub to hide behind and I could watch the baby go about being a hippo.

For the next ten minutes the calf moved around its mother with a wobbly gait. It kept on slipping back into the water, but would pluckily push itself up again and continue circling Blackface's body. It obviously wanted to suckle but couldn't figure out which end had the udder. Blackface was very aware of the calf and at one stage, when the calf was close to her hind leg, she obligingly lifted her leg so that it could go under and smell the udder. Like a cow, a hippo's udder with the two teats is at the back of the body, under the hind legs.

The calf desperately tried to suckle but was just too small to reach, as by now Blackface was standing up in the shallow water trying to help her baby. She obviously realised it wasn't able to reach the teats, for she changed position, lying down so that the calf had easier access. This time the calf found the udder and for the next 30 seconds pulled at one of her teats. I couldn't believe that I was witnessing such an event and cursed myself for not having brought my camera, but at least I would have the memory.

I was constantly aware that I was in a very dangerous position. Not only was Blackface one of the most unpredictable of all of the hippos (or, should I say, predictable in always being angry with humans), but I was also never quite sure just how angry she would be.

On one occasion I had been up on a bank looking down at Bob's family. She had smelled me from more than 18 metres away and charged out of the water, stomping around for some time. Most of the time she wore an expression of total distrust, her eyes tight. Sometimes she would be snorting whenever my scent was on the wind; at others there would be an outright charge without warning.

Blackface had just given birth. The calf's umbilical chord was still present and bloody. This would make any wild female animal extremely protective and dangerous. A female hippo with a newborn calf was something one did not mess with, and from all that I had heard from fellow guides as well as Africans living in the bush, this was one animal with a baby that you avoided at all costs.

Yet I couldn't take my eyes off this little calf. He (or she) was constantly losing the udder and at one stage it was as if it was trying to butt its mother to ask her to help. I named it Cheeky. The name could be shared by either sex and it sure had a cheeky disposition. It seemed angry with its mother for not helping it to drink, when it looked to me as though she had done everything she possibly could to make her baby's life easier.

After about ten minutes of not doing too well at all, Cheeky (a girl, as it turned out) finally got the hang of suckling and then she didn't want to stop. The water was shallow enough for the calf to suckle while being able to rest her feet on the bottom, but she was still underwater when suckling. She would suckle for not more than 35 seconds, return to the surface for air, and start all over again. For a good three minutes she continued to drink, with the breaks more or less evenly spaced. Blackface obligingly lay still and it was only when the calf had obviously had enough and was once more butting at her mother that Blackface pushed herself back a little until she could stand up again. She then moved further back into the water until she could submerge and Cheeky had to move towards her.

This must have been Cheeky's first experience in deeper water, as she went down and then popped up like a cork, moving around to her mother's nose and promptly resting her tiny head on it. This allowed her to remain buoyant and yet have all of her body underwater.

I realised I was pushing my luck. I had been watching for a long time and the wind could change; the last thing I wanted was to upset Lady Blackface. Also, if she charged out of the water after me, what on earth would happen to such a tiny newborn? With a huge smile and an extreme feeling of satisfaction at having witnessed such an event, I crept away.

FOUR

Hippos and crocodiles

The hippos and their lives fascinated me. They were the largest mammals in the vicinity, as the elephants had not yet returned. The flow of the Turgwe River had been affected by a large dam built some 80 kilometres upstream back in the 1970s. This in turn altered the appearance of much of the riverine flora and fauna, especially as far as pools for the hippos were concerned. Their entire existence and survival depended on the water.

I walked the entire stretch of the Turgwe River over a period of a few days to find out exactly how many hippos lived in the river. This covered a 40-kilometre stretch in which I discovered just 27 hippos. The two permanent families that lived in close proximity to us consisted of eight members, including Bob, at a pool called Chlabata. This pool was situated about 900 metres downstream from our camp. Seven, with Happy, lived at the Chichindwi pool, some 450 metres upstream. That pool was adjacent to a tiny river called the Chichindwi, just where its mouth entered the Turgwe.

The remaining hippos lived downstream in the Turgwe at the Sabi River confluence, which was about 27 kilometres from camp. Nine lived in one family group while three bulls lived solitary lives in the channels up- and downstream, which they would do until they could find their own territory, as two of them were young bulls. The older one had probably lost his territory in a fight with another bull; him I named Crooked Tooth. He had one lower canine growing at a strange angle away from his mouth, as if at some stage it had been knocked out of place.

Every day I spent several hours with Happy and Bob's families, splitting my time between the two groups, observing their movements and getting to identify different individuals by their particular marks. I used binoculars to search for something that stood out, a permanent scar or a rip in an ear, as most of the time the hippos were in the water with only their heads visible. There were two black-coloured hippos, Blackface and a young male I named Robin. I didn't know if he was an offspring of hers, but he really looked like her.

As we moved into our winter season, the hippos would leave the water during the morning to lie on the sandbanks next to their pools. Hippos don't like cold water and the months of June and July can be very chilly, the temperature at night dropping to around 3 or 4 degrees Celsius. The dampness of the river caused Jean and me to wear several layers, piling at least two duvets on our bed. Sleeping outside with the elements, the drop in temperature, or any gain for that matter, could certainly be felt. The hippos would leave their pools as early as eight in the morning after a particularly cold night.

On leaving the water juveniles normally took the lead, their bulks already giving them the shape they would reach in adulthood. They would slowly, very slowly, leave the water, taking a long time to travel only a few meters. This was owing to their natural wariness at leaving their water haven, so they had to depart with great caution. They were getting out to sleep and not to graze as they did in the evenings, so they were even more cautious on leaving their pools.

Hippos' behavioural patterns are the direct opposite to ours in relation to the hours that they keep. They eat at night, leaving the water once it is dark. They will graze for a couple of hours and then often find a soft, sandy spot to lie and sleep in for a while, and then they resume grazing. Their main diet is various grass types and, since an adult needs to consume around 45 kilograms each night, this entails a lot of walking during the dry season to find enough nourishment. They return to their pools before dawn and then, by eight in the morning, they move up to the sandbanks to sleep and digest their meal of the night before. Normally they only start becoming active at around four in the afternoon as this is about the time they wake up, ready for their nightly pursuit of grass.

In order to watch the hippos doing something other than sleeping, I would go along at all times in the day to find out their active periods. Youngsters, like any young animal, would be livelier than adults, but normally only for a very short period in the early morning. Like their parents, they would be far more energetic around mid to late afternoon.

I loved the winter months, as that was when they were at least out of the water. This allowed me to see all of them, from the tips of their toes to their noses, unlike the wet months, when it was mainly their heads that showed just above the water's surface. When on land hippos lose their natural aquatic grace. They take slow, measured steps, and then they stop every now and then to rest their heavy heads upon the ground, noses pressing into the sand. They can stand so still they look like huge boulders, and on many occasions my heart has skipped a beat as I thought the boulder I was approaching might be a sleeping hippo. I learnt to recognise a lot of hippo rocks!

Once the hippo has found a comfortable spot in the sand he will sink to the ground in one movement. Such a heavy animal dropping so quickly gives an idea of how fast they can be. In fact, on some occasions when the hippos were startled by something as insignificant as a small bird, they would really surprise me. They could be up and charging back into the river faster than it took me to raise my camera and grab a shot. Their speed is incredibly impressive for such a large animal.

Once the family were all lying on land, they would be touching closely, mother and calf next to each other, followed by an older juvenile, who was probably her offspring, followed by another cow and her family. Bob was often right in the middle of this melee. Most of the time hippos look as if they are smiling. It has to do with the way the mouth curves upwards. Heads would rest on other parts of their family's anatomy and they all seemed to enjoy this extreme close contact. Hippos are very gregarious animals. They really do look like a heap of large mounds on the ground. If another adult cow approached Blackface's calf too closely, though, this would trigger a hippo roar, quickly stopping the other cow in her tracks.

I had never before known the roar of a hippo and was astonished on the first occasion I heard it.

I suppose you could say it sounds a bit like a cross between a lion and an elephant, and not something you would expect from a hippo. Their standard voice is the bellow, which has the deep musical tones of a loud and guffawing laugh. It is noted in reference material that a hippo's voice is called honking. I prefer to say they laugh in a loud gutsy manner, not a honk. Yet the roar is quite frightening and not a laugh at all. It is used between cows or when a cow is cross with a bull. However, a cow will vocalize towards any other hippo when she is very angry.

Within the Turgwe in the two hippo pools I had counted 17 crocodiles, ranging from 'Big Daddy' of around a massive five metres long down to the baby crocodiles born the year before in December.

Between the crocodiles and the hippos there appeared to be a kind of demarcation line. If a croc swam too closely to them, all the hippos' eyes would be on the beast, their collective stare seemingly enough to change the crocodile's direction. If the saurian persisted in his attempt, a snort or even a half-hearted charge from a hippo would normally make it change its course. When a hippo calf was too close to a crocodile, the calf's mother would mostly keep her head under the surface, maintaining a careful watch. An adult hippo can stay submerged for five minutes at most.

While watching the hippos, I began to reach the conclusion that their behaviour resembled that of police officers of the river, as if they were the guardians of less vigorous animals.

A vervet monkey would be hanging from a branch eating flowers or picking fruit. As the branch vibrated with its antics, a crocodile with its keen eyesight (it can see for an incredibly long distance) would notice the movement. Crocodiles' bodies are ideally adapted to their life in the river and they have not changed in overall appearance since the dinosaur age. The croc would start a stealthy approach, at first with its head just above the river's surface. Then it would sink below the water just before reaching the overhanging branches. The monkey, still unaware of the predator beneath its feet, would continue to feed. But before the croc could launch itself out of the water, which is achieved by a flick of its long tail, a hippo would be upon it. The hippo, or sometimes more than one hippo, would chase the crocodile away from the bank and sometimes even pursue it for a short distance in the water. I witnessed this on so many occasions that it could not have been coincidental.

In magazines and even on film a number of similar incidents have been recorded where a croc had actually managed to pull an animal into the water and someone had been lucky enough to catch a hippo's involvement on camera.

In one instance, a man caught the action as an impala was pulled into the river by a croc. Before the impala could be drowned, which is the main way that crocs kill their victims, a hippo intervened. This juvenile hippo charged the croc, which then released its victim. The hippo weighed in at around 450 kilograms. It raced towards the impala as it struggled to return to the river's bank. Amazingly, the hippo opened its cavernous jaws, took the impala into its mouth and, by clasping the main bulk of the impala in its mouth, carried it over to the bank.

There it deposited the impala on dry land and stood above the buck with its own mouth open, as if breathing air onto the unfortunate animal. The impala was too far gone from its injuries, but the hippo remained by its side until it died, like a concerned onlooker.

One morning I was quietly watching the hippos. They were lying in the water, as always semi-submerged, occasionally huffing to expel air and spray from nostrils that had been sunk under the surface of the river. Bob seemed oblivious to a grey heron perched upon his back, the heron having an ideal viewpoint for spotting fish.

Suddenly the hippo heap exploded in sprays of water as if one animal, amid loud snorts and grunts, lunging around in the water. To my astonishment, there on Lace's back was a crocodile of around 1.5 metres in length. The croc's unpaid ride lasted only a minute as Lace launched herself half out of the water and the croc slipped back into the muddy depths.

Was the croc there by accident, mistaking the hippo's back for a convenient rock? Or had there been some other reason? The hippos, after their exaggerated leaping around, turned back to the semi-submerged sandbanks and once again huddled into a gregarious group, where they promptly went back to sleep.

Each day that I walked in the riverbed my senses heightened. With every step I used my eyes, ears and sense of smell to a far greater extent than in an urban environment. Sure, the scents of cooking and coffee shops will linger in one's mind when thinking of a certain street in London or Paris. Out in the bush, it is as though your eyes, nose and ears are like a child's; everything is new, it needs to be tasted or smelled, or is being seen for the very first time.

My nose would immediately sniff out the first whiff of animal dung that had been freshly deposited, or the rank body odour of a waterbuck. I am a vegetarian, but I know many meat eaters who will never eat waterbuck meat as it is apparently rather sour. Their scent is definitely very strong. Hippo dung smells sweet, of masticated grass, not unlike horse dung. Baboons' deposits leave a lot to be desired, the repellent smell probably owing to their somewhat catholic diet. Their dung is more like a dog's than the pleasant grassy scent of the herbivores'. Elephant dung is particularly pungent, having a smell all of its own that is extremely recognizable, even with your eyes closed. As a safari guide, you often stop and pick up dung to show your clients of what the animal's diet consists.

Thinking back to that year and a half of living in Holland with Jean-Roger, we would often join Jean's work colleagues for a blind wine-tasting evening, the two of us in smart clothes. On other evenings we would all go to restaurants. His colleagues thought of themselves as gourmets, so one of us would choose a restaurant and the idea would be to judge it on atmosphere, ambience and, of course, the all-important food. That was certainly a very different life to sniffing shit in the African bush!

Yet it is essential that guides know these animal scats, for they give you greater knowledge of an animal in the vicinity. If they are quite fresh you know that the animal has walked there recently.

My ears are my best sense. I can pick up the slightest noise. Elephants are very considerate, as they will always let you know they are in an area by breaking a branch with a loud crack, conveniently helping you to avoid bumping into one of them. Or, if an elephant herd is in the area, their distinctive communication rumbles echo through the trees, even from some distance away.

On many occasions I liked to belly crawl into thick bushes close to the hippos' pools, moving along their night-time trails and reaching the water's edge. I would go home covered in scratches, but I felt they were well earned. As I reached a position from which to observe them, I could sit quietly for a couple of hours and just watch the hippos being hippos.

In many ways they reminded me of certain overweight people, for hippos are very light upon their feet. As a teenager I used to dance for a disco called Unicorn Sounds with my friend Babs. It was a traveling disco and my boyfriend, Chris, was the DJ. We had a large van that, funnily enough, had been painted with various animals and inside the van a huge hippo face with mouth agape gazed out at the world.

I still love to dance and have always noticed that the person lightest on their feet is often the most overweight. Hippos, when moving under water, appear so graceful, their gait is more like that of a ballerina's. On land they walk with such stealth that you can hardly hear them as their feet press into the earth, like all of the big animals. The only time you hear a hippo is if it is charging at you. Their feet are somewhat cushioned and they leave wide tracks as they walk on land. The track looks as though a mini-tractor has passed by.

I came to know the difference between Bob's spoor and that of his females. His footprint was about one and a half times my size 6 shoe, measuring from the tip of his toe to his heel. I initially took plaster casts comparing all the hippos' foot sizes. Blackface was obviously not very young. Her tracks had many kinds of lines imprinted in the earth, more so than that of other hippos, like wrinkles. Cheeky, at six months of age, had a tiny little footprint. It would have fitted into her mother's track at least fifteen times over. When a calf is newly born, the whole footprint is not more than about ten centimetres in length and the same more or less in width.

When you walk in the wild you must try not to startle the inhabitants. No animal wants to hurt you unless it is a predator, and even then you need to walk pretty close to it and say 'eat me'. Then, perhaps, you may be granted your wish! In observing how animals behave with each other you will notice they have mainly harmonious relationships, often living side by side with predators if the animal in question has already eaten.

As we advance in technology, we lose so many of our natural instincts. To walk with stealth is not something people do any more and noise is a factor that we constantly live with in our daily lives. The tourists I took into the bush would at times make me shudder with the way it seemed impossible for them to remain quiet. They had to cough or sneeze or simply talk, when they would hear so much more if only they could keep really quiet. It amazes me how much noise people can make – I think it is because they are usually surrounded by noise. Nature is full of sounds but it has its own beat, with most sounds there for different species to relate to, and they are always complementary.

A bird's alarm call alerts other animals to danger from a predator. All species have their own vocalizations that tell one another something of importance. Monkeys' and baboons' calls describe whether the predator is a raptor or a predatory cat, or even a domestic dog or painted wild dog. Or a human. Each call has a different pitch depending on which animal they have seen, and they warn the other members of their group about it. Animals regularly tell each other what is happening.

With this in mind, I found a new way to approach Bob and Black-face. Whenever I got close to their pool, I would talk. A one-sided conversation, for sure, but it was a way to introduce my presence. I would chatter away and it felt quite natural to be talking to a pod of hippos.

On my first attempts I would find an irate Bob or Blackface for my troubles, but with time this changed, or at least it did on Bob's side. Instead of his usual snort, grunt or mock charge, he would open his mouth in a large gape but without the angry expression previously visible in his eyes. His eyes were no longer mean and tight looking. He began to relax and realised, I think, that the voice of this specific human was not a threat.

One afternoon near to dusk I returned to camp having spent quite a few hours with the hippos. As I reached our open-plan bedroom/dining area, I discovered Jean-Roger sweating and shivering in bed. Before I even reached the bed I knew what was wrong. I had had malaria myself on several occasions, but this would be Jean-Roger's first time. As he lay there, alternating between sweating and shivering, I gave him the first of the course of anti-malarial medicine.

Poor Jean! How different his life had become since meeting me. Were it not for me he would not have been here, far from any familiar reality. Now he was really suffering. This is a particularly awful disease. As he lay trembling in the grip of the fever I felt so much love for him, realizing how much he had given up, leading a life for which he had never bargained. The malaria had to run its course and it was a week before he was more or less back to normal. Bed rest is the only way to fight off malaria, as the slightest movement or any form of mental concentration can set you right back and the disease then gets a stronger grip.

This was one aspect of living in this part of the world that was not at all fun. Malaria kills more people in Africa than any wild animal. That tiny mosquito is far more dangerous than anything else. It is actually the little guys in Africa that cause the most problems, from mosquitoes to ticks, spiders and scorpions: all of these can make you very sick and even kill you if you cannot get the cures.

Once Jean was fully recovered, he had lost around three kilograms in weight. I thought it prudent that he hung around with me instead of going straight back to work in the bush. I asked him if he would like to come and meet the hippos, as he had left me to my own devices until then.

As we arrived at the pool, I took over.

'Keep upwind of them,' I said, as we pushed through the bush. 'We must be quiet and not startle them. That's when Bob or Blackface can get mad and charge.'

An American scientist, Bill Barklow, had discovered that hippos use echolocation based on sound under water, and I knew that above the surface sound is all-important to them.

We reached the Chlabata pools just before dusk, when the hippos were emerging from the water to wander inland and find grazing. I had observed them already, drifting further and further from the banks of the river. I had previously found that the hippo trails could go inland for up to eight kilometres from the river pools. Tonight, some of the hippos were already out of their pool and disappearing into the bush, but others remained, wallowing in the water. Bob, of course, was still there and so I pointed him out to Jean-Roger, introducing Jean-Roger to the family, one after another.

Though Jean-Roger had never been an animal person, watching them with me seemed to impress him. I hoped that the awful bout of malaria had not put him off our new life. I really did not want to leave here and return to living in a corporate world. I had now found an animal I could live my life with and get to know. I just hoped I could convince Jean that we should remain in the area for much longer than he had previously suggested.

As we stood together, watching the hippos, we were to see, for the first time, an incredible event unfold. I was so grateful that Jean bore witness beside me.

A dainty bushbuck female, nearly identical to the Disney character Bambi, approached the riverside, on the opposite bank to where we hid. Her thirst took her to the river's edge.

An enormous crocodile, possibly Big Daddy, lunged from the

Turgwe's depths, grabbing her between its jaws. No sooner had the crocodile clamped down than Bob gave a loud snort and charged at it.

Self-preservation is a strong impulse, and a crocodile is no match for an angry three-ton hippo. The croc released its vice-like grip on the bushbuck, disappearing underneath the water.

Bob nosed and sniffed the bushbuck, which was now half-lying against the riverbank. It looked in a very bad way, covered in blood. If it was alive, it definitely had not long to live. All the same, Bob moved up to the bushbuck. He rose up in the water and stood with his mouth agape, holding his immense jaw opened wide, looking as if he was breathing life upon the poor buck's face. Just like I had seen in that film.

Bob stood like this for the next ten minutes, opening and closing his mouth as if he was guarding the animal and trying to resuscitate it with his breath. It was all to no avail, as the bushbuck suddenly shuddered in its death throes and then was forever still. Yet Bob remained.

It was getting too close to dark and it would be dicey to walk home at night in hippo country, even with Jean-Roger by my side, so we left Bob to his ministrations.

This was the first time that I fully understood the hippos to be the guardians of the lesser creatures of the river, but it was not to be the last. In only a few short months, and for the years to come, these hippos themselves would need guardians.

It seemed that I had found my place in the world. I just hoped Jean-Roger felt the same way.

FIVE

Drought, death and a plan

Christmas came, and with it, searing heat and skies of endless blue. This was quite unlike the frozen, cold Christmases we both knew as children. Christmas does make everyone remember their families, and in my case family always included animals. I thought about Kuchek the pony, the love of my life as a child, the one thing I still treasured from my English roots.

Still dealing with the debilitating after-effects of his malaria, Jean-Roger did not recognise this as Christmas either. My cold-weather husband was beginning to suffer – and, alas, he was not the only one.

Without realising it, we had arrived in Zimbabwe and moved into the area at the beginning of what would become the Lowveld's longest and most desperate drought in living memory. As Christmas turned into New Year, we began to see the effects of the lack of rain: first, the grass wilted; then bare earth began to take over from what should have been a carpet of greenery. Then, to my great sadness, the first animals started to die from lack of food.

As the Turgwe's water level dropped lower and lower, the riverine bushes died and the whole environment took on a desperate feel. The heat was so intense that everything wilted, including us. Leaves on the trees died before time, nothing was as it should be, and the land lost all its colour.

The first animals to die were the warthogs. Entire families died.

A female kudu I had got to know began to live at camp, even when the labourers were present. Our trees still had green leaves thanks to the water overflow from our tanks, but how long could we keep on pumping into the tanks? This kudu's ribs protruded from her starving frame. I named her Steyl. We realised that our haven of beauty was fast becoming a desert and I knew that I had to do something.

The problem was, what? We were only two people, and we could not summon the rain. I suggested to Jean that his labourers dig holes in the riverbed, hoping to unearth any water hidden beneath. Perhaps, I reasoned, there would be just enough below the surface to see the animals around us through until the return of the rains.

Never one to shirk work, I dug alongside Jean and the guys as we created small pools deep enough for some animals, but not good enough to sustain hippos. I felt a particular need to protect Bob, Happy and all the others. After all, they had just begun to accept my presence. No longer did Bob charge out of the water, although Blackface was still very aggressive. The digging in the riverbed was back-breaking work and we knew the water would not last, so in a way it was futile. As soon as we unearthed some water, the sun's rays greedily gorged upon this new feast.

January arrived. Our clothes stuck to our bodies and we sweated continuously, even at night. In our bed even a sheet felt too hot to cover us so instead we took to soaking towels in our bathwater, using them to try and cool ourselves as we lay upon them on the bed. The very air burnt us. I now understood what Africans meant when they said the sun bites you.

Birds began to die. I would see the odd one falling off its perch, such was their weakened state. No new fledglings survived. I had found a green-backed heron's nest with four fluffy chicks. Three days later they were gasping for air. The nest was situated in some reeds right next to the hippos' resting area, so I could not intervene. They were dead the next morning.

As I walked along the river, I began to find dead antelope lying close to dried-up pools. Alongside the pools some of the predator birds, resident storks and raptors, found plentiful food in the fish stranded by the loss of their pools. Predators in general were OK feeding off the dead, but what about herbivores like the hippos? How on earth could such large animals possibly survive? They would never be able to sustain themselves.

Most of the antelope in our area could browse as well as graze, but not the hippos. Without food, they would all die. Without their water haven would their skin not burn, possibly causing their death? What about water to drink? I knew a hippo had to drink a lot of water, but at that stage I did not know exactly how much.

Hungry porcupines and large baboon troops tore at the trees' bark, effectively ringbarking and killing them. The hippos were beginning to look bad. They no longer had nice chubby bottoms and their backbones stood out. Little Cheeky, who was now over a year old, was too thin. Another new calf, Loner, was far worse off. He was too young and his mother Lace's milk was drying up. Every day I expected to arrive at the pool and find his carcass. One day it happened.

At that stage they had two pools left: one for Bob, and the other Happy's territory. Bob's pool was getting dirtier each day. Without the natural flow and with the hippos constantly defecating in the water, it had turned into a rather oversized toilet. Hippo turds exploded in gassy eruptions from the bottom of the pool as they fermented in the heat.

Loner lay on his side about two metres from the one bank. He was not breathing and had been dead only a short time, as no crocodile or fish had nibbled at his tiny remains.

Tears in Africa do not get spilled. It is such a harsh environment in so many ways compared to the soft life of Europe, and that doesn't only apply to the animals. People born to the continent do not show much emotion. Culturally, an African expresses grief with a wailing cry rather than weeping. These wails can continue for a very long time, according to the size of the grief. I never have forgotten Mushave, the cook at the safari camp where I had been employed, when he first saw me cry.

'Madam, you have flu,' he exclaimed one morning.

I replied that this was not the case.

With an extremely puzzled expression he looked at me for a moment and then replied, 'But, Madam, your eyes are wet. I think you do have flu. You must sleep to make it go away.'

I assume it was the first time he had seen a white woman's tears.

Well, there was no Mushave, or anyone else for that matter, to see the tears that now spilled from my eyes. I had only known Loner for two months, naming him for his independence at such a young age. I realised now that his very independence had probably been due to the lack of milk from his mother. His lethargy and lack of energy were obviously because he had been starving to death, being too young to graze.

Soon his carcass would be food for crocodiles and fish, but I knew

41

it would take some time. Since this pool was the last refuge for the rest of the family, I should somehow remove the body. If I didn't it would rot. I could already smell the first scent of decay. This would not be healthy for the hippos. They had enough to deal with without one of their dead beside them.

I found a large branch and tried to hook his body with the idea of pulling it closer to the bank. Loner was waterlogged and far too heavy for me. I needed help. I ran most of the way back to camp, hoping to catch Jean before he left. Fortunately, I was in time and, once I had caught my breath, I related the sad story of Loner's death and asked him if he could help me remove the body. We returned to the pool with Jean carrying a long roll of towing rope taken from the Land Cruiser.

Jean expertly hooked one of Loner's back legs by turning the end into a kind of lasso, but even with our combined weight we couldn't drag him to shore. I was terribly worried that at any moment Bob or Blackface would charge us, but up until then they had been unaware of our presence. I think most of the animals had lost a lot of their natural fear of man and, as they had to conserve every molecule of energy, aggressive behaviour was kept to a minimum.

Finally, with a great deal of effort, we managed to drag him up next to the bank, but we didn't have the strength between us to get him out of the water. We could only lift him high enough that his hind legs hung a few inches above the water, and Jean tied the rope to a nearby tree. He believed that crocs would find Loner and feed on him, as Jean had used his knife to open up his little tummy to make it easier for them. Nothing is ever wasted in the African bush.

Through all of these manoeuvres I had managed to keep my emotions at bay. But as I turned away from what had been a cute little baby hippo and now would become food for others, I made a vow. I would save the rest of his family. I did not know quite how, but I knew I was going to damn well try.

Either these hippos would all die or we would have to find some way of helping them. Jean-Roger and I had our savings which, if desperate, we could use, but I could not stand to be among them every day, simply documenting their deaths. I resolved that if nature could not feed these beautiful animals, I would find a way of feeding them myself.

I visited Humani Ranch alone, and spoke to Roger Whittall. I said

I had a plan to save the hippos that would involve giving them food in the bush. I knew it had never been done before and would not be an easy task. The drought was affecting people all across southern Zimbabwe, and what little cattle feed people had stockpiled had suddenly become as valuable as oil. Yet I would do the best that I could.

On that first morning Roger looked at me with a twinkle in his eye.

'If you think a Pom like you can do something like this, you can try, but you know you are going to face all kinds of problems. I do have a relative, Simon Hale, my brother-in-law who farms up in the Harare area, he might be able to sell you some hay.'

Before meeting up with Roger I had managed to contact various people in Zimbabwe who worked in the wildlife field. The best way of feeding hippos in their natural habitat would be to use a high-protein hay and supplement it with some form of protein, for example horse cubes or, if any were available, something called game cubes. The hay would be filling and act in some ways like their normal diet of grass, while the cubes would give them those extra vitamins and minerals that they would ordinarily have obtained from their natural diet. A dry hay substitute had to be high protein, and it seemed soya bean hay would be the best, if I could find some.

Owing to the amount of cattle in the Lowveld needing food, all the farmers had upped their prices for this sought-after commodity. No one I had spoken to had ever fed hippos long term in their natural habitat and the zoos that I contacted overseas all used lucerne, which was unobtainable, so we had to find something that we knew would last the course. I would need to start feeding them soon as possible until the next rains, a period of between nine and ten months.

Roger had not refused me permission to feed the hippos; he had just appeared somewhat cynical as to whether I could actually achieve such a long-term goal. I knew he still looked upon me in a most unfavourable light.

Jean-Roger and I then began the 1 500-kilometre circuit of farms and feedstock companies from the camp to Harare, building up a stockpile of horse cubes and hay. To do this I had to persuade Jean to use our own savings. As we drove around the country we came across a lot of drought-related problems. There were awkward moments when the company from which we were buying horse cubes found out it was to feed hippos. They actually wanted to take the food back, saying that the national cattle herd came first. However, I can be stubborn, as can Jean, and we had paid, so we left with our precious cargo.

The problems of a drought, though, are not only animals and the environment; the crops in the fields had failed and as a result humans were going to suffer. I hoped that all of the human charities, which were many, would take care of the people affected. My priority has always first and foremost been animals. There are thousands of people who care for people, but, sadly, only a relatively small number who help animals. I knew I would meet obstacles. The most common statements we heard over the following months were, 'Why do you worry about a bunch of hippos? People need food. The cattle herd needs to survive.'

When we returned to our camp with a full load of soya bean hay and game cubes on the Cruiser and packed tight on a large trailer that we had managed to borrow from the mining company, we were given another bit of bad news.

Lawrence told us that a young English boy staying with Richard Whittall (Roger Whittal's brother) had come to the camp to find me gone. He had reported that a large hippo bull had been found dead over 20 kilometres away. Oh, my God. Which of the bulls would it be? I heard myself screaming in anguish inside my head. I had to keep up a positive, tough front for Lawrence or I would lose face. Please God, I asked over and over again, don't let it be Bob.

I accompanied the boy after meeting up with him over at Roger's. He took me to the place where he had stumbled upon the dead hippo. The hippo lay in the dried-up riverbed against the bank as if he were asleep, but the vulture droppings that not only surrounded the decomposing carcass but also left white streaks of excrement on his bloated body were proof enough that this magnificent bull was gone. It was Crooked Tooth. His ancient jaw had slipped open, and his cockeyed lower canine could not have been more evident. He had just been too old to keep going, and another victim of the drought had been claimed.

With his skin pulled tightly over his bones he no longer resembled a hippo. Vultures and other raptors' droppings covered his pathetic frame. It was so undignified and yet part of nature. His hippo bellow would never be heard again, nor would he ever be able to challenge a younger bull for the right to mate a female.

In an effort to be practical in the face of such a tragic event, and mainly to occupy the flurry of thoughts attacking my brain, I used science to cover the pain, measuring his body, teeth and feet. Yet inside I was howling. How many more hippos were going to die? I had to save them, I just had to.

I knew I could not feed all the hippos along the Turgwe; I had to concentrate on those closer to camp. Maybe some of the others would join Bob and Happy and I could help them, too. Crooked Tooth's death must not be in vain.

Another hippo, a sub-adult male named Robin who I suspected was Bob's son, had left the Chlabata pools the week before and I prayed he was OK. I would still have a dozen enormous mouths to feed.

Jean and I had hit upon a plan to set about building gigantic sandwiches of soya bean hay, horse cubes and molasses, and leaving them by the pool each night. The problem was that we did not own a four-by-four vehicle and the company one was not supposed to be used to feed hippos!

If we had expected Bob, Happy and the others to start munching away immediately, we were in for a long wait. For almost three long weeks, days of worry and fear of another dead hippo, where the sun baked our skins and we continued to find more carcasses of smaller mammals, they would not eat. The heaped hay brought visits from bush pigs and the ever-canny baboons, which would make a huge mess of our tidy stacks of carefully placed hay and cubes. Yet no hippos were eating. I was glad that at least something was investigating this unnatural feed, but the hippos just continued to wallow in their ever-shrinking pools.

Finally, when I had nearly given up hope, I arrived on the twenty-third morning and heard a sound I had hoped to hear for so long. It was the noise of hippos munching and crunching hay. Pushing through the bush toward the feeding station, I hid behind an ilala palm and was amazed to see the whole hippo family busily eating away in broad daylight.

This was the first time I could see all the hippos out of water and I was quite horrified at how thin they had become. Bob's backbone stuck right out, razor-sharp in its prominence. All the others had visible signs of near-starvation, their ribs clearly showing. Yet the most amazing thing was how they were eating: all lined up side by side, juveniles next to adults, contentedly munching away without any shoving or fighting. Even in a state of near-starvation the hippos exhibited an extraordinary lack of self-interest and territorial behaviour. It was something I believed we humans could learn from.

Within a week, some of the errant hippos that had taken off in search of food returned: Robin, who I thought might be Bob's nearly mature son; and Blackface and her daughter, Cheeky. Watching them feed filled me with an elation I had never known before but, always, there was the gnawing knowledge at the back of my mind that we could not afford to pay for this forever. We needed more food and we could not keep using the company vehicle.

As I watched I snapped away with my camera, emotions too hard to express battling in me. I felt joy that they were actually beginning to feed after such a long wait. Sadness overshadowed this as I looked at their emaciated sides. No hippo should be that thin. Now these wonderful animals were dependent on me to survive. I would have to find help financially as they would need to be fed until the first rains, which were several months away.

Having the hippos start to feed was a great stride in combating their starvation, but there was also the other essential part of life for a hippo – water. Water to drink, water to bathe in, water to keep their thick, greyish-brown hides moist so that they do not dry out or burn.

Later that night I sat down with Jean-Roger and told him that we had to do more. There had to be some way to bring water to the hippos, as well as feed. Surely Jean-Roger, with his knowledge of engineering and all the expertise he had picked up while working as a geologist, might have a solution?

Jean-Roger looked at me, his face conveying a mixture of emotions.

'Do you know what it is about you that I love?' he said. 'You never give up. You just keep on pushing.'

I took that as a cockeyed compliment, as Jean was never one to romanticize his words.

'Then you'll help?' I asked.

Jean-Roger smiled and shrugged. 'I love you, so I will do my best.'

In the end, the solution we hit upon was simple. Somehow we would build the hippos a big water pan, lined with rocks and concrete and with a wall at either end. The pan's depth would be enough for even an adult hippo to submerge and large enough for all the hippos to use at one time. Basically, a huge hippo swimming pool. We would speak to Roger Whittall and ask him if we could divert some of his underground water over on Humani, using a pipeline to go the full 19 kilometres to the boreholes. Here they had huge underwater aquifers to which we could attach our piping and pump that precious source all that way to our hippo swimming pool. If we were successful the hippos would never be without water to drink and wallow in for as long as the drought lasted. We would also build the hippos drinking troughs, as their swimming pool would become as dirty as their last river pool, I was sure.

Now I had to go back to Roger with my new idea. Since he was the main landowner in the area, he was, ultimately, the hippos' owner at that stage in Zimbabwe's politics. I cannot understand how anyone can own a wild animal, but that is the viewpoint in Southern Africa.

Once more, Roger agreed and actually offered to lend me the use of his bulldozer to dig the hole we would need to form the pan. He would also provide us with a workforce of his own labourers, on condition that we financed the pan, the piping and the cement, which would make up the bulk of the costs.

I realised that I would have to start asking for financial help soon, as our own savings would not stretch to both feeding hippos for many months and building a large pan.

Fate stepped in as another woman with her own vision, living two hours away in the Chiredzi area of the Lowveld, got involved with the nearby national park. The Gona-Rhe-Zhou is probably Zimbabwe's finest park, both for its scenery and for its huge populations of elephants and, at that time, hippos, as well as all the other animals. Penny Havenor's plan, like my own, was to feed *in situ*, and she had formed a committee of like-minded people. Sadly, though, I have discovered that the more people are involved at an administration level the less actually gets done on the ground. Everyone has an opinion, and animals die while people agree to disagree.

Penny, however, did help the Turgwe hippos in one way. She was dealing with the media as well as overseas animal charities. She had contacted several, and Care For The Wild International sent a representative to meet her and see exactly what she was trying to achieve. She sent Henry Hallward to me afterwards, probably because I had already begun feeding and could show some results, which would help her to get the charity behind her.

Amazingly, just ten days later I received a message from Humani. There was a fax for me.

After driving over I was overjoyed to read that Care For The Wild had raised sufficient funds to help us buy all the equipment we needed to build our water pan. I felt as though I had just won the lottery. This was incredible news. I now could concentrate on raising funds locally for feeding the hippos, knowing that the UK charity would back us all the way to build them their swimming pool!

In Africa people tend to move slowly and with a lot of procrastination when they get together for a meeting, which seems to be a common occurrence. I think it has something to do with the heat; people just slow down in this country. I am still very British in some of my ways even though I live in Africa, and this drives me to do things as quickly as possible so as not to waste valuable time. In the case of saving these animals' lives, it was all go from dawn until I collapsed into bed at the end of an exhausting but often rewarding day.

During all of this, Jean-Roger and I were supposed to pack up our camp as his contract with the mining company was due to finish. However, instead of preparing to move back to the oil world, Jean, like me, had fallen in love with our new home, and he had not written a single letter to find employment. He realised that for me to walk away right when we had the hippos feeding and planned to build the pan would be asinine.

Jean-Roger suggested that I stay behind while he would remain with the mining company for the time being, taking the new posting they offered. We would approach the Whittalls and ask them if I could stay there alone with, say, one employee and continue to feed the hippos. He had four weeks of accumulated leave, so he could stay with me during that time and help me build the pan. I was so pleased, as Jean-Roger is the practical one in our marriage. I have many ideas but he can build and has a logical mind, which has never been my strong point.

I went back to see Roger, since none of this could go ahead without his permission. It could take a month or more to get new piping sent down from the capital, Harare, to the nearest village, two hours' drive from us. I thought we could borrow Roger's own piping and replace it with the new stock when it arrived. The objective was to get this pan going before the last hippo pools disappeared. They were now feeding regularly, but I had a new problem: with Jean's company leaving the area I would not have a four-by-four to drive down into the riverbed and off-load hay. So I had to bring those hippos up to camp.

Easier said than done.

How do you convince 13 hippos to walk more than a kilometre away from their normal habitat and move right next to human habitation in order to be fed? I had forgotten how intelligent hippos are – like any animal, they know where the food is and they will find it. Jean mentioned that one of his workers was now unemployed and keen to help with the feeding.

Eliot had been born less than a kilometre from our camp and his father had worked for Roger's family for over 50 years. Like most Shona people, he was not particularly tall, but his lean, muscular frame and quiet personality appealed. I like to be quiet in the bush and, even if we would be mainly dealing with laying out food and saving animals' lives, I wanted to work alongside somebody who just got on with the job. He seemed to fit the picture. I hoped that other animals would take advantage of the feeding station and allow us to help them as much as possible. Eliot proved to be the best choice. He hardly uttered a word and when he did speak it was always something that made a lot of sense. Having been born in the wild, his knowledge of animals helped in many ways.

For two nights just before dusk, we timed the work to try to deter the pesky baboons from destroying our well-laid-out hay – at night they roosted in the trees and would not disturb the pile of hay. We would place the hay in one area and then move it along towards the base of the riverbank. Here the animals had made a very pronounced trail, which we then followed up the bank to the top. So we continued for the next week, gradually moving the hay closer to our camp.

Finally, after five nights, I had the hippos right at the back of camp. All that separated them from coming in was a rickety old wire gate attached to our bush fence of thorns and debris, acting as a kind of demarcation line between bush and camp. Once I had the hippos there it was easy for me to drive our old pickup loaded to the brim with hay and the sacks of game pellets. Between us we could then offload the truck and lay out the hippos' sandwich, as it had become known.

This sandwich was approximately seven metres long by one metre high. It might have made the *Guinness World Records* for a sandwich, and was an ideal size for hippos to munch away at side by side. I had worked out that the best way to distribute the high-protein game cubes was by placing them in-between layers of hay and toppings of molasses, broken cane tops and cottonseed, which we had found in the next village from Chiredzi. Here the cane-growers' crops had failed and their company was milling all the leftovers for cattle feed. I had booked a ten-ton truck to bring me a huge quantity of this to mix up with the soya hay.

In the meantime I had begun to approach locals for help, as I knew we could not continue only with our savings. Just in terms of transport I would have to have large trucks bringing huge quantities of hay down to the Lowveld. I had been given an initial guesstimate of what an adult hippo might eat by a man who had fed them for a couple of weeks when capturing hippos to move them from one part of the country to another. He believed that 14 kilograms of hay a night per adult would be sufficient, but I had seen that they ate every single scrap and still were not gaining weight. I just kept upping the amounts until they left a bit and their weight change could be verified on sight alone. It worked out that on average one adult ate 45 kilograms of my sandwich a night.

I had managed to come to this conclusion thanks to Happy. Being the less dominant bull, he was now living a solitary life. His entire family had joined Bob's in the very last pool, as Happy's had already turned to a mixture of sticky mud and sand of only about 60 centimetres deep. Bob's was still deep enough for 12 hippos to live in, but was becoming very dirty.

Happy would come along to the front of our camp, so I left his food there. This made it easy to calculate how much an adult animal consumed. I also used an old cement sink that had been lying around the camp as his water trough, filling it by hosepipe from the camp's water tank.

I discovered that Happy could drink up to 200 litres during his visits. As there were no other clean drinking spots in his area, I assumed this must be about what the average hippo drank in a 24-hour period. A lot of water, and without water all the food in the world would not keep the hippos or the other animals alive. We had to move quickly to get the pan finished and a water trough built before the last waters of the Turgwe totally dried up.

Every animal was suffering from drought-induced stress and we needed to build our pan without putting the animals under more pressure with workers, a bulldozer and all the noise and disturbance that would ensue. We had decided that it should be built away from the river, so that if another drought was to occur there would always be this back-up for the animals, readily available and operational. If we built it in the riverbed and got good rains, the Turgwe's floods could quite possibly break up the structure. We needed a place convenient for the hippos to use but near to camp, easy for us to observe and to do maintenance.

We selected a small natural affluent of the Turgwe and then brought in Roger's bulldozer, which would enlarge the area selected. The rest of the work would be done by hand, digging with shovels, by the labourers and us. The plan was now in motion.

Jean took leave and, having designed the pan, we set to work from sun-up to sundown, alongside ten labourers sent by Roger. Eliot and I assisted wherever we could.

Using picks and shovels after the bulldozing, we enlarged an area that was over 22 metres long and around seven metres wide. Its one end was two metres deep and the other about 60 centimetres, so the hippos could move down to deep water to fully submerge and then return to the shallow end to wallow. The sides sloped down with a wall on each end to support the mass of water. We would need to add around 320 000 litres of piped water from Humani's boreholes in order to fill the pan.

The hippos appeared curious about what we were up to. A small depression had been created nearby from the constant cement mixing and had formed a muddy puddle. Bob, I suspected, rolled in it one night, leaving his territorial marking of dung over half of the newly built wall. This caused much merriment the next morning among the workers.

While the pan started to take shape, the builder, one of Roger's employees, completed a large drinking trough that I had him build right next to where I was feeding the hippos. It could hold over 2 000 litres of the piped water. The pipeline was in place, as we had used Roger's existing pipes and just had to lay them the 19 kilometres through the bush to the Humani aquifers. We filled the trough and then the pan, which took three days to fill to capacity.

During the time that we filled it the hippos kept their distance. Just as when I had begun the feeding, they were apprehensive and did not check it out.

Then, one night, I awoke to the sounds of large animals splashing in water. At first light I rushed off to the pan to find Bob's whole family wallowing and playing in their new water home.

You are not supposed to anthropomorphize when watching animals, but I had learnt long ago that this is just some scientists' way of covering themselves. If we see animals as they are, as sentient beings with emotions and sensitivities close to our own, how can we possibly experiment on them or, for that matter, kill them? It is much easier to say animals have no emotions, although, thankfully, that school of thought is shifting now.

There was absolutely no doubt in my mind that Bob's family was having fun in the pan. Even Robin, the younger bull, was being tolerated by Bob as he rolled and lunged around. Within an hour they had all left the pan, returning to their muddy pool in the river where I believe they felt safer, but at least now they had found a much better back-up.

SIX

Saving hippos and other animals

I had started writing a diary for Zimbabwe's local wildlife magazine that had helped to bring in donations. I was making monthly appeals for help to feed the hippos. A few businesses were supporting me and several other wildlife institutions were passing the word to ask people to help financially. In itself, it was a novelty for a woman to be feeding a family of hippos in the middle of nowhere. Now that Jean was due to leave it became even odder for some to accept. How could a young woman live alone in a bush camp just to save 13 hippos' lives?

We were finding that camp was no longer the peaceful refuge it had been in our first year. It was extraordinary how many people found their way to our home in order to view the hippos' feeding, from journalists to concerned Zimbabweans. Happy was often the star of the show. I could take people to the platform where they could easily view him at his food, for often he came along in broad daylight. But Jean-Roger is a very private person, far more so than I am, and this invasion of our privacy was getting to him.

So engrossed was I in the whole exercise and the feeding of the hippos that I had not fully understood how unhappy Jean-Roger was beginning to feel. I would get home after dark, having put out the hippos' evening feed, to find that he had been at the camp for a long time already, had eaten dinner and already retired. In retrospect, I had become so desperate to be a part of Bob's world, so desperate to be loyal to the hippos and the animals that now needed me, that I had lost sight of the sacrifice Jean-Roger had made in being with me here in Africa. He had quit a highly paid and good position with an oil company to live like we lived and be paid peanuts and have absolutely none of the mental challenges of his previous career.

One night, deep into the drought, I got home late. The pan had become the centre of the world for so many animals, and that day Steyl, our camp kudu, had found her way to the water. I stayed until I was certain that she had fed. As well as the hippos, I now had waterbucks, Steyl and other kudus, warthogs, bush pigs, bushbuck and impala, all coming along to eat with the hippos. I would leave specific piles of hay for each species.

In the dark, Jean-Roger was waiting. That night we talked at length. He told me he loved me but that our way of life was testing him to the extreme. He told me what some of his employees and the game scouts from Humani Ranch had been insinuating, saying that I was more a 'wife of the wild' than I was a wife to Jean-Roger. The time that we had been living here had proved in many ways a period of great stress for him. He had endured malaria and back-breaking work to dig up dry riverbeds and create the water pan, all because he loved me.

'It isn't that I don't love it here,' he began. 'It isn't that I don't love you. But …' He paused, clearly finding it difficult to say what he had been thinking. 'Perhaps it will do me good to be at this job away from here, as then when I come home I will not have seen you for three weeks and it will be just like in the beginning when we first met. I just need to get back to my own work and away from these constant visits from total strangers.'

I felt a mixture of emotions. There was guilt that as Jean's wife I should be leaving with him and not staying on to look after these animals. After all, this wasn't our fight. We didn't own the land or even belong here, or so I was constantly being told by Roger, when he would say, "Hey Pommie, so how'z it going and when are you going back to England?'

None of the Whittalls appeared to understand my need to help wild animals. For them the land and the animals were a way of life, but still a business; emotions for an animal were not something they would ever understand. Roger's favourite comment to Jean was, 'Hey Jean, come and eat with us where you will get fed real food, real meat rather than live on lettuce leaves.'

Being a vegetarian when the only people in the vicinity all killed animals for a living in sport hunting made me yet more an oddity that not one of them could understand.

Jean continued, 'I am thinking that maybe I could leave Zimbabwe altogether, go back into the oil world. You know how much I miss the mental challenge of that way of life. I could still come back here every now and then, but I could do some work, real work, work I want to do … and come back to you when I could.'

I must have looked shocked, for I could not reply.

'We always knew it wasn't forever, Karen,' Jean-Roger went on. 'But we could make it work. I could work three weeks on, and have a week a month back here, back home with you. That is, if I can find the right position.'

I realised that I had no option. I could not walk away from the hippos at this crucial time. We had just made a pan for them and there would be many more months before the new rains hopefully fell. I loved Jean-Roger more than any person I had ever known. We had already been through so much. Surely our love could survive separation? I knew that I could not desert Bob and all the others.

The following day I managed to persuade Jean to accompany me to the pan at dusk, so that the two of us could climb up a tree to watch the hippos when they arrived. As it was full moon we would be able to slip away and back to camp without bumping into a hippo or any other animals.

It could not have been a better night to watch them.

When they arrived we saw an amazing sight, much to my astonishment. Bob mounted Lace, mating her in the water while we sat up our tree. It was the first time I had seen hippos mate and I realised that, if Jean-Roger and I had not been here, this thing might never have happened. Without us, Bob and Lace might both have been dead by now. Yet here they were, with luck conceiving a new life.

This was a miraculous thing, and surely a sign of life going on. Hippos normally mate during the wet season and the idea of them mating, here, in the middle of a drought, was terrific, a testament to the success of my feeding programme and the water pan. I knew that the gestation period was around eight months. I wondered what Bob and Lace would produce, a male or a female calf.

I could not have been more excited at the thought of a new calf. Would I be able to keep up the feeding until the rains so that Lace maintained her health and could support her unborn calf? The responsibilities that I felt at that moment were probably the largest of my life. I couldn't leave these hippos, I knew that, and so did Jean.

Together, holding hands, we went back to camp and even Jean had a smile on his face that night.

In the beginning of my relationship with Jean he had asked if I wanted children and I had shrugged, saying I had not really thought much about it. My mother had never wanted children and I had been an accident in more ways than one. I had told Jean at that time about my upbringing and that for me a child was really not a priority. He had been very relieved and told me that he had never wanted children. Unbeknown to me at that time, I had endeared myself to him even more. Yet here was I now with an even bigger family than any human child, 13 hippos needing a ton of food each night, as well as all the other animals that had joined them.

I did not believe, as some women had suggested to me, that my love for animals had anything to do with maternal needs. I had loved animals since I was around four years old. I had been raised by a mother who had felt the same way. My natural father had been a vet. My mother had worked as a manageress in the small zoo at Woburn Abbey, the stately home of the Duke of Bedford, so I grew up with exotic animals as well as ponies and cows. My passion for animals started at a very young age; in fact, as far back as I could remember.

I did not understand why so many people automatically assumed that my maternal side nurtured this passion. Living in Africa, I knew that I was viewed with pity in some cases, especially from Africans' point of view. Families and lots of children are very important to the traditional African way of life. In the rural areas the men normally take several wives. One man often has as many as 20 children by his different wives.

One of Jean's employees, Silas, had told Jean that when he was in his late teens his family kept asking him when he was getting married. He had not wanted a wife as he was afraid of contracting Aids. He thought that the first time you went with a woman you would get it, so he had remained a virgin.

His family accused him of liking boys, which in Zimbabwe is illegal. To stop the rumours he found himself a 15-year-old wife, knowing that, being a virgin, she would be free from Aids. In African culture and in the view of many people, having a big family and lots of children was the normal course of life. In the rural areas, the more children you had the greater status you assumed. This was especially true if you had girls, for *lobola*, the bride price, would be paid to her parents on a monthly basis well into their old age, and so she became a valuable commodity. Often the father would be most displeased if his wife kept giving birth to boys and this would prompt him to take another wife, hoping that she would provide him with daughters.

Our white neighbours had a hard time understanding my love for animals and I think both black and white people felt I was replacing children with animals.

Early one afternoon Eliot and I learnt to be very aware of Robin, and it certainly reminded me never to become too blasé with the hippos.

We had been checking on the previous night's old food and cleaning some of the hippo dung that was starting to pile up around their feeding station. No more than 15 metres from us, I suddenly saw a large hippo approaching. It was broad daylight and a time when the hippos should be back in their last river pool.

At first I thought it might be Happy, as he would appear early, but on the other side of the camp where I fed him. It would be a first for him if he came around to Bob's feeding station. Then I realised it was Robin. This made me slightly apprehensive as he was fast approaching maturity. I clapped my hands to deter him, but to my astonishment he kept coming.

I suggested to Eliot that we back off towards the gate, as the vehicle was on the other side and we could not take refuge inside it. We started to walk slowly backwards, keeping an eye on Robin, and when we reached the gate we quickly dragged it closed, fearing that Robin would come straight into camp. Instead, he stopped at the drinking trough and started gulping water as if his thirst was unbearable, though he still had a somewhat malevolent glare in his eyes.

I realised that I had forgotten to take the sacks that held the last traces of the cane tops, which we would still need. He was so occupied with drinking I felt I could sneak back out and grab the five sacks, as they were at least nine metres away from him. I suggested Eliot join me, but he shook his head and so, not wanting to lose face, I slowly walked back towards the sacks.

Before I had gone more than three metres Robin's head abruptly lifted from the trough. He snorted once and then charged at me.

A hippo on land is an awesome sight, in full charge even more so. His mouth was slightly agape and he meant business. In those seconds I had only one chance. I threw caution to the wind, turned my back and pelted back towards the gate to find that Eliot had gone. He had taken flight at the first sign of Robin's anger. I leapt for the clasp, knocked the gate to the side and fell into the vehicle, seriously expecting to have Robin lunge at me at any moment. Panting and shaking, I looked up to find him happily drinking once more at the trough. He had obviously stopped once I took off. He had made his point!

The hippos' differences in character were something that became very clear during those months of feeding them all. Happy was literally as his name implied: a gentle hippo who never in all those months showed anything but a nice disposition. Of all of the hippos at that time, Happy was the one who met the most visitors, as he always ate alone at the front of camp. He spent most of the daylight hours living on a bush island in-between the two channels of the Turgwe River, just upstream from our camp. His pool was no longer large enough for even one hippo to live in. Happy had his own trough and pile of hay but his skin had become very dry, unlike Bob and the rest who used the pan but did not allow Happy, as another mature bull, to enter.

Jean had built me a wooden platform at the back of the camp facing Happy's feeding station. Here I would spend a few hours each day watching Happy feed and taking photos of him. Once he realised that the food was always there, he would come up to camp in the early afternoon in broad daylight.

Bob's family I could watch only during a full moon. Often I would be sitting in a tree while they walked mere feet below my perch. At first this was a scary moment, as having the huge bulk of a hippo pass directly underneath adds a certain element of danger. The mind can trick you and say, 'Hey, what if the branch breaks?' and such nonsense. Also, by the glow of the moon, their bodies seemed even more massive than in daylight.

I would be quite nervous having three-ton Bob close enough for me to touch if I leaned down far enough, yet the more times I sat in the tree the more I began to relax and to just enjoy these special moments with the hippos. Here I sat up a tree being able to watch hippos feeding at night and they were aware of me but not afraid; the food was the most important thing and so they went about their business.

Later in the evening I would hear our vehicle rev up and then Jean would drive out in the pickup. Just this small disturbance was enough to move the hippos away from their feed. They never panicked – once they got used to the routine it was accepted as part of the feeding programme. Then I would climb down the tree and join Jean in the pickup. I obviously would not be able to do it once he left, so I took advantage of nights where the sky remained light enough for me to watch Bob and his family.

The behaviour of the hippos when feeding never ceased to amaze me. They were much calmer and far kinder than many other species. I had expected them to act like cattle when feeding. Cattle do a lot of pushing and shoving, with the larger ones dominating the younger. This was certainly not the case with hippos. Not only are they, to my mind, the gentlemen of the river in the way they help other animals, but when eating in a drought situation they just happily stood side by side, Robin often right next to Bob with the rest of the family, all eating without any kind of greedy behaviour. As a family they worked together. The only hippo they would not tolerate was Happy. He was a mature bull and hence competition for Bob. Robin must have been Bob's son since he always teamed up with Bob against Happy.

When hippos are in the water they can be afraid of a tiny family of Egyptian geese, backing down in the face of the mother's quacking call and protectiveness as she glides past with her babies. The same applied at the feeding station, where many other animals appeared to dominate the entire hippo family.

The first time I watched a family of bush pigs challenge the hippos over a pile of food by squealing and making little rush charges at the hippos, who actually backed down from these rambunctious squirts, I thought it was mere coincidence, but then it became a regular event. There was no doubt in my mind that the hippos would back down from any animal that postured in a strong way. They just did not want the fight. Where was this savage, aggressive killer of man that everyone talked about?

Yes, I did see that when a hippo was startled it would often retaliate with a charge, but in general they only acted that way if caught off guard. Another animal showing dominance was enough for them to back off. Perhaps their eyesight not being the best made them nervous of movement and hence the snort and rush forward in defence, which came across as attack mode. Blackface, of course, was another story altogether, but I was still convinced something awful had hap-pened to her in her past.

Rhinos are notorious for charging anything that moves and their sight is the worst of all the wild animals. As I watched and studied the hippos I began to come to the conclusion that most of their threat behaviour was due to their inability to see what was in their way. So I always made sure, when approaching the hippos in the river during daytime or even at night, to talk to them. I did not want them to see me as a threat, and by their becoming used to my voice I might just win their confidence.

The feeding stations for Bob's family and all the other species, as well as at the front of camp where I fed Happy, fast became the central meeting point for many animals in the bush around us. One male warthog, which I called Arthur, became a daily visitor and then brought along a female. She had somehow managed to keep three of her five babies alive. The family of five always arrived before all of the other animals that fed with the hippos. Steyl was only the first of many kudu that would appear from the fringes of the undergrowth to eat and then go to the hippos' drinking trough to drink. For Steyl and her fellow browsers, I was hanging cabbages donated by a vegetable grower in Harare. I hung them in branches so the kudus would be able to lift their heads to browse the cabbage leaves, as they did with normal leaves. They loved the cabbages.

I also built large bird tables from slabs of tin taken from old Rio Tinto structures. Eliot and I fixed them onto the branches of dead trees and then the kudus could eat as they would normally, with their heads raised. We made a mixture of corn and some of the cane tops along with the cabbage leaves and I watched their condition improve rapidly. They had all been very mangy, with loose skin and ribs sticking out. Within a month or so they started gaining weight and their skin returned to a healthier state.

The only animals that did not come up to the feeding station from the nearby area were the crocodiles. Big Daddy and the rest of the gang that had once lined the banks of the Turgwe were able to bear the heavy drought better than the other animals. They still lurked in the dry riverbed, seemingly oblivious to the perfect hunting grounds only a short distance away. They had tunnels into the banks and packed themselves into these like sardines. So instead of living in water they could stay in the moist soil of the riverbank tunnels during the heat of the day. Food was no problem, as the many animals that died would always be found by a predator. Fortunately, no animals were dying now in our immediate vicinity, thanks to the success of the feeding stations.

This was not the case only a few kilometres away.

My mother had taught me a valuable saying that I rolled around inside my head whenever I saw a dead animal away from the camp. It was that one can only help what is in your own garden, and thus you must concentrate your energies on this. Our garden, admittedly, was pretty large as it encompassed several hectares, but I tried to live by this. I could not save all the animals, but at least I could try to save the hippos and animals that ate alongside them. One of the other characters that fed with the hippos was a chacma baboon, which soon became a regular. While others would come in groups, startling flocks of birds drinking at the pan's edge, Sid always came alone. Much larger than his fellow baboons, he had dark beige fur and a patch of rough hair at the nape of his neck. His teeth, especially his canines, looked bigger than a lion's.

I was beginning to lose a lot of weight in the unbearable heat and, with the daily exercise of laying out a ton of food as well as the stress of finding money and organizing the transport, my weight dropped from 55 kilograms to a mere 50 kilograms. Jean was also thinner than normal after that first bout of malaria.

Although Jean-Roger had freely admitted to me that he did not feel for animals as I did, I did see one animal that really touched his heart. This was a vervet monkey, which, alongside her troop, began visiting camp. After a while all of them moved in with us, spending their entire day in the trees next to the caravan or even, with time, playing on the tiny lawn that still existed by our water tank. They numbered over 30, but Jean named this particular female Biscuit, as she began to associate him with her favourite titbit.

It seemed that every vervet in the Conservancy had heard about this new, strange food and water facility where hippos could wallow in an artificial water pan, waterbuck, kudu, bushbuck and warthog families ate food supplied by people, and no savage crocodiles waited to break through the water's surface and snatch an unsuspecting monkey away.

Biscuit was the smallest of the vervet monkeys and I am not sure if that wasn't what Jean found so endearing about her, but as his contract with Rio Tinto came to an end I would increasingly find him with Biscuit.

One evening, just before dusk, I watched incredulously as she climbed on to his knee while he squatted next to her and he gently, oh so gently, stroked her head. Instead of fleeing she allowed this contact between man and a wild monkey.

The day of Jean-Roger's departure eventually arrived. He had paid off all the labourers but I would keep Eliot and Patrick, Patrick to help around our camp home and with the animals and Eliot as my main assistant with the hippos. The labourers' camp had been dismantled, Lawrence had moved on to the next base and now my man was leaving. We drove to the nearest village of Chiredzi, a two-hour drive of which more than half is off-road. I was dropping him at the local airstrip.

I tried to appear confident, but as he left me the tears fell. We were both aware that this was a huge step. We had not been apart for even one night for nearly two years and now we would only see each other one week in every four.

SEVEN

Hippo fights and problems

That drive back to camp left me feeling very depressed. The worry about finances to keep the feeding going, the loss of Jean-Roger's much needed support – both emotionally and physically – and with the worst heat approaching, all seemed a bit too much for me. One of my worst nightmares had also occurred: the hippos had had a fight.

With so many creatures forced to live in such a confined area, I had known there would be conflicts. Before long, the hippos started to become territorial again as they regained some weight and energy, with their natural behaviour coming to the fore.

The first rumblings of unease were when laid-back, reserved Happy was forced into a fight by the belligerent younger bull Robin, the two hippos contesting who had rights to the last scraps of food at Happy's feeding station. Happy – who, I imagined, would have done anything for a quiet life – came off the worse.

But worse still was to come. Several days later, I arrived at Happy's feeding station at dusk to find Bob now back to his former weight and all the more monstrous for it. Suddenly I heard a loud snort as I saw him charge at Happy. Happy ran off towards the dry riverbed with Bob in full pursuit.

The following morning I found a broken part of a hippo's lower canine, and I was not sure if it belonged to Bob or Happy. It was obvious that the fights were becoming serious. This behaviour of large gapes and then lunges at each other can often result in the death of a hippo. If the one bull is stronger and manages to cut a vital blood vessel, the other can easily bleed to death.

Over the next days, I watched Happy constantly being picked on by both Robin and Bob. I felt desperately sad for him. He had already lost his females at the little Chichindwi pool where he used to be the dominant bull, and I found the thought that he was systematically being pushed out of his own feeding station unbearable, especially as he had such a timid and gentle nature for a bull.

On one occasion I did something that was not really appropriate but was all I could think of to save Happy from a serious beating. Bob and Robin had ganged up on him and had him cornered against our camp's grass fence. Happy had nowhere to retreat to. I ran to the caravan, grabbed over a dozen oranges that had been donated by a local shop for the monkeys, and began throwing them at Bob and Robin. Twice I actually hit my target and all the time I was hollering and shining the torch right in their faces. Well, this certainly stopped them in their tracks. I don't think any hippo in history has had an irate woman yelling and cussing and throwing oranges at him. It did the trick, for they both backed off, moving back to their respective feeding places. Happy then managed to move away, this time without a single scratch.

Then the evening came when he was not at the feeding station. Whether it was Bob, Robin, or the two together I could not know, but Happy was gone. I wondered if he would ever return.

Not one to be beaten so easily and knowing that Happy would die out there, for there was no more water or food for kilometres around, I spent my days and early evenings searching for him. I explored tracts of bush I had not followed before. I made the journey along the dry riverbed to the Angus Ranch upstream and downriver to the Humani Ranch, but Happy was nowhere to be found. Even the game scouts who worked for Roger Whittall could bring me no good news.

All pain at Jean-Roger's departure was stored inside me as I continued my quest to find Happy. I could not face up to the fact that Happy was gone, that only an amazing bit of luck would save him out there in the dry, dead bush.

Happy was such a character. On so many occasions I had found him holding the hosepipe in his mouth. I used the pipe to fill his trough from the camp tank and when the trough was empty he used to pull the pipe out and stand there with it dangling from his mouth, as if telling me to move my butt and give him some more water.

Only problem was that nine times out of ten he would drop the pipe away from the trough. I could not just walk out to him and put it back in – after all, he was about two and a half tons of hippo bull.

So I would drive out in our pickup and he would calmly walk a few paces away from it. I would get out, gingerly at first, until I grew more confident of his gentle nature, go to the trough, put the pipe back in and admonish him for his new party trick. Then I'd return to camp and fill up his trough once more.

It was different at the camp with Jean-Roger gone. I still spent my days writing letters and stories for the local wildlife magazine to raise funds, as well as walking the bush and organizing feed for the evening for all the hippos and other animals. I would then watch Bob, Blackface, Lace and the others wallowing in their pan. I still fed Arthur and his bristly piglets, which had all gained weight and looked nearly normal. I still took scraps of food to give to Biscuit and all the other vervets. Biscuit was not particularly happy that it was now me and not Jean-Roger who gave her food; this was abundantly clear as she would never sit on my lap.

I had Patrick around in the daytime to keep an eye on the cats, darling Sammy having died two months previously from cancer at nine years of age. He had died in my arms and, as with all my pets' departures, it left a huge hole in my heart.

I had Eliot to help me each night to lay out the food for the hippos, but at night in the bush camp alone I would think about my life and how people were right that I was more a wife to the wild than a wife to Jean-Roger. I wondered if he thought the same way as he, too, camped over 300 kilometres away without any kind of comfort or companionship. At least I had the animals.

With Jean-Roger gone for weeks on end, suddenly the bush seemed to turn against me. Out following a trail one day, I was charged by a hippo bull I did not know, and spent long hours up in the branches of a tree until it was safe for me to climb down. I kept thinking that nobody knew where I was and nobody would come looking for me. I never saw that bull again, but heard that a hippo had arrived at a ranch some 30 kilometres away and moved into their tiny dam. I hoped he would survive.

Soon after that incident, I was bitten by a violin spider. Without Jean-Roger there to look after me I let infection set in, only raising the alarm with the game scouts at Humani when it was almost too late. I passed out, two days after it had happened, and on coming to had to shout for Patrick to help me stand as my leg was so painful.

Patrick eventually heard my cries and I asked him to bring the camp wheelbarrow and help me to the bedroom. Seeing that the leg was turning a bit blue, I sent him all the way to one of Roger's safari camps to get help by locating the game scouts, who in turn could radio the Whittalls. I realised that living in the bush one needed a backup and the support of a like-minded person.

Africans like Patrick and Eliot, who were both born on communal lands adjacent to the Conservancy, took illness and even death stoically. When someone was sick they would be taken to the nearest clinic by wheelbarrow, if possible. If this was not possible, the sick adult or child would just lie by their hut or in a darkened room and either recover or die.

I no longer had Jean-Roger to drive me to a hospital. Neither Patrick nor Eliot could drive and the nearest hospital was over three hours' drive away. I had no communication with the only neighbours since we were not supplied with radios. Africa does one thing for a person: she makes you extremely tough. You learn to adapt to her ways. In fact, if you don't adapt you should leave, or Africa could easily kill you.

I was lucky the games scouts found one of Roger's white hunters, Hilton. Hilton arrived at camp and in no uncertain tone told me I had to go to hospital. He had to carry me to his vehicle. Hilton then drove me over to Humani, where Roger gave Matt, another young hunter, the job of driving me the three-hour trip to the hospital.

I was diagnosed with blood poisoning and the following day the doctor had to cut the spider's bite to remove the accumulated puss and poison. I am not one for hospitals, having only been admitted twice in my life. I was also very worried about the feeding of the hippos, so I managed to persuade Matt that he should spend the night. After a lot of persuasion on my side the doctor finally agreed that I could go home that afternoon. With the poison removed the pressure on the wound was far less extreme and I would be able to hobble about and feed the hippos.

Perhaps it was only that I had more time alone to dwell on it, but the drought, too, seemed to intensify. Soon after Jean-Roger's departure an incredible wind built up and with it came a dust storm of gigantic proportions. It practically blotted out the sunlight as the earth was so barren and the wind just scooped up all the topsoil. This all seemed to end up in my camp, covering not just me but the camp, the cats, even the sparse bit of vegetation around the camp. We were all blanketed in a fine, all-pervading silt.

In the storm I had managed to walk smack bang into the hanging gas bottle and had literally seen stars as my head connected with the hard metal casing. I had hit it with such force that I broke the mantle and I found myself dabbing at a sticky substance pouring from the bump. I staggered to the caravan where there was a small mirror. The wound looked a lot worse than it actually was as head wounds do bleed a lot, but even so it looked pretty disgusting.

I heard a noise while I was dabbing disinfectant on the wound and realised that there was a large animal at Happy's feeding station. With hope in my heart I battled the wind and, with eyes half-closed, made it to the platform.

To my absolute joy, there stood Happy. He had his back to the wind, just like my pony Kuchek used to do on a rainy day in the UK, but this was Happy, no doubt about it. He looked a bit thinner, but he was home and hungry. He was really munching away at the hay that I still put out each day for him. I said a silent prayer of thanks, and it made the bump on my head and my feeling of uselessness fade away as I watched him eating.

Whenever I am blue and feel the need for attention or help, I find that work clears the head and stops me feeling sorry for myself, so I made a pact to keep Happy safe. Somehow I had to get him his own watering hole, just for one hippo. Perhaps with his own safe haven, the other two bulls would leave him in peace.

From that day, guarding Happy became a daily priority. Often he would come up to camp in daylight hours to feed and drink from the trough. I am sure he knew that Bob and Robin would only come up at dusk. Having the young calf Cheeky and the family to take care of, they acted more like normal hippos by eating at night. I still stayed close to him, making sure nobody was around. I kept a box of oranges as missiles.

I would chuckle, imagining what people would say if they knew that I had oranges as ammunition against two very large bull hippos. Bob and Robin would still try a sneak attack at night and then my torch and the oranges would come into play. Nine times out of ten Happy got away to the river and the bush island before having to face a stronger and more determined competitor.

I persuaded Roger to bulldoze one of the old pools that Happy used to use and the driver managed to scoop out enough of a depression for a small amount of water to seep through. At least Happy could roll in the muddy water and get semi-submerged. It was nearly 48 degrees Celsius now and Happy's skin, was not looking good: red around the thighs, anus, neck and ears, dry and cracked over most of the rest of his body. His condition alarmed me, but there was nothing else I could do. Care For The Wild, the UK charity, had paid for the first pan, the piping and the main water trough, but it would not be able to raise funds for just one hippo. It was up to me to do my best for Happy with the materials we had around us. Eliot hit upon the idea of our building a sort of dip like they use for cattle, but instead of it being treated with a mixture to kill ticks, we would fill it with water.

For the next two weeks I carted bricks from over 40 kilometres away at a kiln made by Africans working on Humani. The builder, Thomas, who had helped us with the pan, agreed to help me again. Between Thomas, Patrick, Eliot and me we built up what I thought would be a big enough dip for Happy to enter and submerge. Only problem was, when I piped in the much-needed water it never rose in depth to more than about a metre.

I kept telling Thomas to heighten the walls, believing that this would increase the depth. Needless to say, my lack of practicality was glaringly obvious to Jean-Roger when he first came home and viewed my work of art. He could not stop laughing. I have never boasted of my practical skills, having been banned from any class at school that required that sort of workings of the mind. I was much better suited to the arts.

Jean-Roger explained to me amid his laughter that, irrespective of how high I built the side walls, the water would only rise as high as the lowest open point. In the case of Happy's dip, the two entrances into the dip were at ground level. Even building an extra half a metre of wall on either side would not deepen it. So this white elephant remained and, believe it or not, Happy did use it, but more as a paddling pool than as I had intended. To empty it and continue digging down would have been counter-productive in a time of water shortage.

I had managed to make a deal with the farmer selling the soya bean hay to pay him at a later stage, so any cash that came in could be used to pay for the game cubes and the survival rations. A man who owned trucks up in Harare had kindly given me the use of his 30-ton trucks on a monthly basis, which allowed us to bring down over 50 bales of hay each month. As each bale was over 220 kilograms, this allowed us to feed. We alternated the soya bean hay with ordinary small bales of Rhodes grass and star grass, as well as the survival rations of cane tops and cottonseed.

The drivers seemed to enjoy arriving in the middle of the bush and finding a large hippo – Happy – that was often feeding when they arrived, or meeting an assortment of other animals at the back gate. I took each driver along to the feeding station so that he could see what his cargo was being used for.

One guy in particular was not amused, but he was a real townie, born and bred in the city. He arrived at dusk and got out of his truck at the entrance to the camp just as I was heading towards him with a torch. Next minute I heard a shriek, then the sound of running feet and the door of his truck crashing open. I found him halfway down in the driver's seat, peering out into the gloom and looking worried. When I asked him what the problem was, he replied, 'Ish, ish, this place is too dangerous. I drive here for eight hours and get out and there are wild animals all around me, animals everywhere wanting to kill me, one was right by my feet.'

I was somewhat surprised as I couldn't imagine any animal having been right by his feet, not when he had just driven up in a 30-ton truck that made so much noise. I then realised that the animal in question was Arthur Warthog. Arthur, who had smelt the new food, was trotting back in my direction as I spoke to the guy. The man, having seen me standing quite safely by his cabin door, made a move to join me, then let out another screech, launching himself back inside. Pointing aggressively at Arthur, he repeated to me, 'Ish, ish, too dangerous this place. Look at this hippo.'

He asked me to sign his forms from the safety of his cab and told me he would not be getting out again as he wanted to leave before he was eaten. I tried to explain that none of the animals would want to eat him, but he would not listen.

In general, though, most of the drivers and, once, the actual owner of the company found the whole experience very exciting, and it gave them something to talk about to friends and family on their return to the 'big city'.

During the first week of October the weather changed. For the first time in nearly a year the sky turned overcast and a forgotten sight began to form: clouds. Pushed by a steady wind, they passed uninterrupted over my head. By mid-October they had turned into the wonderful white fluffy candyfloss marking them as the cumulus clouds that herald the rains. The African sky turned into an exceptionally beautiful artist's palette. I stared at them in wonder. Could we be blessed with early rains?

EIGHT

Rain and new life

On the night of 12 October as I sat in camp alone as always, I heard a long-forgotten sound – thunder rumbling somewhere in the distance. Then the cold flashes of lightning could be seen far off in the darkened sky. Eventually there it was, the scent that had lain dormant for so many months, the sweet smell of rain. The storm hit camp without a minute's warning. The tin roof above my canvas bedroom echoed with the pelting of large raindrops. The wind came up once more in full force, but the dust was kept to a minimum by the water pouring from the skies. My God, it was really raining!

I rushed out into the weather dancing around, head up to the sky, and within minutes was saturated. I could not be sure if my eyes were wet from rain or tears of joy. After that awful heat and the smell of death and decay, the welcome sweetness of wet earth assaulted my senses, one of the most beautiful perfumes one could ever smell.

I had forgotten what a really big storm sounded like. That night was one of those nights. The rain drummed onto the tin roof and ran down the canvas sides, collecting in large puddles that seeped into my bedroom-dining area. Great sheets of water seemed to spill from the skies. After such dryness, it was as if the heavens had truly opened huge doors and poured water onto the earth's floor. The downpour was endless.

As I stared into the grey nothingness, I wondered what everything would look like in the morning. Or would the water never stop, to compensate for so many months of nothing?

The rain fell for over two hours and then stilled. I was so excited by it that even my damp bed was welcoming.

I was awake before dawn and so were the guys. Patrick arrived with a huge, beaming smile, telling me that now everything would be all right again. The rains would fill up the rivers, the grass would grow and so would his family's fields, once planted. He and Eliot said that God was happy again. We all had ridiculous grins that just kept lighting up our faces. When I thought back to my British upbringing and how we British tend to complain about the weather, especially the rain, I realised how far removed I was from that life.

I wanted to see if the land had changed, so I slipped on wellington boots, knowing that the soil would be muddy. As I was about to leave camp I heard a roar; a noise that at first I could not identify.

Then I realised exactly what the sound was: it was water, a lot of water rushing over the rocks and crashing trees in its path. The river was coming down in a great big flood.

This was incredible, considering the day before all had been dry, but every single stream and small dry riverbed adjacent to the Turgwe must have built up into their own small torrents and then filtered into the main river. She was in full flood, and although it lasted for only two hours, once more she became a river where life could grow.

Two hours passed while the three of us watched in awe as debris rushed by in the river that had steadily risen up the bank. So many trees had gone by, dead from the drought and swept into the waters as the river crept up on to land. So much had died and amid my happiness at this unexpected early bonus, I worried about the hippos. Would they have been caught up in the flash flood?

I had forgotten that nature and her inhabitants have senses far superior to ours. The hippos had known before any of us that the rains were coming and they had taken themselves away from the main channel, moving into bushes inland from the Turgwe's banks.

By late morning I headed for Bob's old pool area. The waters in the Turgwe had risen well past the spot where I had first laid out food for the hippos many months before. Debris covered the banks now that the water had receded, and amid the debris in the sticky mud my eyes were caught and mesmerized. I saw the tracks of one, then two hippos. They had moved here quite recently, heading back in a straight line towards the river. A river that now ran from bank to bank, brown murky water filled with sand deposits and silt.

I slipped and slid as I followed the tracks. I knew one set was Bob's, as he had the largest feet of all the hippos. I tried to get as near to the river as possible, while being extremely careful as the bank was soft and crumbling, having been lashed by the flooded waters. I might find myself part of those dirty waters if I was not careful, where I am sure Big Daddy and the rest of the crocodile clan were having fun.

Then I saw them: 12 hippos, minus Happy. Even Cheeky the baby was there by her mother Blackface. They were playing like puppies – not just the young ones but the adults as well. It was the first time I had ever seen the entire hippo family jumping and leaping around in the water all together. Cheeky leapt over her mother's bottom and Blackface in turn followed her daughter in a game of tag. Blackface, much to my surprise, was pushing herself up in the water, placing her feet on the riverbed and then launching herself in the air and flopping back into the water. Even Bob was full of movement, rushing around from bank to bank and every now and then bellowing out his oh-so-recognizable laugh. The hippos snorted and looked more like mischievous children than adult hippos. Lace rolled in the water and all four feet for a moment came up without the rest of her, then her upside-down head appeared and she rolled back to her normal position. This seemed to set the others off, as two more rolled and then my beautiful Bob followed everyone else. How could people say that animals never experience emotions? These hippos were so happy that surely even the most sceptical would see it.

I stayed and watched them for over three hours, my face awash with my emotions, for once allowed free rein, as there was no one nearby to witness my tears. A crocodile passed by. In my imagination, it had a smug look on its prehistoric face. Two Egyptian geese, survivors of the drought, stood on the opposite bank, clacking and squawking and having a great noisy time. A green-backed heron and a pied kingfisher passed by. Hadeda ibis flew overhead, making their distinctive call. Silas calls them *Nderera nderera*, a very appropriate name as it is exactly how the bird's call sounds. The local people are wonderful mimics of animals and people and the names they give both often resemble the way a person or an animal communicates.

That first day the dry riverbed had surged with new water. A great flood rampaged down it, churning up the dead earth at the bottom of the channel and bringing Big Daddy and the rest of the crocodile hordes out from the tunnels in which they had remained hidden. In places the river seemed to cut a new course, carved by the fast-rampaging floodwaters.

Once the first wave of rain had abated, the hippos stopped using our pan and stayed in the river. They still had to come up to feed, but our artificial pan could not compete with their natural home. It had served its purpose, but until new grass grew they would still have to be fed.

Even though the drought was over, the animals that had become so close to me during the year did not disappear. Every evening, Arthur, the warthog, would appear at the camp, looking for food. Sid, the chacma baboon, would linger in the fringes of bush by our home, sometimes followed by a troop of other baboons, all calling out to each other. Steyl, the kudu, seemed to travel a fixed path, so that she would pass us every evening, and Biscuit was a regular guest, among dozens of other vervet monkeys that had come to know us.

Several months into the new season, when rain had fallen in abundance, the devastation of the drought could still be seen as many trees had succumbed and there was a shortage of a lot of animal species. Yet the Lowveld's grass is one of the sweetest in Zimbabwe, probably owing to the low rainfall in this area. Nature likes to compensate by improving the proteins of the grasses. The animals would soon put on weight and, much to the amazement of the locals, both black and white, would recover and breed prolifically to make up for the loss of their kind.

On my side, I had kept the last 13 Turgwe hippos alive. Every other hippo that had once lived in the Turgwe River was gone. During those harsh months we had found seven dead hippos, including Crooked Tooth and little Loner. Five hippos that had lived in other parts of the Turgwe had disappeared but we never found their carcasses, and two others, a bull and a cow, had found their way to the one man's dam 80 kilometres away and survived.

The first hippo to be born after the drought was the result of Bob and Lace's mating in our pan. I was privileged one morning at the Chlabata pools to find Lace on her own in a tiny channel, nursing her newborn calf.

The tiny grey barrel then moved around to lie on Lace's semisubmerged body, hitching a ride as baby hippos will do. Even this young the calf was the spitting image of Bob. I remembered seeing them mating in the pan. If ever there was a symbol of life going on, here it was. I named the baby Tembia.

Tembia's birth really lifted my spirits. After the deaths during the drought and the demise of Crooked Tooth and Loner, his arrival brought new hope. This is the way one has to look at life in Africa. We are constantly assaulted by death, living as close as we do to nature, so birth is celebrated in more ways than one.

Tembia's first weeks of life were lived alongside his mother in this smaller channel adjacent to the main river pool where Bob and all the others claimed residence. Lace spent 12 days there so that he could have that vital imprinting lesson necessary for him to know that she was his mother. Where young animals live in gregarious groups they need to know from day one who is their natural mother. Male hippo calves are more at risk of being harmed by the bull or another young male than a female sibling. Only one bull can be the territorial bull and he will suffer no other male within his family. Young male calves can even be killed, either by the bull by accident or by one of his sons still in the family group. Sometimes an adult female can attack a male calf when she herself is protecting her own son. In ideal situations, where hippos have plenty of habitats, the males leave the family at anything between two-and-a-half and five years of age. This departure time depends on when the mothers are due to give birth again and when their udders begin filling with milk for their unborn baby.

The mother will then attack her male calf, pushing it away from her and at times even chasing it out of the pool in order to teach him that he must soon live a solitary life. These attacks are not gentle and the young juvenile can be cut quite badly by his mother's insistent stance. Although it appears cruel, she is helping the male to become independent and remove himself from the family before his father views him as competition. However, it is a sad time for a male hippo and some do not survive.

In their first few years they are accepted in the family like any of the females, allowed to play open-mouthed pushing games with similarly aged hippos or even occasionally with their own mother, but more often than not with younger calves or juveniles in their age group. They mount the other youngsters in playful games, chasing each other like dolphins as they plunge and jump in the river, filled with fun. The mother is normally far more protective of her male calf than of any female offspring. Perhaps she knows that the male's time with her will be much shorter than her daughters', and so she makes the most of her relationship with him. She also uses a lot more of her energy with a male calf than a female. Her daughters are allowed from an early age to spend time on their own or move freely around the family, but this is not the case with a male calf. She nannies him and is constantly aware of what he is up to.

Tembia joined the group when he was 12 days old and Lace was exceedingly protective. Whenever a youngster tried to approach the new baby, she would give a loud snort or a half gape and the calf or juvenile would move quickly away. On the sixteenth day of Tembia's life, Bob the bull came towards Lace. My heart was in my mouth, afraid that his intentions could prove aggressive. I should have known my Bob better. He gently pushed his huge nose towards Tembia's tiny one and they touched noses in what could only be called a welcoming into the family.

Bob was the first hippo allowed physical contact with the calf. I was to discover this was always the case with a newborn: the bull was introduced first and then the other young members of the family. Other cows could meet female calves when they were around two months old, but were normally not allowed physical contact with a male calf until it was at least six months old, as its mother would chase away any adult that came too close to her son. Tembia on this morning wiggled around in the water towards his father, looking more like a small puppy or a seal cub, and the next moment he was right by his dad, nuzzling into his side and twisting and turning his little body. Bob could not have been gentler.

On the fifty-second day after Lace had given birth, I happened to be on the way to the pool when I heard a commotion. I was accompanied at that time by a 15-year-old nephew of Julia Whittall's. Lloyd and I rushed forward, thinking that a crocodile had captured an animal. We found Bob trying to mount Lace and, as she backed into him, I saw to my absolute horror tiny Tembia stuck right between the two massive bodies, very close to Bob's front feet. Lace was doing her utmost to attract Bob's attention, lifting her tail and shaking her bottom in front of his face and pushing herself towards him by reversing in the water. Bob was being extremely dominant and throwing the water all around him as he tried to heave his massive weight up and onto Lace's hindquarters. Lace was frantically trying to get Tembia to join her closer to her head, so that he was not in the way of Bob's heaving body.

I don't think Bob had any intention of hurting Tembia, but his huge weight and the movements he was making as he tried to mount Lace could easily have pushed the calf into the water, drowning him. He was far too close to this action. When a baby is as young as Tembia, they can remain submerged for a maximum of one minute. The water was so churned up by Bob's attempts to mate that at times Lloyd and I could not even see the baby.

There was nothing I could do but trust in nature, hoping that some how Lace would get her calf away from the activity and into a safer position. Eventually Bob gave up. It was just too much effort, so he moved away to rejoin the rest of the family. The clock ticked slowly as Lloyd and I waited for a tiny head to appear. The longer the seconds passed by, the more I feared that Tembia had drowned. A minute passed and there was still no sign of the calf, yet Lace seemed undisturbed. I kept talking out loud, saying to Lloyd surely she knew the baby was OK to behave so calmly. Sure enough, a second later Tembia's tiny head broke the surface and was at last moving towards her head, where he promptly pushed himself onto her nose and rested. Tembia had survived his first introduction to a bull behaving as bulls have to do. Both Lloyd and I let out sighs of relief.

At that stage I had no idea that Tembia was a little male. I probably would have been even more nervous of the outcome had I known. For the next few months I watched him daily. On one such day I saw Lace and Tembia go onto the land and realised he was a male. I wondered if he might grow to be as bold and dominant as his father or if wanderlust might take hold of him, as it did so many other bull hippos when they came of age. Then he would leave this area altogether.

He had been conceived during the worst drought in our neighbours' lifetimes and the food that I had fed to his mother had allowed this new life to be born. I had named him after an orphan female cow that I had hand-reared many years before and loved very much. Tembia may have been a male, but I hoped he would stay with the family and allow me to chart his life. As the first to be born after the drought, he was a very special hippo.

NINE

The Turgwe Hippo Trust

Jean-Roger and I realised how much we loved living in this area, so we decided to approach the Whittalls to see if they would sell this tiny plot of land to us. We saw that even though Jean could only at present be at camp one week each month, he now thought of our camp as home. He loved the space and the freedom of living in such a natural environment. We needed roots and what better place than here in the bush? This tiny plot had its own title deeds and was set in the midst of a massive tract of land. Surely the Whittalls might allow us to buy it? They had thousands of hectares. Surely they would not miss those nine?

Jean-Roger negotiated with them, but it was not an easy road. I believe in the end it was thanks to the hippos that they let us lease the land and eventually, for quite a large sum of real money, not Zimbabwean dollars, have the plot on the condition that we built our own house at our cost. This amount of money would finish off any savings and meant Jean would have to sell a pension he had started when joining Shell. In later years this would have provided nicely for us, but when you are young the future is a long way off and so we gambled.

Jean was desperate to put down roots after first camping for so long and now having to live in a caravan where he worked. With a house to come home to he would be in a much happier frame of mind. We drew up a design for our house and, thanks to his father's background in building, Jean proved more than competent at making up the plans and starting the foundations of our home. We would build it with our own hands and with the help of just one man, Thomas, who had helped us in the drought with the pan and water trough. He had never built a house either, but had some rudimentary knowledge of how to work with rocks, cement and bricks. We wanted a house that fitted into the surroundings, so we chose the natural rocks from the riverbed and the koppies. Once again we would collect them with the ever-useful wheelbarrows. We made a deal to have bricks made at the Humani kiln by two men and Jean took time off work to start the foundations. Our plan was for a simple thatched house with an A-frame design, a spacious living area and a big bedroom that could double as an office. No windows, just mesh gauze, and a small loft as a spare bedroom. That was, if anyone were ever to visit us, which seemed pretty unlikely.

I was not sure whether I could sleep in a house after living all this time in the open, but the house would have more windows than walls, and since the windows had no glass we would have plenty of fresh air, as if we were still outside. At least if we wanted to we could escape the numerous insects that always arrived with the rains. I loved where we had been sleeping and living for three years, so we decided to turn the area into a thatched gazebo and leave our bed out there.

The house, I hoped, would give Jean a feeling of stability, while it would allow me to continue my life with the hippos, a life that was near to perfect.

Every morning I woke up with a huge smile as I breathed in the sights and smells of this unpolluted land. Each day for me was a day shared with the hippos, learning about their lives. As I chatted away to them I realised how much they responded to my voice – even my bad singing didn't seem to faze them.

Instead of the anger and apprehension of the first couple of years, Bob would now open his mouth in a huge gape and show off for me. I could call him and, even when he was far upstream in the river, sometimes up to 300 metres away, he would lift up his head at the sound of my voice, and slowly submerge. A huge tidal wave would then roll towards me and out of the wave a form would take shape as Bob reared up in the water. He would open his mouth in a huge gape and then splash back into the water, looking at me the whole time with what could only be described as a humorous expression, as though he was laughing at me. He did this every time I saw him, as if it was his way of welcoming me to his riverine home.

His eyes opened wide and, if a hippo can smile, it was there in the way he looked.

When Bob was angry, like any other animal, he showed it easily:

tight eyes, sometimes snorts, and as often is the case with hippo, by scooping water. This is when a hippo gulps at the water as if he is eating it. He mouths the water in this way to show displeasure. These days Bob was hardly ever angry with me and it was such a joy to be in his company. I had no doubt he recognised me and had absolutely no problem with me spending each day with his family.

Blackface I always had to watch out for, which was good as it kept me on my toes and stopped me from becoming too blasé. With any animal, even your own domestic dog, you always have to recognise their moods. There are bad hair days and emotional moments, and when they are out of sorts they can turn on you, just as a friend or relative might do if not in a particularly good mood. Blackface was always my wakeup call, reminding me that all these hippos were wild and freeborn and that I must never overstep into their own territory without being sure that I was welcome.

Early one morning I was walking close to the river near thick reeds. I had just peered into the vegetation when I noticed a hippo tunnel joining the river through the thick reeds. I softly began to call out to the hippos.

'Come on, Bob, hello Lace, how are you Cheeky? Where are you, my guys?'

There was an explosion of sound, a flash of movement: lunging through the tunnel came a hippo. I had a fleeting glimpse of an enraged animal and realised to my horror that it was Blackface; then my survival instincts took over.

I took off towards the bend in the river, managing to turn into the bend and head for the trees. I scrambled up a mopane tree whose welcoming branches definitely saved me, as Blackface was less than a metre behind. Just as I clambered up into the tree, she hit the tree with all of her massive weight behind her. Unbelievably, she had pursued me out of the river and onto land and would, I am sure, have bitten me had I not made it to the tree.

She was snorting furiously and swinging her head around as my scent made her even angrier. I was afraid that the branch I was hanging on to would crack and send me hurtling down. I was bleeding from scratches and I knew I would have a few bruises. I had definitely strained the muscles in my arms from hauling myself up the tree, but I was ever so lucky.

From this lofty viewpoint, I watched her stomping about in the sand. Finally, she tired of this surveillance and gave a huge hippo bellow, which was immediately answered by Bob and the others, and then she left me and returned to the river.

My mouth was dry and my breath came fast and furiously loud inside my head. I tried to calm myself, calculating how long I should remain in the tree, but I was quite sure she had re-entered the water as I had heard the splash. I did not believe that she would be malicious enough to go around the bend and then come back again to finish me off. After all, she was not a buffalo. I had to find out why she was so angry with people and what had been done to her in her past. She seemed to hate anything human and, even after I had been with them for a few years, was still totally unpredictable.

The next day I went over to Humani and spoke to some of Roger's relatives, hoping to get a picture of what had occurred in our area in the past. I had got to know Roger's sister quite well. Jane was quite a bit older than me and I knew she must have disproved of both my ways and my appearance, as I was always in a singlet and short shorts or skinny jeans. Her ideas and mine differed greatly when it came to dress, for Jane was always the image of a colonial lady. Long dress, practical, no-nonsense haircut. A lady who made tea every afternoon for her husband and any hangers-on, the cakes lovingly baked with her own hands. But even with our differences she had become a friend. I looked on her as a motherly figure and, although she was very different from my own mother, it was nice every now and then to talk to a woman about womanly things. She would always be either working in her garden or cooking in the kitchen and catering to her family's needs, or she would be out at work in her store. She never lazed around and was forever thinking of the family, a perfect matriarch. She gave herself completely to her husband, Arthur, and her four children; she really was a poster woman for motherhood.

Jane was as tough as her brothers, having been born to the land and from pioneer stock. All of them had been born on Humani, where their parents had started from scratch, building a ranch and a home in the wilderness. If anybody would know the history of the land and its people, it would be Jane.

As I had hoped, she did have some stories.

Apparently, many years before, a man and his wife had lived in a house that was now just a roofless and windowless broken-down building three kilometres from where we camped. This man had tried to farm a small area next to where he built the house. He had leased the land from the Whittalls, but had failed dismally as the wild animals ate any crop that he tried to grow.

Like most white Zimbabweans he was an entrepreneur and so had this idea to capture a baby hippo, as he had found a man who wanted to buy a hippo for his game park near Harare.

He had sat up a tree very much as I had done during the drought and watched the hippos' movements for a few weeks. He worked out that they regularly moved along certain trails close to his home, so he thought that he could lasso one of the calves, tie it to the tree and, during daylight, once the other hippos were back in the water, retrieve the baby. He obviously did not take into account the protective instincts of a mother hippo or, for that matter, any mother, animal or human.

Blackface must have been the mother of that calf. The man managed to lasso the baby, but then everything went pear-shaped. He was lucky to survive. He had captured the calf and begun dragging it towards the tree when Blackface charged. She hit the tree with such force that it cracked and he had mere seconds to climb higher. The impact of her two-ton weight on the tree had loosened the main roots and the tree was bending perilously close to the ground. He really thought his time was up.

Fortunately for him, as the tree bent towards the earth, the young calf freed itself from the loop, which had broken with the impact of the mother hippo hitting the tree, and started running towards the river. The mother abruptly turned and ran after her terrified baby.

He later told Jane that looking down into the throat of an enraged hippo would probably give him nightmares for the rest of his life. Those lower canines would have snapped him in half, just like a knife cutting into butter, his soft skin no match for those razor-sharp edges. It was only the fact that the calf was calling out to the mother that saved his life. He had remained up the tree, which had not broken, for the rest of the night, as he was too terrified to come down in case Blackface returned.

He had described the hippo to Jane and mentioned she was black like Satan. No wonder Blackface did not like people. The interesting part for me about this incident was that, just like an elephant, she had never forgotten. What had happened to her calf that night had made her forever distrustful of humans.

As I continued to live with the hippos I kept thinking of ways to be constructive for their future.

I came up with an idea.

I would form a non-profit organization, since starting an animal charity in a country where the people were often in need of outside help would be very difficult. To my knowledge there were no actual animal charities in Zimbabwe, but with a trust I could expand my ideas and hopefully get financial backing to help the hippos, not just Bob and Happy and their families, but perhaps eventually hippos throughout the Conservancy. At least now I had the drought experience and knew exactly what hippos would need to survive a prolonged period of feeding.

The Turgwe Hippo Trust, as I named it, became an official non-profit organization in October 1994. Funnily enough it was gazetted on my birthday, another auspicious beginning, just like the first day when we had arrived in the Lowveld, and a sign to me that fate was on my side.

The trust that Bob extended to me, a mere human, formed part of my motivation to create a means to supply the remaining hippos with habitat and security. The Trust would keep reserve funds to be able to face the worst scenario: another severe drought. In such an event, money would be readily available to initiate immediate feeding, as we would not again be in a position to dip into our own savings. All of our money had now gone into the building of the house and the payment for the plot.

With Jean-Roger's initial advice I then completed another 'emergency pan'. This time it would be for Happy and his family, as once more he had females who had joined him in a new pool. I had obtained the money to build the pan through two organizations, the Summerlee Foundation in Texas, and the World Society for the Protection of Animals (WSPA), also in the United States. I continued to raise funds locally and managed to have two boreholes sunk in our area free of charge, using the funds to buy the pump and equipment needed for the boreholes. This was in order to give the hippos their own backup water source, rather than depend on Humani's good will.

Safari clientele from most of the properties in the Conservancy were now coming over to the camp on a regular basis. The owners of each safari camp realised that they could leave their clients with me for a day at no cost. Foolishly, I did not ask for payment but suggested that they tell their clients they could make a donation to the Trust. This was fine when they mentioned it, but on many occasions tourists would pitch up with their driver, not knowing that I was not part of their safari tour. I had left the safari business to get away from having to deal with the public and here I was, back to back with tourists and with the Trust only benefitting occasionally. I was to discover that many of the operators in the Conservancy thought that I could be used in such a way.

Jean-Roger was not impressed by this new turn of events. He would come home for his week off each month and find tourists taking over his home for three or more of the seven days he was there. I couldn't afford to tell them not to come as the little money that some donated helped, and it also spread the word to the operators that taking a photo of a hippo was far more beneficial than hunting the animal, or so I hoped. As many of the safari camps had sport hunting as well as photographic clients, I desperately hoped they would realise that a dead hippo made them money only once, but happy tourists coming along to the Trust regularly would make that animal worth far more to them alive than dead.

This was especially true of our two main neighbours, Humani to the south and a safari set-up called Mokore to the north. The family who owned that piece of land were the biggest hunting operators in the entire area and, to our bad luck, they were our neighbours, living across the river. Their safari camp was a 45-minute drive away. The hippos would often cross the river and graze on their lands, which made it easy for them to sport hunt one of the bulls even though there were so few hippos that they should not even have considered hunting one of them. I had to find a way to show them that the hippos were more valuable to them alive and that the Trust could benefit their safari set-up.

I found, though, that the majority of hunters who came along to see what the Trust was all about already had the same bias as most of the Zimbabwean professional hunting guides, who would influence their clients before they set a foot through my door. In their eyes I was just a 'bunny hugger', as they loved to call me. A crazy girl who talked to hippos.

Some of the sport hunters coming from overseas were men of education: lawyers, doctors, even, much to my amazement, the odd vet. How could a vet hunt? Those men would spend the time allocated to their hunts with white Zimbabwean hunters whose very job was to promote the dangers of Africa, basically to boost the client's self-esteem by telling him how wild and ferocious this world was. How his prowess as a hunter in taking on a lion, leopard, elephant or whatever animal he had come along to kill was commendable. They puffed up their client's ego, making him more of a man in the eyes of his wife. The Zimbabwean hunters were experts in this. I was so used to all the bullshit that these white hunters spouted that it was kind of laughable, and yet, when the same hunter or his wife came along to meet the hippos, I found it extremely hard to remain objective when I listened to them talk.

I would be telling them how Bob would come to my call and show them the evidence when we arrived at the river, as he would come racing down to where we gathered by the edge of the bank. I would see the fear and apprehension not only in some of the clients' eyes but also in the eyes of the white hunter from Zimbabwe. His hand was never far away from his rifle. I never ever carried a weapon to the hippos or, indeed, anywhere in the bush. We did not even own a weapon. Of course, when I had worked as a safari guide I had to have one as a supposed protection for the clients when I took them walking in the bush, but I much preferred to use common sense and not threaten an animal by carrying a rifle. At home we had no need for a weapon.

Then, while we were in front of Bob, these hunters would discuss his trophy value, his teeth and his size. How could they be so insensitive?

Safari clients were not the only visitors. A film crew from Australia asked to come along and film my relationship with the hippos. They agreed to pay filming rights and make a donation to the Trust. As they seemed to be quite genuine and their programme was to promote animal/human relationships as opposed to animals of the 'red in tooth and claw' variety, I agreed.

I had always employed local black people for any jobs concerning the hippos. These people had no permanent jobs and so, on employing them, I would explain that the hippos' welfare and their protection by the Trust allowed me to help them with money at the end of the working week to take home to their families. When I built the second pan, I employed 12 men, with Silas, who was Elliot's younger brother, as a supervisor. Silas had taken over from Elliot after the drought, Elliot having married and moved to a different part of Zimbabwe.

Silas was in his twenties, never having worked for anybody, and I found him to be an ideal assistant and very keen to learn. Patrick still ran our homestead and now with our house Silas could help me quite a lot with general duties. The second pan gave three months' work to the men and at the end of it I was pretty proud of myself, as the only help I'd had from Jean-Roger was in the initial design and advice on how to bulldoze the area. After that, it was totally up to the guys and me. We carried rocks as before from the nearby koppies in wheelbarrows; and this time we did not just cement the bottom and top walls, but had learnt that doing this created leaks and problems. This time we would need to plaster and, as there was no emergency as in the drought, we could take more time to iron out any awkward building moments.

I did have to fire half of the first group of men I employed, as they tried their luck with me. Many Africans, be they white or black, tend to look at women as barefoot and pregnant in the kitchen and not on any kind of equal footing. As a woman you constantly have to prove your worth in a harsh environment. Even then, there are some who will never accept a woman as their employer in a bush environment. It was a hard learning curve, but I needed the men to realise that I would work shoulder to shoulder beside them and try to be their equal. Although my size made it impossible to have the men's strength, at least I got dirty alongside them. Eventually I had a team and we completed the pan and the day came along to fill it with water, this time from our own piping. The piping was laid in a trench we had dug from the pan to the house, a distance of about one-and-a-half kilometres. Seeing the water gradually filling the pan made all the trials and tribulations worth it.

I had various goals for the Trust and I hoped to be able to help hippos in other parts of Zimbabwe, where they may be classified as a 'problem animal'. If a hippo entered private or communal lands in search of food and damaged farmers' crops, the Zimbabwe Parks and Wildlife Management Authority would often be called in to shoot that hippo. My idea was that the Trust would step in and capture and relocate such animals to areas within the Conservancy where suitable habitat existed. Ideas continued to breed in my mind as I learnt more and more about the hippos' behaviour and their needs.

Bob was my hippo guide. He was teaching me so much. If he was in a mating mood his eyes showed his intentions and I would not approach him too closely. Respect was the vital factor of our relationship.

Wish, one of Happy's permanent females, honoured me with a unique experience, which proved to me yet again how the hippos were accepting my presence. Yet it was always the sound of my voice that somehow seemed to be the key to this acceptance.

Wish had given birth to her second calf after the drought, having weaned Flame, her son born in 1993. With her new calf, all fear of me had now vanished. When the calf was just two weeks old Wish came to within four metres of where I was standing next to the river's edge talking to her. She then moved onto her side, allowing her baby to submerge and go to her udder to suckle. This unbelievable behaviour, allowing such close human contact, decided me on the calf's name. He would be known as Trust, a twofold meaning combining this incredible bond between a wild hippo mother and me with the future of the Turgwe Hippo Trust.

TEN

Hunters and heartbreak

The animal side of working for the hippos was always a pleasure and with each day I learnt something new, but the people side was sometimes very hard to understand. People thought because I loved these animals and enjoyed their company that I wasn't a people person. This was not entirely true. I loved being with fellow-minded people and am as interested in human behaviour as in any animal's, but I have found that criticism and insults have often been thrown at me by people who dislike what I try to achieve for animals.

This became most apparent in the hunting world that surrounded us. There was one white guy who was employed by Mokore. Tony was related to the owner and had previously worked in photographic safaris. So, unlike some of the other guys, he had not always been a hunter. He had changed over to the hunting profession as it paid far more and appealed to his character, but he had never been offensive towards me and I gave him the benefit of the doubt.

I had decided upon a new project, which would entail having up to two paying volunteers regularly coming along to stay with me and spend about two weeks helping with projects for the hippos. I would have these volunteers staying over during the time Jean-Roger was away. The Trust had bought a pre-fabricated wood building, which Jean in his time off had turned into a lovely cottage, building on to it an open-plan bathroom with a loo that looking down on the wonderful view of the Turgwe River.

I received a letter from an Australian woman, Sharon Pincott, who had read in a magazine of my work with the hippos and was interested in a voluntary position. She would become my first paying volunteer. She had already worked with cheetahs in Namibia and chimpanzees in Uganda, and was prepared to make a decent donation and pay for accommodation and food. She had been to Zimbabwe before and had made some good friends, one being the warden of Hwange National Park, so she was not a total novice to the bush.

I picked her up from a safari camp in the south of the Conservancy to where she had managed to hitch a lift. She was a high-flying IT executive, financially secure but wanting to do something more with her life. She had caught the African bug, falling in love with not just the wilderness but also having a very similar dream to my own. I had mentioned to Tony that she was coming along and was to be my first volunteer, and so I hoped the hippos and I would make a favourable impression.

At the time of Sharon's arrival, I had an awful lot going on in my personal life. Jean-Roger's father had recently died. Jean had flown back to France after being called by his sister, who told him that his father was dying. Sadly, his father died while Jean was still in the plane and about to arrive in Lyon. Jean had come back home a changed man, his grief tightly wrapped up, and I was not allowed to console him. We had not been in a position financially for both of us to return to France. In fact, Jean's sister had paid for his ticket and I think being alone over there had been very hard for him. As the eldest, he'd had to make most of the funeral arrangements. So I had an unhappy husband who was not at all himself and at the same time the important role of being with Sharon, as well as my plans for a new building project for the hippos.

Sharon fitted in well, adoring the monkeys, especially Boon the troop leader. Much to my astonishment, Arthur Warthog, who now allowed me to touch him, let Sharon stroke his head at the back door. Arthur had been a permanent evening visitor ever since the drought days. Sharon had an instant empathy with animals.

At times Arthur would not come along during the rainy season, but in the winter months he could be found every night eating his cubes at the back door. One evening I accidentally knocked his large lower wart as I was laying out his food. Instead of lunging at me, like a wild warthog would normally do, he pushed the full weight of his head against my hand. It was quite obvious what he was asking for – a scratch. I obliged and this became a nightly affair. Arthur would eat and then ask for his scratch and a rub.

Another day he collapsed in front of me, lying on his side and presenting his by-now rather fat belly. I gingerly leant down and rubbed his tummy. Well, this was exactly what he had wanted me to do. This now had to be an evening event, as after eating he would collapse in front of me, demanding the highly desired tummy rub. I loved Arthur and he meant as much to me as the hippos.

The following day, after Sharon had stroked Arthur, we took a hike of a few kilometres since I needed to look at the area where I felt the Trust should help with the building of a new weir. There was a small river there that always dried up during the winter and I thought that if we paid for some of the cement it would help Mokore, the owners of that piece of land, to once again look upon the Trust favourably. The weir would contain water during the dry season and give the hippos another pool area.

They had increased in number since the drought, but their own pools were minimal owing to the sand and silt clogging up many parts of the Turgwe every year during the rains, when it was washed downstream from the communal lands that bordered the Conservancy. In places, erosion of the riverbanks and crop cultivation had caused this immense amount of sand and silt to gradually find its way into the hippos' habitat. The weir would be yet another artificial cemented wall, but if built with the environment in mind it could not only sustain the hippos but also provide all the other animals in the area with a new water source during the dry period.

On arriving back at the house, we were met by Silas carrying the raw and bloody thigh of a warthog.

I stopped in my tracks and stared. Hesitantly, he came over.

'Tony just came here. He said this is Arthur and that he had just killed him.'

Every hunter in the area knew that there were two animals that influenced me more than any other and that I loved them with all of my being. One was Bob, the other Arthur. Now Silas was telling me that Tony had shot Arthur and this lump of bloody meat was him. I had the presence of mind to examine the thigh and realised that Tony was lying. It was far too small to be Arthur, but even so, it had been brought to my home, either to fool me or as some kind of sick joke.

I was shattered. Tony, out of all the white boys training to be professional hunters, had always been the most reasonable one. He talked of other things instead of just hunting and killing. Most of the men and boys were forever hurting me with their barbed comments about having just shot Bob, or in their behaviour when coming along with clients. The boys and men pumped their clients full of talk about the mad girl who communicated with hippos, the ultimate 'bunny hugger'.

This event pushed me close to the edge. I let rip in strong language to nobody in particular, telling Sharon I was going to drive to Humani to phone Jean-Roger as I had had enough. She was, I am sure, wishing she were somewhere else at that particular moment.

I drove those 19 kilometres in record time, taking out my anger on our poor old pickup truck, pushing her to her limits, my foot flat on the accelerator. Barging into Roger's house and finding it full, as usual, of his white staff, all of them watching cricket on his satellite television, I forgot my manners, demanding of Sarah, his daughter, to use their phone.

I finally got hold of Jean in Bulawayo, where he was living with a colleague in a suburb. Between sobs, I explained what Tony had done. I asked him whether what I was trying to achieve here was worth it. Surely these hunters would at some stage shoot Arthur and Bob, or some of the hippos, and everything I was working for would be for nothing.

Jean calmed me down, trying to restore some pride and confidence, but I was way over the top, tired of the constant battle to keep the Trust going and raise funds. Carrying out projects and at the same time having to put up with behaviour like Tony's was too much. I was overwrought, but eventually Jean told me he would drive all the way back the following day. He was not pleased and his tone was curt, but I was his wife and I think he realised that this latest business was really the last straw.

Jean drove in the next evening. His face was expressionless and there was no welcoming embrace. He told me he had sorted out Tony and a few more guys who had been over at the Mokore camp, telling them that in future if they had a problem with me they should first talk to him about it and leave me in peace. This was the first time in nine years that I had asked Jean to intervene on my behalf and I hoped it would be the last. Apparently the boys were very deferential to Jean-Roger, with Tony, who was over two metres tall and no weakling, cowering when Jean shouted at him.

Jean informed me that he was going to South Africa on his next leave and so would not see me for over eight weeks. He said he had business there. I knew immediately he was lying, but being so emotionally drained and tired I didn't question him. I knew, though, that for the first time my marriage was on shaky grounds. But I still had Sharon staying and so could not fall apart.

I achieved this with difficulty. When the day came to drop her off at Senuko she left with a smile, but I wondered what she really thought. She went on to follow her own dream. She now runs a project in Zimbabwe studying the elephants of Hwange, known as the President's Herd. Through her knowledge of these highly intelligent animals, Sharon has managed to have physical contact with some of the wild elephants. From her vehicle she can touch quite a few of the females. Her love for the elephants equals my own for the hippos.

Another film production company had been in contact with me for nearly a year. They wanted to film my relationship with Bob as they felt it would make an interesting documentary. The plan was that it would be filmed over several months, and on the phone at Humani we had had many conversations. I had agreed to the requests of the English producer, a woman who certainly seemed to be very dominant in her own field.

Bob and his family were so amazing these days that all I had to do was call his name and he would move to where I was standing by the river's edge and then show off to whomever I took along to meet him. He would gape, opening his mouth in a huge display of all of his canines. At times you could even count his back molars, so impressive was his wide-mouthed stance. He would then close his mouth, crash his head back into the water and do it all over again. It appeared to be a kind of game and he was having fun, as anyone could see. For tourists and the media alike this made our relationship even more special. So with the hippos all was wonderful, but in my personal life everything was grinding to a halt.

Then Jean told me he had met another woman and that he would not be coming home again.

To say that I fell into total despair is an understatement. I took stock of our relationship, realizing that I was as much at fault as he. I hadn't been unfaithful, but I had been in another way. 'My hippos', as they were called locally, had taken over my life. I had warned Jean in the early days of our courtship that the one thing that mattered to me more than anything or anyone was animals. If he married me he had to understand that my priorities would always be first and foremost any animals I was connected to. I had said at the time that an animal was not a human and so nothing to be jealous of. He had laughed and told me not to worry. As long as it wasn't children I wanted, he could handle anything.

Why was it that I now faced losing my marriage because of my dedication to a family of hippos? What was I to do?

I had spent my entire childhood dreaming of working with animals and that goal had grown with me. I was now doing exactly this, working in conservation for the protection of not just the hippos but of all the wild animals that surrounded our home. As my mother had said, 'Look after what is in your own garden.' The one hippo pool was actually on our property.

During all of these problems, yet another hunter employed first at Humani and later at Mokore was really working against everything I was trying to achieve. Frikkie was like a bad smell in his obnoxious ways. He would often bring his clients to hunt right next to our property, crossing over the border (up to which he was allowed to operate).

Those not involved with the hunting world or who have not seen it on the ground often think it is an admirable old activity from colonial days. In Southern Africa, where the policy of sustainable utilization is the foremost way that people 'manage' wildlife, hunting is part and parcel of this policy. In Kenya, thanks to visionaries like Richard Leakey, there is a far superior attitude; they have banned sport hunting. The Kenyan government had been advised by Leakey to burn stockpiles of elephant ivory to make a public statement, saying no to the sale of ivory and the massacre of Africa's elephant herds.

Frikkie was the epitome of an unethical hunter, a man who would tell his clients long stories into the night of the dangers of wild animals and in this way boasting of his own prowess. He deliberately upset the animals that he hunted with clients, making the animal appear aggressive and dangerous. In reality, he just pushed the animal's tolerance level by getting too close to its comfort zone and thus provoking aggression. His radio call sign said it all: Blood.

When we had first met I had been about to go out riding with Julia Whittall and a couple of her friends. She kept over 25 horses on Humani as she hoped to start a horse-riding safari business, eventually involving her daughter, Belinda. Of the Whittalls, Julia, being of English background, was the one I could relate to the best. She was highly intelligent and very welcoming in the true blue British way. Once in a while, just to get a break from being with the hippos all day, I would arrange to ride with her in the bush. There is a real pleasure in being on horseback in a wild terrain. The animals no longer fear man, as they relate to you and the horse as one. It is easy to get up close to the animal without causing disturbance and I loved nothing more than to ride for pleasure.

On this particular day, I was to meet Frikkie for the first time. I should have followed my instincts. He rode a horse without kindness. Holding the reins far too tight, sawing at the mouth, he used his legs as a weapon instead of as a guide. It was like watching a robot on a horse. Yet he spoke pleasantly on that day and I tried not to look at his actions but just listen to his words. I was to learn in later years that my first instincts about the man could not have been more correct: he was a control freak, a killer and an evil personality.

I had tried to be civil with all of the hunters, but it did not last for long. They were placing unrelenting pressure on the places where the hippos lived and around our home. They had thousands of hectares to hunt in, but for some reason they had to come and shoot the animals where I was looking after the hippos. Time and time again, Bob and his family would be happily asleep on the sandbank adjacent to their river pool, large ones and little ones all huddled up next to each other, snoozing soundly. I would be sitting peacefully nearby when the report of a rifle shot, and often more than one, would explode on the opposite riverbank, directly behind the hippos. The hippos, as if one animal, would panic and charge straight back into the water. The times that Bob in his flight or even one of the cows nearly knocked over a tiny new baby were more numerous than I could count.

I had tried going over to the main hunting camp and explaining to the owners that this kind of behaviour was counter-productive. By frightening the animals in such a way it would not be long before a panicked adult killed one of the calves by accident. Surely, with all the places they hunted in, they could leave the tiny area of our home and the hippos' pool hunt-free? My words fell upon deaf ears. Frikkie in particular seemed to step up his hunting with clients around the hippos' pools.

At that time my relationship with the hippos had grown to such an extent that even Blackface had calmed down considerably. The crocodiles living in the river also acted as if they knew me. Although I studied the hippos' behaviour I could not help but be interested in the lives of all the other animals using the river and the hippos' pools. The crocodiles lived with the hippos in relative harmony; in some ways there was a kind of symbiotic relationship.

Many photographic safari clients asked me about the dangers of crocodiles and how aggressive they were towards hippos, yet a lot of what I seemed to witness were positive things. I managed on several occasions to photograph and film hippos grooming crocodiles.

It is completely normal for a hippo to groom another hippo, a behaviour that can be seen clearly when they are on land during the winter months. A juvenile normally licks the hide of another adult at the hindquarter area – usually the bull, but sometimes its own mother. The youngster will lick at the hide for up to 15 minutes and at the end of this he or she will give a huge gape, the saliva that has built up from this exercise dripping from the hippo's opened mouth.

I would also watch regularly, year after year, hippos grooming crocodiles.

The hippo would be on its way out of the water onto a sandbank where a crocodile had already found a sunny spot to warm up in. In winter, crocodiles will leave the water to let their bodies heat up in the sunshine and will lie on the sand all day during the coldest months. The hippo would approach the crocodile. At first the hippo would sniff the crocodile with his nose, moving around the lower end of the crocodile, mainly its tail area. The hippo would then start licking this area of the crocodile, often for as long as when grooming another hippo. They would also give a huge gape after some minutes of licking and then resume. All of the time that the hippo groomed the crocodile it would lie there apparently enjoying the attention, as not once did I see a crocodile object to this behaviour and try to move off. If a crocodile gets angry it will emit a roar or a loud hiss. This never happened during these grooming sessions.

I was very curious as to why the hippos did this.

When I was a little girl of five, my mother's husband, Jack, moved to Iran for work reasons and my mother and I joined him there for a year and a half. Our home was rather grand. As an engineer, his company provided him with a large house with staff and a beautiful swimming pool. A natural stream ran into it and there I spent many hours collecting live frogs. At the end of the day I would smuggle them into my bedroom, setting them free on the floor so that I could continue to watch their antics and learn about their ways. This came to an abrupt end when one evening my mother was tucking me in and a frog leapt from the pillow on to the sheets. Then, as if on cue, frogs came leaping out from every hiding place, be it under the bed or from behind the cupboards.

Later, after Jack had died in Iran, we returned to England and moved to the Buckinghamshire countryside. As an only child I would amuse myself for hours walking in the woods, finding streams filled with stickleback and minnow fish and whiling away the time watching them. Nature was my constant companion and if ever my mother needed to find me all she had to do was walk outside and look for the nearest animal activity. As a teenager, I would often sit in public places like railway stations and watch people. Their behaviour also fascinated me. I would make up little stories in my head as I saw a loved one kiss another, or friends laughing as they boarded a train. My favourite word then as it is now was 'Why?'

So I asked myself, why did the hippos groom crocodiles? Why did they save other animals in the river?

With the crocodiles, I did have a couple of theories.

The importance of hippos' sense of smell made me believe that grooming came about owing to a scentrelated trigger. When grooming another hippo, they always groomed the hindquarter area and ap peared to spend more time grooming the bull or another young male hippo. Males and the odd dominant female spray their dung when they defecate, as in the San people's fish story. When swishing their tails to launch the dung on to some nearby protrusion like a boulder or a bush, a lot of it ends up flying about and sometimes lands on their own bottoms. Young males in a subservient position will approach a bull by slinking next to the bull with a lowered body movement. As he defecates onto one of his mounds of dung, they often get sprayed as well.

At times crocodiles can be found lying near one of these regularly sprayed-upon bushes or boulders. If a bull hippo sprays, the crocodile will also be covered in dung. Within the river, crocodiles spend a lot of time at the bottom of the water and the dung of hippos can stick to the serrated edges of the crocodiles' tails. The crocodile, like the bull hippo, will now have the scent of hippo dung all around its tail area. Perhaps this is what attracts a hippo to groom it: its smelling like one of his own. It could also be due to some kind of secretion on the crocodile's leathery hide that might attract their taste buds.

Bob and I had made some kind of connection, as he began to warn me of danger lurking in the Turgwe's depths. At first I believed it to be just a coincidence, but I was to learn there are rarely coincidences in nature. There is normally a good reason why an animal behaves in a particular way. Sitting watching the hippos for hours on end I easily fell into a light slumber, seduced by a combination of the heat and the constant buzzing of insects, with the occasional splash and plop of a leaping fish. This, together with the gentle breathing noise of dozing hippos, made it easy to forget to pay attention to the water. Crocodiles have bucketloads of patience and they watch for routine behaviour by animals. I, too, became a regular routine as they grew accustomed to my daily visits to the hippos.

The first time Bob intervened I had a huge fright.

It had been well over two years since he had last charged at me. To have him come full steam directly towards where I sat, without his customary happy look, had really given me a moment of alarm, mixed with sadness that he had returned to his old ways. But before I even had time to run to a nearby tree I realised it was not me at all that he was charging.

Directly to my left, a huge crocodile surfaced. It was more than three-and-a-half metres in length and its intentions were clear: it had been stalking me. As Bob charged at it the crocodile propelled itself away as fast as it could by swiping at the water with its tail. Bob was in hot pursuit. Could Bob now regard me as part of the pod? Or was it coincidence? After Bob had repeated this behaviour on four occasions, I realised that it was no mere chance. He really seemed to want to protect me like he did the other animals using the river.

Over time the crocodiles, just like the hippos, became used to my voice and studiously began to ignore me. One in particular became quite my favourite. His dark skin announced his gender, as normally the darker-shaded crocodiles are the males. He had a favourite rock that he would be found lying upon and if I spoke to him as with the hippos he remained on his rock without taking fright and returning to his river home.

One morning I had a class of local schoolchildren coming to our home. At that time an Australian girl, Nicky, was helping out at Humani and her passion was to help the children in any way that she could. She had suggested they visit for a safari, which I readily agreed to.

The idea was to explain to them first the importance of hippos in the ecosystem and then take them along to meet Bob and the rest of the family. Nicky had suggested that after the trip they all draw a hippo and write a short essay on hippos, and then we would have a competition for the best story and the nicest drawing and give the kids a Turgwe hippo T-shirt as the prize. The children, aged between 10 and 12, were very excited and extremely well behaved throughout the entire day's visit, telling me that their favourite moment was seeing Bob moving towards us at speed when I called his name. They also were fascinated by the crocodile on the rock and on our walk back to camp, one boy, Epheas, pointed out a huge python curled up sleeping underneath a bush. It was a huge success and Nicky and I planned to carry on with other children while she remained at the school.

After they had left, I decided to go back to the hippos to thank Bob and the crocodile for being such wonderful ambassadors.

As I reached the bank and began the descent to the pool, a shot was fired, then another.

I froze, my heart hammering in my chest. I imagined an animal lying dead and wondered if it was a kudu or an impala that earlier in the day I had met on my walk. All the animals that shared our lives within the riverine area were regular visitors and so I knew each of them as individual animals, and those that lived in herds I would recognise by the ram or bull that led them. I had noted different things about all of them: one kudu with a broken horn, another bushbuck whiter than others of her kind and similar signs of their differences.

I knew the shots had come from the direction of the river, so my fears for the hippos were at maximum pitch as I ran towards the pool. There I found Frikkie and an American client with two trackers. They had a huge length of rope with a hook attached and were pulling something from the water.

For a second I feared for my hippos, but realised that four men could never drag a hippo from the river. Then I saw it was a crocodile, and not just any crocodile. It was the dark male from the rock. Through his lack of fear of my presence and having just had a visit from 15 schoolchildren, he had become too blasé around humans. Now he had paid the ultimate price. Frikkie had let his client shoot him. How on earth could they call this sport? That crocodile had been lying on his rock not more than four metres from the bank. It would have been like shooting at a stationary target.

The guilt I felt at that moment was tremendous. Surely, if the crocodile had not become used to my daily visits he would never have stayed lying on a rock in the sun when humans came along? Now he was dead and it was all my fault. Frikkie was on the opposite bank on the Mokore side of the river and, on seeing me standing there, gave one of his smirks and saluted me in a dismissive way. His client seemed somewhat surprised to see a woman in the bush unarmed, but Frikkie said something to the guy and the two of them looked at me and laughed and continued to pull the poor crocodile towards the bank. I had to leave, as I knew if I approached them my temper would take over and then all hell would break loose.

Occasionally in the past I had lost my temper with him and it had always backfired. He would go back to Mokore with big stories about the mad woman with the hippos and how she was disrupting his hunts and upsetting the clients. This was counter-productive in trying to instil in the owners the conviction that the hippos were worth more to them alive than dead, and I always lived with the fear that they would shoot one for a trophy. I had to walk on eggshells and yet my emotions at that moment were right up there. If I could have shot Frikkie right then I might have felt some relief. He was a lazy hunter and a man who would do anything to get the trophy for the client. The dollars he received as a tip would be much higher than his salary.

I walked back to camp reflecting on the life I led. Here I was, yes, living my dream, but would it be at the expense of my marriage and even my sanity?

I had learnt by now that it was by talking to the hippos that I had become accepted. I had learnt how they responded to words. I had learnt that this was the way they distinguished humans from each other. Even Bob, so familiar with me, would not recognise me as an individual human if I did not talk to him. Over time, and with much trial, error and observation, I had learnt the intonation to tell the hippos that it was me approaching, the tiny inflection that told them they could come closer, the soothing call to placate a hippo I had startled by accident, and who might have been considering a charge. There was intelligence behind their eyes, and I felt as if I was getting closer and closer to this as the time passed. Yet was I sealing their fate like I had with the crocodile? Would they lose their fear of humans, only to let Frikkie or another like him end their lives?

I could not understand why the hunters always had to hunt right in our area. They were not allowed to hunt directly in front of us as that was our own land, but surely they could leave the animals around the hippos and the hippos themselves alone?

But some people are exceedingly greedy and, like Frikkie, lazy. It was easy to shoot a 'tame' crocodile. The other crocodiles further up- and downstream in the river would demand more effort on his part. He wanted that tip from the client and most of the clients who came to hunt were content to get their trophy with as little work as possible on their part. They would go home with stories of bravado and how they walked for hours tracking the animal they had killed, but the reality often was quite different.

Little did I know as I sat in camp that night, feeling the pain of the loss of the dark crocodile and running over and over again in my mind the negatives of what had happened, that these problems would appear minor compared with what soon would occur.

ELEVEN

The flood

I knew I had to face my crumbling emotional life and find out if Jean-Roger wanted to continue with our relationship. In one way I was afraid to confront him in case he made the decision to quit, and in another I knew I could not continue working with the hippos with my heart in so much turmoil.

I was being pressurized by the TV production crew to make the documentary that had been discussed for a long period now and they wanted an answer. The producer had the idea that the crew would live with me for a few weeks every couple of months over perhaps one year and film my relationship with the hippos. However, if Jean and I were to survive his infidelity and find each other again, it would be impossible with a crew around the home invading our privacy.

I drove over to Humani to phone the producer and tell her of my decision. At first very polite and kind, she tried reasoning with me, telling me how her own marriage had collapsed due to the career she had chosen. She said being divorced had made her a lot happier and that this film could be the making of the Turgwe Hippo Trust. The publicity it brought in would help me to help the hippos. I would be able to set into motion many of the plans for them that I had in mind. She told me not to close the door and to go home and think about it.

I returned to the camp and headed for Bob, as I knew I could talk to him about my troubles. No longer did he show any aggression with me. He enjoyed my daily visits, or that was how it appeared. He always came close to me when I called his name and would bring along the rest of the family. His gaping and showing off for the tourists made their trip to the Trust the best part of their safari, or so they told me, and they all made donations or bought merchandise. Some adopted a hippo, Bob being the favourite, even beating adoptions of his younger son, Tembia.

I cried, unleashing all the pent-up emotions that Africa somehow stores inside your body. The fears for the hippos' safety thanks to the hunters, the pressure of constantly trying to find funds for projects for their benefit and, most importantly, tears for my marriage. Jean-Roger, I believed, was in many ways my soulmate. He had given up his life as a high-flying oil geologist to follow his wife to Africa. He and I were friends in so many ways, with the added bonus of being married. We never ran out of conversation, he always made me laugh and normally we agreed to disagree on subjects that he was not interested in.

Though I knew Bob could not understand my words, perhaps there was something in the tone of my voice that conveyed how I felt, for he came closer than I could ever remember until he was only half a metre from where I sat at the river's edge. Tembia, too, started coming a lot closer, curious at this human who was a friend of his father. I told them it was just us now, but that I would never leave. These two magnificent animals, the supposed biggest killers of man, were commiserating with me, of this I was 100 per cent sure.

I knew that my passion for the hippos and putting them before our relationship was half of the problem with Jean and me. The other factor, I believed, was the death of his father. This had been the catalyst for his affair, as the woman in question had been there for him when I was hundreds of kilometres away. She was very attractive, an independent woman, a stills photographer for movie productions in South Africa. A typical Dane, tall, blue-eyed, with long blonde hair. As I was but a pup joint, as Jean always called me, she was totally different in every way. She lived with a guy and had paid to fly Jean down to South Africa and put him up in a five-star hotel so that they could be together. What man could say no to such an offer?

He was in such a mess emotionally at that time that even his appearance had changed. He had grown a beard and looked quite awful, with dark circles under his eyes. He had lost weight and this time it was not due to malaria.

Jean and I cut the apple in two. Our futures discussed amid tears, we eventually decided on a trial period of six months back together again. Jean would give up his work, reasoning that if it worked out he would have to find some other way to make a living so that he could live at Hippo Haven, as we had called our home. He said he wanted to rekindle our love and our life together. If it did not work, he would leave Zimbabwe anyway, probably for South Africa. We both, though, believed in our marriage vows and what had happened had come as quite a shock to his friends in France and some of my own back in England.

It seemed as though in the First World, as soon as things imploded people just moved on and called it quits. We wanted more for ourselves and thought it best to try to give it another go. For my part, I promised to cut down on my work with the hippos. Jean-Roger was adamant that I should not stop the Turgwe Hippo Trust in case things did not pan out, but he was happy when I told him I would give up the tourists and the TV production company and just be with him at home. I would continue studying the hippos and organizing the hippo adoptions to raise money for projects, but these would be projects purely for the hippos' sake that did not involve having loads of people at our home.

The next day I phoned the producer.

'Sorry, I have to stick to my original decision. I have to cancel this programme. My husband and I need to work at our marriage. I am dreadfully sorry to let you down, but I am afraid I have to say no.'

To give her credit, she tried everything from kindness to threats, but she rubbed me the wrong way by saying that no man was worth this and that there were plenty more fish in the sea. Here I was trying to work something out between my marriage and the hippos with not one thought for another man in my life. I firmly said no thank you and goodbye, aware that I had rather blotted my copybook.

I then started tidying up my life, removing all the hippo merchandise from the volunteers' cottage and taking it over to Jane, so she could sell it in her store. The Trust would get the proceeds, minus a percentage to her. I rang and radioed all the safari operators in the Conservancy saying that I would no longer be available to take their clients to the hippos. This shocked quite a few of them, but I didn't give them a chance to argue. I knew I couldn't stop the Adopt a Hippo scheme, as it was the Trust's main bread and butter and also made a lot of people very happy.

I had not met many of the hippo supporters, as I called them. They all lived overseas, but had heard about the Trust through magazines or newspaper articles or even watched Bob on television. They would write to me and tell me how my life and what I wrote about the hippos made their own problems seem so small and that I inspired many of them. They loved the hippo that they had adopted, and on the odd occasion when a hippo left the family, or worse still, died naturally, they were as devastated as I was when I wrote to tell them the news. I couldn't let them down. Some of them had been supporting the hippos as adoptive parents for several years.

Jean came home and, as we had chosen each other for better or worse, we both hoped that just by being in this wonderfully pure and spiritual place our love and marriage could be restored. We would put our heads together to sort out the mess.

Africa, though, had other plans for us.

Within one month of Jean's coming home, a terrible cyclone hit the Mozambique interior, causing massive flooding. People and their livestock drowned and thousands of Mozambicans were left homeless. Rumours began to circulate that our area could catch the tail of the cyclone; then the rumours became reality.

The flood that hit the Turgwe in February was beyond anything we had ever seen.

We were both fast asleep in the gazebo as we still slept there, preferring the fresh air and the outside environment to being in the house's bedroom. A deep rumbling roar had awoken me and I shook Jean awake. The roar was becoming so loud that I had to raise my voice. It was a pitch-dark night without a single star to light the way. The crash and crack of trees being uprooted seemed magnified in the darkness – and then we heard the sound of rushing waters roaring below us.

In the dark of the night it was really frightening. My first thoughts as always were for the animals, especially the hippos. Surely, if this flood was as ferocious as it sounded, even they would not have got away in time? No animal could stand up to that amount of water, not even a hippo. Water must be pouring into the Turgwe from every single tributary. As the roar of the waters intensified we were shouting at each other to be heard.

For a few minutes the sheer volume of noise cast away any sensible thoughts, but then I leapt from the bed. Hurriedly pulling on my clothes I shouted to Jean. 'Will we be swamped? Is it possible for this river to run as high as the top of the bank? Is the gazebo going to be swept away?'

A million questions and no answer. Jean-Roger had already run off towards Silas's house. I realised he must have gone to pull out the river pump before we lost it.

Fortunately, dawn began to break. I ran to check on the cats, which seemed totally unconcerned. At least inside the house you could hear yourself think, as the rock walls acted as insulation against the thundering of the river below. The house was about seven metres away from the riverbank. As only the gazebo had been built near the bank I removed the chairs in the gazebo. On Jean's return we took out the bed, moving it into the house, so at least if the bank collapsed or the waters rose to the very top we would salvage the furniture.

As it became lighter, the voice of a river in full flood grew.

Our first sight of the Turgwe was unforgettable. This medium-sized river had become an almighty sea of waves as the waters swelled over rocks and trees. It had risen more than 18 metres and I knew that nothing could survive such a torrent. Huge trees were swept along, rocking and rolling over submerged rocks. Waves of over six metres high smashed over the same submerged boulders. I asked in my head for the hippos to be far from any danger. I was afraid to look at the water in case I saw an animal swept into its embrace. Nothing could save anyone caught up in such a fast-flowing mass of destruction. Two new hippo calves, Tacha and Misty, were less than two months old, but even Bob would be unable to manoeuvre in such a torrent.

In previous years the Turgwe flooded with each rainy season. Occasionally I would come across Bob during those floods. He would be tucked up against a bank with the whites of his eyes showing, just like a frightened horse. He did not venture into the main current, as even with his three tons I am sure he would have been hard-pressed to stay in one place. The current would have swept him along.

This was like no other flood and, as the waters steadily rose, the markers we had taken on the trees left in the river became submerged and we had to take a new marking point. The water was not going down at all. It was now not more than four-and-a-half metres from the top of the bank. Most of the large trees that had stood for years in the river system had toppled and been swept away.

I wondered if the people living some 50 kilometres upstream had survived, as many of them built their brick and mud thatched huts very close to the banks of the river. Fortunately, Silas's family lived inland, but he suspected that many huts would be swept away.

I had a desperate urge to try to find the hippos. Jean said he would stay at home to keep an eye on the steadily rising water, but warned me to be extra careful as any riverbanks might crumble. The pressure of the water pushing against the soil could easily weaken them.

It was impossible to take the normal route along the riverbank as all the paths were under 15 to 18 metres of a brown sea of fast-flowing, froth-covered water. The river had a somewhat hypnotic effect so that I constantly had to check myself from being pulled by vision alone towards the current. Less than a kilometre later, I reached the Chichindwi mouth where it usually joined the Turgwe. It was no longer recognizable. Now it covered an inland area more than four times its normal size. It would be impossible to cross this normally tiny river and I had to halt my search for the hippos. I tried to gauge the depth with a long stick, but it was way deeper than the stick and the length of my arm, so I had no option but to return home.

The Conservancy had allowed us the previous year to have our radio system join up with theirs. At home, Jean radioed around to find out if other areas had had heavy rains. He learnt that two safari camps built near small river systems like the Chichindwi had been flooded, with all the furniture, bedding and everything else in the chalets washed into the river. Fortunately, because of the time of the year there had been no loss of life. It was not the tourist season and so the camps had been empty apart from one or two guards, who were OK.

Over at Humani the three main homesteads had river water in their gardens. The Turgwe's floodwaters had extended to their homes for the first time in the Whittalls' memory. About 800 metres between river and home were normally sufficient to keep any floods at bay, but not this year.

Julia's husband, Richard, had taken their small rowing boat into the flooded plains, managing to rescue sheep stranded on a rapidly flooding bush island. They had passed three partly submerged trees teeming with rodents and snakes. Larger mammals had taken to higher ground, but they had seen the floating carcasses of snakes, tortoises and some small antelope. Half of the safari camps close to river systems had lost all their pumps and equipment that they used to get water from the river. We had been lucky, as Jean had built a pulley system when putting in our pump and so had been able to remove it without getting close to the waters. He had removed the main pump down in the riverbed when he had heard about the floods in Mozambique.

Three man-made weirs built to cross the river system, including one into which the Trust had put over 30 tons of cement, had been breached or broken. The only weir that had survived was the one I called Bob's weir pool, as it was out of the main current of the Turgwe. This weir wall was on our own tiny piece of land, but the wall crossed the river in the one channel. In that place the river split into two, with the main current across from the hippos' bush island. These weirs provided pools in the dry season for the hippos. Now they would have only one dry season pool instead of four.

We heard that the cemented causeway that crossed the Turgwe River, the access route to the north of the Conservancy and the road out to Harare, had been washed away. The other exit point in the south, which entailed crossing another river, the Mkwasine, had had another bridge smashed and was not at all crossable. It was under a mass of raging water, just like it was at home.

We were trapped.

We and everyone else living in the south of the Conservancy now had no exit by road to either the north or the south. The only way out would be by using a boat and having someone pick you up on the other side, but even a boat could not be used while the waters were so dangerous. We knew the Whittalls had a couple of boats and many friends and contacts in the Chiredzi area but, needless to say, we had neither!

I tried to look on the bright side, as only three days previously we had been to Chiredzi and bought our monthly shopping. I could not, though, look on the bright side for the hippos. I was deeply worried about them.

The river finally stopped rising almost three metres from the top of our bank; the gazebo would survive. The outside buildings used to store fuel, tools and all the paraphernalia one accumulates for living in the bush were also fine. The wild animals had become noticeable by their absence. At first I feared that many had drowned, but then, gradually, all the old favourites started to reappear.

Arthur and his mate Jeannie and their four piglets pitched up in broad daylight, as if to prove to me that they were all OK and let me check them out properly. Steyl and her kudu family, the familiar waterbucks and bushbucks that normally lived in the river were OK. It was only the hippos I had not seen and that became a daily worry, as I had not heard even one call or the voice of my beautiful Bob.

Finally, five weeks after that first night, when we were down to absolutely the last remnants of food and trying to ration Silas and ourselves, I took a walk back to the Chichindwi mouth. There to my relief were several hippos, all tightly packed up against the bank. I moved in as close as I dared. I was afraid of startling them and having the calves, of which I could see at least one, swept into the faster flowing waters of the main Turgwe channel.

There were Tembia, Cheeky, Blackface and Lace, Abe and her tiny calf, Tacha, who was only six weeks old, and right in the middle of them was my magnificent Bob. Only seven hippos when there should have been 15 but, surely, if tiny Tacha had survived, the other eight must be OK.

For the next couple of hours I sat as close as I could without worrying them. The roar of the Turgwe was still loud and I could not talk to them as I normally would, so I preferred to remain hidden and just watch how they fared. Lace had two new large cuts on her hide; one of these wept blood but it was not life threatening. Blackface's back, or at least the part of it that I could see, was as scratched as if a lion had leapt upon her. The criss-cross of scratches was not deep, but it made her look somewhat battered. I assumed it must have been from debris knocking against her wherever she had taken refuge. Tacha, the youngest, actually had the fewest wounds. I believed her mother, Abe, who is very gentle and protective, must have placed her in such a position during the main floods that nothing had touched her. She was full of life. I had my heart in my mouth more than once when she tried to move away from the bank towards the fast-flowing current to investigate, but Abe always forestalled her by shoving her back, using her bulk to keep the baby safe.

Bob had a huge cut near one eye, but other than that he looked fine. At one stage he ventured into the main channel, the current dragging this huge bull along, but he just went with the flow, waiting until he could pull himself out and push himself back towards the bank. For a few moments I had felt quite faint watching his struggle. Once he reached the bank he hugged it while he ponderously resisted the current and returned once more to his family. None of the others had attempted to follow him so I felt sure this had been a trial run, so to speak. Obviously it was not safe. It had taken Bob with all his great girth over 30 minutes just to return to his family.

On the sixth week of the flood we heard on radio that they had managed to fix the Mkwasine bridge 80 kilometres to the south, which meant that if we could negotiate the dirt roads from home back to the main Conservancy road we would be able to drive out and restock our larder.

Jean had tried once or twice to drive out, but the dirt road had been under more than half a metre of water, so it had been pointless to attempt a trip to Jane's store. She would have some basic food for the locals – maize meal, cooking oil, sugar and beans – but it had not been worth it. If our vehicle got stuck, nobody would have been able to come and help us. We did not have a four-by-four, only our old pickup truck.

Eventually Jean borrowed Silas's bicycle and, by carrying it over his head in places where the road was not negotiable, managed to cycle to Humani on the higher ground. A two-hour bike trip took him just under four hours and another four to come home, but he at least brought back some maize meal, sugar and beans.

A week later Jean managed to drive out to Chiredzi, where he caught up on the news. Sadly, there had been loss of life, with the bodies of ten people who had lived on the communal lands upstream of the Turgwe never being located. They were presumed drowned.

Of the Turgwe hippos, seven out of 24 hippos had disappeared. It was possible that they had moved away altogether to a completely different river system. This had happened before with juvenile females and, as three of the missing animals were adult females and two of them had calves, I tried to convince myself that all had survived. Not a single hippo carcass was reported, while many other animals' carcasses were found once the floods receded. The remains of a couple of cows from the communal lands and other animals were seen, but no hippos. I had to believe that the seven hippos were alive somewhere else.

Cheeky and Tembia were OK, as was Tacha, who had been only six weeks old, so the others had a good chance of having made it. Once again, I kept the pain of not knowing inside and tried to fight off the worry, focusing on those that I could help.

We had our work cut out, which made me extremely thankful that Jean-Roger was back at home with me, even if the circumstances that had brought him home had created another wound that would take a lot of effort to heal. At least now I had his logical brain and strength to help me to work out what to do.

The river and the hippo pools had completely changed in appearance. Three weirs were broken, mountains of sand had been washed into the river and in places the channels were clogged with both silt and sand. No natural hippo pools remained, just the one weir pool. We had to find a way to remove the excess sand.

Happy had lost his pools and was living in the reeds in the main channel, but in the dry seasons he would need a pool as the channel would be too shallow for his family. Jean-Roger had an idea that came from working in the mining world. He remembered that at one mine they had used a sand pump to pump water from the river. Perhaps it could also be used to remove sand. A machine that size would not be practical, as you would need heavy machinery like a tractor and a lot of workers to operate it and the Trust could not afford to buy a tractor. He figured we should try to hire one to find out if it would work in the river to remove the excess sand. Then perhaps he could make a plan to design one that was smaller and easier for us to operate on our own.

Once the plan was set in motion and the hired machine on its way from halfway across the country, we interviewed over 25 men. We took on ten to help us with the work, once again explaining how this work gave them a salary and was only possible because of our trying to save the hippos. In this way we tried to instil into them the realisation that hippos living in the river systems would benefit them and their families financially.

We hired a tractor from Mokore and when the machine arrived we were prepared, with Jean choosing the best place to take it down to the pool, which could only be done by using a four-by-four tractor. The machine weighed over three tons.

Jean-Roger devised a rota system. Each man would enter the river pool for 20 minutes, his job being to hold the huge suction pump pipe while Jean-Roger held the end, sucking out the sand and water. Then it was all drained through 90 metres of PVC pipeline onto dry land, well away from the river system. The amount of sand we hoped to remove had to be far enough away so as not to be washed back into the river in another flood. The water would drain into the soil, but the amount of sand turned out to be even larger than we had thought, creating mountains of up to six metres high as the suction pipe did the trick.

We kept moving the pipes so that the sand hills did not become too much of an eyesore. As the sand was removed, the pool began to gain depth. It was back-breaking work, with Jean-Roger doing the longest stints in the pool. Three guys quit, saying the work was too hard and too dangerous, for as soon as the pool became bigger the crocodiles moved in. Jean-Roger again came up with an answer. They took a roll of chicken wire and each morning they would gingerly get back into the river pool and place the wire upstream of the previous day's work, keeping it taut with wooden pegs cut from the dead trees. The wire could have been knocked over easily if the crocodiles had tried, but the barrier did the job of keeping them at bay. They were not too enamoured of the roaring of the sand pump, which helped to keep them some distance from where each man worked. I did not have the strength to lift either the pipes or the suction part so my job was to keep guard, make sure everyone had drinks and stoke the fire.

It was surprising how cold Jean-Roger became in the water. We had not realised that even though the sun beat down, the water became very cold after a long session. At times Jean left the water with his teeth chattering and his skin an unhealthy-looking shade of blue. None of the workers could do the actual dredging. You constantly had to remove rocks or large lumps of sodden hippo dung blocking the suction pipe and the men were not diligent enough, as we found out, so Jean had to stay in the water for up to 40 minutes at a time, then take a break by the fire for five minutes and return.

Eventually the workers were on a rota system of 15 minutes in the water and one hour off. Jean ended up staying in the water for an hour at a time. Had we not managed to get him a wetsuit, I think he would have ended up with hypothermia. For a guy who was not that bothered about animals he really impressed me with his determination to reconstruct a pool for the hippos.

Our relationship had taken a beating, but there is nothing like shared hard work to stop one dwelling on the negative. By helping the hippos Jean was coming back to me in more ways than one. He was now part of the whole project and at the end of each day he had

113

something to be proud of. Without him I would never have been able to operate the machine or find a worker who would do the work. The only reason they stayed in the pool was because Jean did, or so Silas told us when we all returned to camp. They had told him that the white man had special magic to keep the crocodiles away and so they were prepared to work in the water. None of them knew how to swim.

For the next five weeks Jean-Roger and the men worked at the pool. From a minuscule pool measuring only six metres wide by 30 centimetres deep he created an area of water some 75 metres long, one-and-a-half metres deep in places and around 22 metres wide. Natural river water still flowed into the pool from the channel, but now at least the pool was big enough for the hippos to live in for all of the dry season.

Jean was fine. The work, though, had been exhausting; he had lost almost five kilograms in the five weeks he had worked on the pool. But without his help, the hippos would not have had a dry season pool to live in.

Our relationship once again felt loving. We would hold hands and kiss without anger or resentment. Jean was surely being tested; after all, I was the one dedicated to the hippos and now all he seemed to do was work for me by helping the hippos. Yet he seemed happier than for many years.

Not only was the pump expensive to hire but labour was also required at all times. Jean felt sure he could design something far more user friendly.

We had no idea that our problems had only just begun. The water and sand in the river would be a minor setback compared with the political moves that would change everything.

TWELVE

The land invasion begins

In April 2000, over on Humani so-called war veterans – men who had supposedly fought in the Rhodesian liberation war – were sent into the Conservancy to take over land belonging to white people. Everyone on Humani suddenly found themselves threatened by large mobs of people who had moved onto part of their land. The war vets were accompanied by hundreds of men from the communal lands. They began to build huts all over the bush, cutting down trees.

Then they started killing the wild animals.

On our next trip to Humani we could not believe our eyes. In the centre of the ranch, instead of wild bush and animals there must have been over 100-odd people, all clearing the natural vegetation. The leaders of this movement were easy to recognise as they had bearded, unkempt faces. As we drove past them, they scowled and shook their fists in the salute of Zanu-PF, President Robert Mugabe's political party.

Within days, Roger found delegations of up to 30 people at a time coming to his home, demanding that he and his family leave. The men carried beating sticks cut from hardwood trees, sticks that could easily kill a man. They went about in large gangs and shouted political slogans as they walked. Their eyes were filled with hate and animosity. One man had even put a hand-painted sign on a large baobab tree reading 'Dealers in death'.

Roger said he would stand fast, that his father had pioneered the land. This was more than land to him. His parents were buried in his garden and he had absolutely no intention of turning his back and walking away from his birthplace.

Over the following months his perseverance and commitment to his land and the wildlife were sorely tested. The people who had invaded began a free-for-all grab-and-destroy. There was no police backup for Roger and the other members of his family. The people who had invaded could do exactly what they wanted.

Roger and his game scouts found dead animals by the thousands; animals caught and dying in long lines of wire snares. The land invaders had cut away large sections of the Conservancy fence, using it to make these snares. There were so many of these that his scouts often came across as many as 20 animals dead in just one snare line, counting up to 150 snares when they were removed. So many animals were killed that the people did not even gather up the carcasses; it was wanton destruction. From leopards and painted wild dogs to baby elephants, nothing escaped.

The scouts were completely outnumbered. And then the violence began.

Poachers working with the war vets first attacked the game scouts, using bows and arrows, sticks or any weapon they could get their hands upon. Several scouts were badly wounded. Again, the police did not arrest the people who instigated the attacks. They were all living on Humani and were part of the invasion force. The police told Roger that their hands were tied as it was all politically motivated; they were not allowed to interfere. Law and order had deserted the country and politics now ruled us.

We lived only 19 kilometres from the Humani homesteads, but at that time nobody moved into our area. All of the land invaders were concentrated around the Whittalls' homestead and on land adjacent to their houses.

Then some scouts were abducted by the invaders and very badly beaten up. Roger's headman, a tough character called John, was one of the kidnapped scouts. They beat his feet with wooden sticks and broke a couple of bones. Yet despite the escalating violence, Roger's workers and scouts remained loyal to him. Many of the people living on Roger's land had been working there since his father's time. Humani was as much their home as the Whittalls', and they had no home elsewhere.

Years before the Whittalls had a school built for their workers. Now the people who invaded took it over, moving their own children in. They did not chase out the children already at the school, but they overloaded the classrooms. Instead of 20 children to a class now up to 40 could be found in one tiny room.

The slaughter of the wildlife was beyond imagining.

The small caravan and our open-fronted bedroom and dining area where we lived for the first three years. From our bed I could look up at the stars, or across the Turgwe riverbed at the 'pregnant lady' hill.

Jean-Roger, myself and an African builder, who had never worked on a house, built Hippo Haven. We wanted the house to fit into the surroundings, so we chose natural rocks from the nearby koppies and from the riverbed to build it with. The only professionals were the Ndebele thatchers who came from Bulawayo to thatch the house. Our open-fronted bedroom is in the gazebo.

Courtesy Joan White

I had loved being with animals since I was tiny. Here I am, age seven, at Edinburgh Zoo in Scotland, feeding an African elephant. Jean-Roger, on seeing this photo, said that I have been gutsy all my life!

Courtesy of Hervé Morand

Jean-Roger and me in the Gamba area of Gabon.

Author collection

A dung scattering from young hippo bull, Kuchek, as mentioned in the San story. The hippo, having asked God to live in the river, showed him, by scattering his dung and by swishing his tail in a sideways motion, that there were no fish bones in it. This was proof that the hippo did not eat the fish, and so he would be allowed by God to live in the river.

Courtesy Jean-Roger Paolillo

One minute Blackface would be watching me, the next an immensely powerful and really angry hippo would be rushing straight at me, often just on a whiff of my scent.

My beautiful Bob gaping for everyone to see his splendour.

Bull hippos fighting. Robin is the bull on the left and Tembia (Bob's son) is the smaller bull on the right. Robin won this fight and Tembia eventually found his own territory six kilometres upstream from Hippo Haven, where he lives with his own family.

Courtesy Jean-Roger Paolillo

Here I am delivering food to the hippos' feeding station during the 1992 drought. The stack of hay has the survival ration with molasses added to it and horse cubes at the top of the stack. It is also mixed into the hay. All the hippos would line up next to each other and consume nearly one ton of food every night.

Author collection

The hippos' pan we built in 1992 when the Turgwe River dried up completely. It is sixty centimetres deep at the shallow end, two metres at the deepest and over seven metres wide by twenty-two metres long. It was big enough for all the hippos to be fully submerged in.

1992 drought: Happy the bull, who lived by himself when his own family joined Bob's. He was very dehydrated because he could not use the main pan, as Bob and the rest of the hippos had taken it over. His only water came from a trough with which we supplied him. He drank 200 litres every day. His skin shows each individual hair, not usually seen on a hippo, and the reddish parts are where the sun has burnt his skin.

The birth of a new calf always brings hope and joy. This is Tacha with her two-day-old calf, BonBon.

Tandee, a one-year-old male, grooming a crocodile. Hippos groom each other by licking each other's hindquarters and then, after about fifteen minutes, they gape. Here, at the Turgwe Hippo Trust, I have also watched them regularly groom crocodiles.

Left to right: Silas, with game scouts – Herbert, Chengetai, Libarty and Edson.

Courtesy Jean-Roger Paolillo

February 2003: Paying my respects to my beautiful boy, Bob – dead at the Majekwe weir.

Courtesy Silas Matyarutsa

Jean-Roger and me in the gazebo at our home, Hippo Haven, with the Turgwe River in flood behind us. 31 December 2013 – our wedding anniversary.

For years I had been strongly opposed to the white hunters who made their living from killing animals with their overseas clients. Now, when I visited Humani and saw the amount of dead animals that the game scouts were bringing in from snare lines I felt sick to my stomach.

This was not controlled hunting: this was mass slaughter. The poachers set so many snares that hundreds of animals lay rotting in the wire while the poachers were busy taking down dead animals in another area. They just continued to kill and kill, as if it was a race against time to destroy as much of Humani as possible.

The game scouts were amazing. Some of them did quit, but the nucleus remained loyal, fighting back in any way they could. However, if Roger or any other man's scouts attacked a poacher after the poacher had tried to hurt them, they, the scouts, were the ones who were arrested.

Within a couple of months of these invasions, the people began destroying buildings. One of Roger's hunting safari camps was burnt down. A mob of over 100 people, led by two war veterans, arrived at that camp. The 12 game scouts who lived there valiantly tried to negotiate, but the mob got angry. The men realised they were vastly outnumbered so they turned to leave. The mob, seeing that they were backing down, ran after them.

The scouts ran as the mob gave chase, rapidly catching them up. They fired their weapons into the air but to no avail: the mob kept coming. The scouts realised that if the invaders caught them they would be lucky to get away with their lives. Eventually they shot at the crowd and three people were wounded. They were using bird shot for their shotguns so it should not have done too much damage.

True to the bullying nature of a mob, the minute the 12 men showed courage, even with such small-calibre weapons, they panicked. They stopped giving chase and ran off in the opposite direction.

Of course, not more than a day or two later all of Roger's scouts were arrested by the police, who told him they would be charged with attempted murder. Roger tried to discuss the issue but was told, 'This is political. You have nothing to say to us.'

The men were released on bail, but morale among the scouts was now at its lowest ebb. Roger later had to pay a considerable amount of financial compensation to the mob and his scouts all got huge fines, which Roger also paid.

This was just the start of many similar incidents.

Jean-Roger and I were still living in a kind of cocoon. To try to remain focused, Jean concentrated on designing our own sand pump for the river. I kept studying the hippos and working for the Trust. Every week or so we took a drive over to Humani and heard from Roger and Anne yet another horrendous tale of the deaths of animals and destruction of the environment.

On one trip I was driving alone to Humani when I came across about 20 men. Five were bearded; all were very dirty looking and had deranged expressions. They were carrying sticks and machetes and were heading in the general direction of Humani. They did not want to get off the dirt track and I wondered if they intended on attacking me. About a second before I reached them they grudgingly moved off, but they shook their fists and screamed at me as I drove past.

These people were intent on destroying, harassing and spreading fear not only into the whites' hearts but also into those of their black employees. Violence was a strong persuader and it was not too long before Roger heard of nightly beatings in his employees' quarters, with Humani people beaten in front of their own families in order to subjugate them.

Then Roger started to receive death threats. Either a mob would come to his door or a note would be delivered. Anne said this used to happen back during the Rhodesian war, but she had thought that those awful days were over. Now Roger was often told he would die if he remained on Humani. Roger and the other families held fast; after all, they were from pioneer stock.

At that time Richard and Arthur were not under as much strain as Roger. The invaders concentrated on the wildlife, which was Roger's department. Both he and Anne aged in front of our eyes and my heart went out to them. I wanted to help and so offered to do snare patrols on Humani. I did one or two, but the scale of the snaring was just too great. Roger could not afford to have other scouts protecting me while we walked and it was too risky leaving me with only a couple of guys in the bush because of the invaders. He hired more men to train as scouts and increased the number to nearly 50, but they were still fighting a losing battle.

At that stage five properties in the south had been invaded and all of the owners had moved out. Roger and his other family members at Humani were the only ones to have stayed on their property. The people living on the other invaded lands were mainly managers, with the owners living elsewhere. Without the backing of their employers, how could they be expected to stand up to the invaders? On those properties the wildlife was wiped out indiscriminately. There were no Rogers there or scouts like his, who were fighting daily to keep the animals alive.

Strangely, not one ranch in the north of the Conservancy had been taken over, and although most of the ranches had only managers life in that area continued almost as normal. It was as though the south had been targeted, so of course we wondered if we would be spared.

Roger's informers warned him that the mob was coming and this time they were going to kill him, then burn all the Humani homesteads. In a situation like that, with no law and order for a man with a white skin, Roger had only one option. He had to leave his home for a short period and hope that, if the mob came along and found nobody, they would go on their way.

While the Whittalls were considering their options, Richard was attacked at the workshop by a mob of about 30 men. At that time Richard was in his early sixties, very fit, as he kept himself in trim, but when a mob of men start to beat you and one after the other hit you as you are held down, you can only take it and pray that they will eventually stop. While they were hitting him one of them suddenly shouted out, 'Oh, this is the wrong man! We want Shumba, not this man. This is the brother, let him be.'

The men stopped their attack and walked away as if nothing had happened. Richard dragged himself up from the floor. With two badly bruised ribs, a black eye and bruises to most of his body, he could just about walk. He believed he was fortunate, as it could have been far worse. His daughter, Belinda, was probably even more upset than her father; the shock of seeing him so badly battered really unsettled her. Yet in true Whittall fashion, Richard and Belinda even managed to joke about it the next day.

Later that day the Whittalls evacuated their homes for the first time, moving 40 kilometres down the road to another property called Hammond Ranch. This was owned by an American family who lived in the United States. The Schenks were there at that time and kindly let all the Humani families, plus four of their employees and all of their dogs, move into their safari camp for a couple of days.

Roger's theory was that they had to remove themselves while tempers were at their most volatile. Once the overheated anger of the mob calmed down they would go back home again. These evacuations became a regular occurrence and they had to leave their homes five times that year. On one occasion Jane and Arthur came along to us for the day.

Jane had left her two cats and Jack, her Jack Russell, at home, as she felt they had more chance escaping a mob than the family did and she did not want to unsettle her cats by moving them over to us. Richard always took his five dogs when they evacuated but not his cats, and Roger left all his animals at home. Everyone had their own idea of what they should do in this kind of situation. As it had not happened to me at that stage, I had no right to judge.

I had to hold back my tears at the incredible braveness of Jane. She was trying to keep Arthur and Janet, her youngest daughter, bright and cheerful, using all her courage and humour to make it seem like a huge silly game. She was so much like her brother, Roger. She proved to be an extremely courageous woman and would stand up to anything. Let anyone dare touch her family and she would become more dangerous than a wounded buffalo. Roger was exactly the same.

The Whittalls were made of the same unbelievably strong stuff that had helped their father and mother build an industry out of a wilderness, an industry that had not only provided them with a good living but also housed and helped nearly 700 people enjoy a better way of life. Roger and all the families were carrying on this legacy and would not let this new lawlessness turn them away from their homes and their children's future.

I felt guilty that in many ways our own lives were still relatively normal, but that was about to change.

Jean had found a company in Harare to make the sand pump. When we got it, Jean worked in another pool. After three weeks of hard slog the hippos would be fine for the dry season and this pump could be operated by Jean alone. He only needed to have Silas, then our only employee, help him set it up first thing each morning.

At times, as Jean worked in the pool, he had up to ten crocodiles alongside him, some of them over three metres long. The only thing separating these predators from a meal was the thin chicken wire fence. The most dangerous part of Jean's day was in the early morning when setting up the pump. He had to get into the water to erect the fence and put back the poles for the wire. At that moment there was no fence surrounding him and he was standing in the deep water of the pool he had opened the previous day.

Either Silas or I was always present as extra eyes to keep watch, but it was nerve-racking. The crocs to date had not tested the strength of the wire, which even a kitten could have knocked over. Jean's theory was that the crocodiles saw it as a barrier and didn't realise it was so flimsy.

One particular morning things got complicated.

I arrived to start videoing his work. It was my new project to make a small movie of the hippos and the work, and hopefully sell it to our hippo supporters. Suddenly a movement caught my eye and, to my dismay, I saw Abe, a mature female hippo, entering the pool slightly upstream from where Jean was working.

I whistled like crazy to attract Jean's attention. If I rushed forward this could startle Abe and create more danger for Jean. Whistling had no effect, as the noise from the engine obliterated other sounds. Jean-Roger was also a bit deaf if there was background noise, a result of flying gliders with bad flu and bursting his eardrums on a couple of occasions.

Luckily, second sight kicked in; he had noticed Abe.

When we discussed it later on Jean said that he knew it was Abe as she is very easy to identify, having a light-skinned body with quite a lot of wrinkles around her face area. Jean knew that she was one of the most passive of the mature females and, unlike Blackface, was unlikely to be aggressive.

Jean was near the bottom end of the weir pool and Abe was not more than 12 metres away. She was definitely curious, lifting her head high. I assumed that Jean was a strange sight; it was a first for her to have a wetsuit-clad human in the river with her.

Jean continued operating the pump. This entailed his bending down and using the suction pipe to suck up the sand, every now and then straightening up to stretch his aching back muscles, and repeating this performance over and over again. Abe lowered herself back into the river and moved closer until she was only six metres away.

Once I realised she was not going to attack I videoed the whole interaction between man, machine and mammal, and I must say it made good footage. I hoped that Abe realised this was all for her and the families' benefit.

Jean and I continued to help the hippos while mayhem and madness carried on just down the road on Humani. Shortly after our respective birthdays, in late September for Jean-Roger and October for myself, everything crashed down on us with an almighty bang.

I was walking along the riverbank when I bumped into two game scouts from the nearby hunting safari camp. They explained they were on their way to tell me that they had just found a dead hippo about nine kilometres upstream. It was in a tiny pool adjacent to the Turgwe River.

As I stood listening to them, I saw a bearded man leading a group of about 15 men and one child in our direction. I knew without needing to ask who they were. I was so concerned over the news of the dead hippo that I had no time to feel fear over this group's arrival. Instead, I asked the bearded one politely what I could do for them. In a gruff voice he responded, 'I am Job Mangula, a war veteran, a liberator of the Zimbabwe people. I have come with my men. We are now the owners of this land. We will sleep with your worker, Silas, and you will go and get your husband. Tell him to come here now and report to me. You will not go anywhere around here without first reporting to me. I will decide where you can go in my area from now on.'

I replied without any real thought, 'Mr Mangula, sorry but I have no time to talk with you now. These scouts have just informed me that one of the hippos under my care is dead, so I have to go with them. You had better go and see my husband yourself as he is at home. Sorry, but I am too busy to listen to you now. Goodbye.'

To his amazement, I walked off. This must have been the last thing he expected. He was totally baffled.

I arrived back home, quickly told Jean what had just happened and headed for the Land Rover. My immediate priority was to check on the dead hippo. I called Silas to accompany me, then I picked up the two scouts and we drove off, leaving Jean to handle the war vet.

I was so upset by the news of the dead hippo that I had no time to worry about this new headache. I was afraid that either a poacher or one of the professional hunters had killed it.

Arriving at the area where the scouts had found the hippo we slid down a quite steep riverbank slope to approach a stagnating pool nearby the river. All that could be seen of the hippo was its upper body, the head and shoulders; the rest was in the filthy water. It was more or less in a normal position, as if it had died in this place. The carcass had been in the water for at least two weeks so I knew it was not a member of the regular family that I saw daily.

Happy, though, was missing, as were two of his females, but the teeth of the animal belonged to a bull. I also knew that there was one other bull that lived several more kilometres upstream; it could be him.

Gingerly, I tried to examine the body, but the water was so dirty and the animal too heavy for us to move around. One scout was brave enough to put his hand under the water, searching every limb for signs of a snare; there was nothing. There were no physical signs of the hippo having been shot. We all believed that it had either been in a fight and the wound was in a place we could not see, or had died from a natural cause. As it was quite possible that there were crocodiles in this water, we couldn't just wade in and examine it further.

It was a bull and later, by aging his teeth, I found out he had been in his prime, around the mid-thirties. It was possible that it could be Happy. The other bull had always remained hidden in reeds and had arrived after the drought, so I had not fed it and knew little about it.

I was incredibly upset that the animal was dead, but I hoped that out of the two animals it was not Happy. The animal had been dead for too long to be recognizable and where Happy had scars the body was hidden from view. I had to hope it was not Happy, as he had been such a wonderful, gentle hippo during the drought days. It did, though, appear to be a natural death.

It was necessary to remove the animal's head for positive identification of the teeth for aging purposes. As it had been in the water for a time the skin had rotted, so it was not too much effort on the part of the game scouts and Silas to remove the head. I had to remain in control of my emotions, as the scouts would note any sign of weakness on my part.

On driving home I saw that the group of men had moved in next to Silas's thatch hut. They had built a cooking fire and put their sleeping mats right on top of one of the hippos' evening paths. I wondered if they were looking for a quick dispatch from the world or if they were just plain ignorant of hippo behaviour.

Jean had the bearded leader at home; both were sitting in our gazebo and chatting relatively amicably. What was to happen to us now was anyone's guess, but I knew we were not going anywhere. If they wanted to hassle us like they did Roger, they would find that we, too, would not retreat.

The man finally returned to the others. I rushed over to Jean to tell him where these guys had put their sleeping mats. He said he would go over and talk to them about it. In the meantime he quickly told me that they had said they were claiming all the land around us and intended setting up camp next to our home.

I explained to Jean about the hippo, but obviously he was more than a bit worried about this man. He went off to talk to them again. I decided to follow him and tell them a little about hippos. They looked at me as if they thought I was joking. All of them were scowling. People who act in such a manner have to look the part, surly and aggressive. All they did was grunt in response to my words about the hippos. Only the leader actually conversed.

We found out later that this man was Silas's blood relative, an uncle. He was also a war veteran, but was quite young during the Rhodesian war, so was not one of the 'heavy' brigade, being quite low down on the war veteran ladder.

He had told us that they were all war vets, but that was utter bull as not one of the others was over 30 years old, which would have made them all under ten during that period of the country's history. One was a child of no more than eight years. He, like the others, scowled and grunted, trying his best to look as evil as he possibly could. Jean attempted to use humour, saying to Job, 'Surely he is not a war veteran? Is he not a touch too young?'

Job, we were to learn, had no sense of humour. He replied that the boy's father and grandfather were war veterans and so he was entitled to carry this title.

Well, good luck to them. If they were keen to die being squashed by a hippo then that was their choice. I walked away as I knew losing my temper would not do any good at all.

Jean suggested they move their belongings, but they refused, so he, too, came home. Then we talked and talked and talked.

It was October 2001 and we had 17 men and a child on our door-step. We had had over 18 months of peace and quiet, but now what had happened to Humani was happening to us. None of these men was friendly, and how many more would arrive? I had a dead hippo bull and did not know who it was. It was all becoming a little bit too much.

We had been aware all the time that there was a chance that our area could be invaded, but we had hoped that this would not happen. The approaching storm had arrived and it would turn out to be one hell of a hurricane, but little did we know then how bad it would become.

The following day we had just got up and were sitting in the gazebo, our bedroom. It was five in the morning when, to my astonishment, I saw 15 bearded men coming through the garden, along the top of the riverbank. All carried machetes and were walking along as if this was a daily occurrence. I leapt from my chair and rushed towards them, shouting.

'What the fuck do you think you are doing? This is my garden, and if you want to see us you do not just walk in here like you own the joint. This is our property. Who the hell do you think you are!'

Obviously they had not expected this reaction. Jean caught up with me and took over before things could get ugly. He was polite, unlike me, but he did not budge, explaining that they were walking through our bedroom area and that was not really well mannered. He then politely suggested they follow him to the front entrance, which, although not fenced, had a kind of boundary mark around it that was obvious to even a city dweller's eyes. He pointed out the other men sitting near Silas's home and without another word they went over to them.

My attitude had so startled them that they were not in the least aggressive. The fact that I had stood up to them appeared to have had a better effect than showing fear. Like all bullies they thrived on fear, and I was not afraid. I was hopping mad.

Zimbabweans, I had always found, were friendly, smiling, never abusive or showing any kind of racial aggression. I had visited a few other African countries and concluded that Zimbabweans were some of the politest and most pleasant people I had met. These 'invaders' were nothing like this. Now there were over 30 people next door to us, and I wondered what next to expect.

As one group, they all headed for the pools near the hippos' weir. They carried fishing lines, nets and spears, and then proceeded to decimate the fish population. We decided to act as if nothing was wrong and instead walked among them looking at their catch and complimenting them on their ability to catch not one fish, but ten in one go. We were making a point of being right in their faces.

If they were going to kill every single fish in these pools we would make sure they knew that we knew they were doing it. We were in their presence, so they could not kill other animals at the same time, or so we hoped. We spent the day wandering among them, which certainly annoyed them, but they did not know how to get rid of us. At that stage they had not been told to harm us.

I was so worried for the hippos and all the animals around us. My darling warthog, Arthur, was wild, but he was exceedingly old and often slept in the bush by small rock koppies, instead of safely down the warthog holes. He would be very easy to kill if these men came across him, and so it would be for any wild animal that we had protected near our home.

In previous years I had constant battles with professional hunters wanting to kill a kudu bull or a bushbuck, because we had many with big horns living close to our home. These invaders would prove to be far worse than any white hunter with his foreign client. The hunter was normally looking for one specific type of animal; these people would kill anything, from a squirrel to an elephant.

The beginning of the slaughter had started mildly with the fish.

For two nights they stayed and then one morning we got up and they had all gone. We were amazed, asking Silas when he arrived for work what was happening. He explained that his uncle, who was truly his blood relation, had decided that it was too dangerous to stay where they were as the hippos were too many and kept coming over to their fires.

I had to hold back a smile.

Apparently they had moved less than a kilometre down the road to an empty house belonging to the Whittalls. That house was locked, with a wire security fence all around it, but that was no deterrent. They had told Silas they would break any lock and move in. We gathered that they had initially decided to do this at our own home, but had not expected us to behave as we did.

The house was close to us, but at least they were now no longer in sight. The relief was tremendous. I knew that it did not mean the end of our problems, but it was a slight improvement. Silas then told us their plans.

Job was apparently now the new chief of around 100 people who would be moving into our area. They all had their own farms and land in the communal lands adjacent to the Conservancy. He and some other war vets had employed them to come to white-owned properties and do whatever was needed. In this case they intended to clear the bush of trees, plough the land and plant crops. This in itself was ludicrous, as the land was useless for any kind of farming. The white owners, with all their technology and money, had not been able to farm these bush lands and had realised the only sustainable income was in wildlife.

It was obvious that their real reason for coming was to poach. They would kill all the animals and make a lot of money from meat, at the same time plundering and destroying white people's properties, as they had been doing over on Humani.

Jean and I decided that the best policy for the moment would be to continue to behave as we had always done. The only thing he was not happy about was allowing me to go alone to the hippos, since they were at the pools close to where the men had moved. He was not sure if a woman on her own would be safe, so he insisted on accompanying me.

On our first trip over to that pool we found 15 new wire snares set on one of the hippo paths. As they were all treble strands they could easily capture a hippo, so we removed the snares and took them home, cutting them into tiny pieces and throwing these down the long-drop toilet.

On returning to the pool that afternoon we decided we would drive to the house to talk to Job to try to reason with him. I felt that if we explained the importance of the hippos for tourism and money for Zimbabwe, then maybe, just maybe, he might listen.

Wrong. Never think you can negotiate with a hooligan; it does not pay.

As we drove to the house a dog barked. There were three skinny hunting dogs within the fenced area, as well as a bunch of chickens. They had even brought a couple of cows. Silas had told me that Job was a very rich man. Apparently he had been a customs officer for years at the Zimbabwean side of the Beitbridge border post with South

Africa, and he owned over 150 cattle, making him a very wealthy man in their culture.

As we stood looking at the house, which still had a padlock on the gate but had been broken into through the one fenced area, I heard wood being chopped. I turned to Jean, telling him I thought that they were blocking the road and we were about to have hassles.

We returned to the Land Rover and, as we started the engine, we saw Job and five men coming towards us. One was carrying a rifle, and the others had their usual machetes. Across the road, sure enough, they had laid two medium-sized mopane trees. We could no longer leave.

Jean, as he had no option and before they could become aggressive, got out of the vehicle, held out his hand and politely said, '*Masikati* (Good afternoon).'

He asked why they had blocked the road, as we were there to have a chat with Job and were surprised that they would do this. I tried to bite my tongue and keep my big mouth shut, but I was once more getting angry. I looked away so they would not see it in my eyes. Job stared at Jean with his normal scowl.

'Mr Jean, I am telling you now something for your own good. We are the owners of this land. We have always been the owners, but Whittalls stole it from us, now we take it back. You have a house and an area, you stay there. This is our land, you are not welcome. You can no longer come here and you keep away or we will not be so good to you.'

Well, as always I felt I had to intervene.

'Mr Mangula,' I said curtly, 'as we told you at our home, I look after the Turgwe hippos. I fed them in that terrible time of no rains in 1992. Since then I have worked on many projects to help these animals. Hundreds of tourists have come to our home to meet these hippos and they all help Zimbabwe by bringing money to this country. Now you tell us we cannot come here. Mr Mangula, this land is where the hippos live at certain times during the year. That weir down below this house we, with the Trust's money, repaired, using cement and builders after the time of the terrible floods. The hippos use that weir now for a few months, and I have for the last 11 years spent every day of my life studying them.'

He cut me off before I could continue, saying that the hippos would either have to leave as well or die, as the land now was for farming, not wild animals. Then the other guy with the rifle suddenly opened his mouth, spitting venom and anger in my direction.

'I am here to kill Roger Whittall and when I have killed him, I am going to Afghanistan to kill Americans!'

Jean and I looked at each other. I could not help it. I was so amazed to hear such dribble that I leapt out of the vehicle, walked over to the man and hit his rifle up in the air.

'Mister, I don't know who you are, but you are not a Shona man. What do you think you are doing, talking about killing people? Don't you know that is against God's will?'

He screamed back at me, 'I am a Christian!'

I in turn screamed back, 'Well, mate, if you are a Christian, those Arabs will take you out anyway, and what the hell do you want to go there for? It is not your fight.'

This was getting us nowhere. He was now furious and all the others were muttering, so Jean, who had followed me out of the vehicle, gave me a huge nudge and loudly said, 'Woman, get back in the car!'

Now, Jean does not speak like that, but I got the message. I had overstepped the safety threshold and this was now out of hand. He was playing the macho man bit, shutting up the silly woman, as was his right. This was the only thing they would understand. I got in and looked away from them.

Jean, as always, used his head and pacified them. Eventually he even had Job agreeing that we would be able to go to the hippos' pools. Job said that if we were in any way doing something he did not like, he would send a messenger to Jean so Jean could report to him. Jean flattered the idiot's ego and agreed, which he had absolutely no intention of doing, but he has always been a good diplomat.

We drove away once they cleared the road of the offending trees. Only when out of sight did I start shaking, realizing that it could have turned very nasty and that I should learn to curb my temper. I kept saying to Jean over and over again, 'They are going to kill the hippos,' but Jean told me not to panic, that somehow we would beat them at their game.

I should have bitten back my words. The very next day there was a lot of smoke on the horizon and we realised they had set fire to the bush. The smoke was less than a kilometre off and the fire was approaching at speed. There was at least another month to go before we could expect the first rains and what grazing was left was going to burn, unless we could stop the fire.

Jean drove fast to Humani, hoping that he would find one of the Whittalls. As it was a Saturday, most of the staff would be off duty. Luckily, he found Richard and explained the situation. Richard kindly organised for one of the supervisors to get as many men as possible and come out to us in the lorry.

At home, Silas and I cut a firebreak around our thatched home. We had never bothered in the past to cut the grass for the chance of a bush fire had been so remote, but things had changed.

Jean arrived and within half an hour the lorry was outside our home. Unfortunately many of the workers were drunk. We all cut branches from nearby trees and set off towards a small dry stream that cut one part of the land in half. I believed that was the best place to fight the fire.

When a bush fire is running, you first need to back burn. You find an area with a natural divide, preferably a road or a riverbed. Then you burn on the other side of the barrier, letting the flames burn back to the approaching fire. You organise people to beat out the flames if they start to cross the barrier so that the fire cannot jump into the area you are trying to save.

It all sounds easy, but when you are out there fighting one of these fires it is a terrifying experience. Much depends on the time of the year and if there are heavy winds. If, like then, it is the height of the dry season and extremely hot, with everything dried out, a fire can be very dangerous, as the trees burn and the flames can reach great heights. You get covered in soot and it is exhausting beating at the flames to keep them at bay; with drunken men attempting to put out the fire, the problems were numerous. As I knew the area well because it was one of my hippos' grazing lands, I told Richard where his guys should back burn, but had forgotten the Zimbabwean mentality. Men do not listen to women about such work and so they did what they thought was best and ignored my idea. We lost more grazing than necessary because of this attitude.

For the next five hours we fought that fire. I was at one end of the approaching flames with ten or so men. Jean-Roger, Richard and about 25 others were spaced out from me, moving along the entire length of the little stream. At times the fire jumped over the barrier and then we all rushed to put it out. So it continued. At one stage I had inhaled so much smoke that I had to stop for a while to recover. I had even singed my eyebrows.

I found 12 of the invaders walking towards me as I sat on the ground. Richard saw them approaching and got into his truck, ordering me to get going as they might attack me. I told him that I was sure they were OK, but as these people had beaten him he was understandably wary.

As it was, they asked me if we wanted help. I in turn asked them why somebody on their side had started this fire. They all shrugged, but still offered to give us a hand. The situation was quite ludicrous: here we were fighting a fire started by them and they were offering to help. It made no sense at all.

I told them we were fine, but thanked them for their offer. Then I got back to fighting the flames. There was too much animosity between the Humani workers and the invaders to let them work together on the firefighting.

Soon night fell and we were still beating at the flames. The fire burnt about 400 metres from the house and had burnt all the grazing on the other side of a small range of koppies.

Although a fire at night can look spectacular, I kept thinking of the tiny mammals and reptiles that would die because of it. One thing was for sure: the animals had lost a lot of grass and leaves that were left on trees for the browsers. Now many would go hungry, thanks to these people.

By the following week we found that the snaring of the river was just their first bit of poaching. Everywhere we walked we were finding snares, with the invaders inundating the area. Initially we found snares but with no animals trapped in them, but it did not take long before we came across the first impala dead in a snare. She was near the path down to the hippos' pool.

She had been caught around her stomach area, having walked into the noose and somehow managing to get half of her body through before it tightened. Obviously, she had panicked at the feel of hard wire around her body; leaping around had caused the wire to tighten and restrict all blood flow. She had died a slow, lingering death.

The snares were always attached to a strong tree, so being only an impala she had not had the strength to break the wire. She must have fought for her life as the ground was scuffed up by her frantic attempts to break free. The wire had cut into two centimetres of her stomach skin from the tremendous pressure she must have put on the noose, fighting it. She had died in terrible agony.

Jean cut the wire away from her belly, using pliers, which we now always carried with us. I gently stroked her soft skin, looking into her large brown eyes. I apologized silently for her being caught in this fight of man against man, and I wondered how strong I was going to be. If we came across such sights every day, could I survive this pain? What would I do if we found one of the baby hippos caught and killed in such a manner?

Fortunately for hippos, they are much harder to snare than other animals unless the poacher is singling them out. An adult hippo normally walks through the bush at night with its head carried low. As they walked quite sedately their chances of walking into a noose and being trapped were pretty remote. If the hippo came across a snare, its body should deflect it.

The only problem was the little hippos, although normally the calf followed its mother when on land. She hopefully would displace any snare, since she would change direction if she felt something alien against her body, avoiding the object.

It was only when their actual exit points away from the river were snared in number that there was the possibility of catching one of the youngsters. It would be up to me to check all the exit routes daily. As poachers often set their snares just before dusk, I had to locate these snares and remove them before they could do any damage.

What was happening here had been carried out on every farm, ranch or wildlife area invaded in Zimbabwe. The wildlife on farms had been or was still being destroyed on a massive scale. Jean now accompanied me on any long walks I took in the bush. He believed that there was too much chance of bumping into the poachers and, as we were unarmed, he felt a little happier when he was with me.

Jean had initially planned to take a six-month sabbatical from his geological work. He would then find another job, but would make sure he sometimes took me along and try to be home a little more often, so that we would not be living separate lives as we had for seven years. With the invasions on Humani he did not want to leave me alone again. We had hoped that the madness that was happening all around the country would stop and life would go back to normal, but it never did. Instead, we were invaded 18 months later. We had some savings to live on, but they would not last forever. We didn't know for how many years this crazy situation would continue, or that it would get far worse than anything we had experienced to date.

My own Trust work of correspondence and trying to raise funds for the hippos and ongoing projects had to be cut by half. We now had to spend more and more hours out in the bush in search of snares. We had not yet encountered any of the poachers, and were learning how they operated.

We had six places we covered weekly, walking for around two hours in the morning and another two each evening. We patrolled an area of about seven kilometres long by five kilometres wide. We were the only people in the entire Conservancy doing our own anti-poaching patrols. The others all had gangs of game scouts, but we had never had the need for such people and were not in a position to start our own force. We had no weapons or any kind of legal standing to hire armed men and employ them as game scouts.

When we searched for snares our eyes got very tired. Often the snare is set under bushes where a warthog or a smaller mammal will move through, or in thickets and heavily treed places, so the wire was sometimes difficult to see. The wire mainly came from the Conservancy's boundary fence. The invaders had cut kilometres and kilometres of this fencing.

They would then make up a snare and noose, using around three metres of wire for a single strand snare. In general, they used single strand, which would easily hold an impala, with double and treble strands used to capture larger antelope like a kudu or waterbuck. Sometimes they used four strands plaited together; these could catch a buffalo, an adult hippo or even a young elephant.

A lot of the larger mammals got caught in the smaller snares. They then broke the wire where it was attached to a tree, but the offending noose would still be attached to one of their limbs and could kill if gangrene set in. It was a never-ending war between the people now living less than a kilometre down the road and us.

In one area the snares belonged to people who had invaded another property in the south called Angus Ranch, which was about an hour's drive upstream from our home. They were using this area as their snaring ground. Job's men had the area immediately around our home and behind the koppies, and of course near the hippos' pools.

We found that Job used his cattle to hide the tracks of the people setting snares. He would send his nephew or one of his workers with a herd of 20 cattle. While the cattle grazed the men set snares among the trees as they walked along. They would then move the cattle away from the snared area and return the following morning, bringing the cattle back while they recovered any dead animal caught in the snares.

Soon there were just too many snares and we could only remove about half of them, if we were lucky. They kept sending more and more people further inland to set these wires.

We realised that these people were not just poaching for meat for their families. This was a large-scale operation. The dead animals were being loaded on to ox carts pulled by two of their cattle. At night they took the meat to the neighbouring communal lands.

Roger's informers had managed to find out who the buyers were; they were not ordinary villagers. The meat went to several specific places where businessmen affiliated to the ruling party organised its resale. The talk in the Conservancy was that the land invasions here had not been authorized by the President; instead it had been done by another government faction lower in rank that had known of the wealth of animals in this area. Trouble was, nobody was stopping it and the animals were dying in their thousands. It was worse than the '92 drought.

THIRTEEN

Violence becomes part of everyday life

We quickly learned that there were different bands of war vets all around the conservancy recruiting locals, telling them that they would be given extra land and meat; an incentive too good to turn down. Though the war vets were supposed to be taking over land for agriculture, in reality their aim was to exploit it for meat. Even they realised that crops could not grow in such a dry area. Over the weeks that followed we were to find more and more snares set for wild animals. We found dead kudu, impala, warthogs, waterbuck and, once, a young buffalo. When we found snares we removed them, destroying them at home by cutting them into tiny pieces. We fed what dead animals we found to the crocodiles in the Turgwe.

Our daily patrols were bringing in around 800 snares each month and those were only the wires we found: for every 100 snares we stripped away, 100 more seemed to appear. I could spend less and less time with the hippos, and less time at our home – though we still found the time to see Arthur, Steyl and Sid the baboon every day at dusk, when they appeared close to our house looking for food.

It was not long before we had our first run-in with poaching war vets ourselves. As we understood it, they were not poaching simply to sustain themselves, but for meat to sell into the illegal bushmeat trade – a trade every bit as lucrative as dealing in illegal drugs.

Out on patrol one morning, a movement ahead of us suddenly caught my eye. I saw two men coming from a koppie range. One had a huge wooden bow and arrows slung over his shoulder; the other clutched a panga (a sharp steel machete). I gripped Jean-Roger's sleeve, using the sign language we had developed over the previous harsh months. The men had not seen us, but they would soon enough. We could not back away, for they were here to kill all the animals we had fought so hard to save from the drought. It was only a matter of time before they killed one of my hippos.

Yet we were unarmed, at the mercy of an armed man. The bow he carried could easily bring down a buffalo if hit in the right place and these guys were extremely good at their trade. Game scouts had been shot and one fatally injured by the same kind of weapon. There seemed to be only one thing we could do. If we ran away, these men would chase us; it would be too tempting. If we charged at them, like a charging hippo, perhaps they would run away.

We set off, making thunderous noises as we charged, but in seconds we skidded to an abrupt halt. The taller of the two had drawn an arrow and strung the bow. It was pointing straight at Jean-Roger.

In that split second I knew I had to react or my husband could die. I had learnt about tribal beliefs and superstitions long ago, when I first arrived in Africa, but I had never thought that I would end up relying on such things. Here, with the arrow twitching over Jean-Roger's heart, I knew that I would have to act a part. I would become a witch. I would reach out to his superstitions.

I threw myself to my knees, beginning to wail. I was swinging from side to side, insane sounds poured from my mouth. I hurled my arms about while my long hair flicked from side to side. To the poachers I was a wild woman, quite unlike any other white woman they had ever encountered. The man with the bow kept his eyes on us, never lowering his aim. Yet, my plan seemed to be working, for the younger man was clearly afraid. His eyes were huge, the whites showing. He spoke rapidly in Shona to his partner, desperate to leave. The older man replied sharply, instructing him to remain.

I forced my voice to rise, made my gestures wilder and more drama-tic, summoning up every bit of madness I could find within. If I was to work on their spiritual beliefs and make them fear me, I had to look bewitched. It was our only weapon and the only thing that might save Jean-Roger.

At last the older man let his bow go slack. Then, suddenly, he leaned down, taking a melon-sized rock between his hands. He hurled it with all his might at my head – but, somehow, it missed.

I knew what this meant for him. Children of the African bush learn from a young age to use catapults to kill birds and reptiles. They

136

are extremely accurate with any kind of missile. They can hit a bird in flight, crush the life from a venomous snake or even grievously injure baboons with the accuracy of their catapults. Yet, this rock, unaccountably, had somehow missed. It even seemed to have altered direction in flight, veering right to miss my head and shattering on the trunk of a nearby tree. Terrified, now, that I really might have magic on my side, the men shared frenzied words and then disappeared back into the bush, using the path they had just come from.

With all these problems, Jean-Roger knew he could not go back to work. He had to be here if he wanted his wife to remain in one piece and for us to keep the house. It was only a matter of time before these people managed to kill all the animals. We could never beat them at their game; we could only hold back the eventual outcome, and yet neither Jean nor I was prepared to give in and walk away. While there was fight left in us and air in our lungs to breathe we would remove their snares and try to keep Arthur, the hippos and all the animals around us alive.

Then Jeannie, Arthur's mate, and the babies disappeared.

We had heard dogs barking in the distance so we knew there were poachers. Their dogs were so badly treated and so thin that it was amazing they could survive to hunt and track the animals. Many of the dogs were just skin and bone, with not an ounce of flesh on their bodies. Yet they were used until they were killed by an animal, shot by a game scout, or just died from lack of care.

The dogs located a warthog down its hole by scent and then the men blocked off all the exit holes, bar one. They would proceed to dig from above with *badzas* (hoes) into the soil, reaching the chamber where the pig was hiding. They then lit a fire at one other exit point, so that the warthog had no option but to leave its refuge.

With smoke pouring into the holes the warthog had only one escape route. As it dashed for freedom the dogs attacked, and the men finished off the animal. They usually hacked at it with a machete if it was small enough, or shot the warthog with bow and arrow. If they had enough dogs and there were at least two men, they could easily wipe out an entire warthog family, up to five animals, in one go. This, I am sure, was what had happened to Arthur's family.

From that day on I lived in fear every night until I saw Arthur's familiar shape at the back door. He was such an amazing wild animal. He allowed me to scratch him, stroke his warts and take many liberties, but I always respected his space. I never approached him away from the house and if he ever saw me walking in the bush he always trotted off. I did not call to him, not wanting him to lose his fear of human beings.

Once he came along with a huge abscess on his neck. He not only allowed me to treat it with tea tree essential oil, but when it was close to bursting he let Jean-Roger cut into it with a scalpel blade while I rubbed his tummy. This completely wild animal, which was capable of harming us quite badly with a slash of his one good tusk, just relaxed and let us help him.

For nine years he had come along to our home. My nerves had been at breaking point on many an occasion during the safari season, knowing that one of the white hunters would dearly love to shoot him just to make a point. Somehow he had survived the hunters; and then, one night, he did not come home.

We searched for him in all his favourite spots, but there was nothing. This meant that the poachers, if they had killed him, had taken all the evidence, which was quite strange. Normally they left behind the head and often the legs of the animal they had killed. With warthogs, they usually only took the entire body if it was a tiny one.

I tried to convince myself that he had moved to another area. This was unlikely, as he had lived around us for years and years, and warthogs have their own territory. I then tried to make myself believe he had died a natural death, that some predator had killed him. I could not allow myself to dwell on it for too long, as he was so very important in my life. The bond we shared was so unusual, such a special relationship, and I missed him terribly. Pictures of his face would daily pop into my mind. I stored the pain and anguish deep in a hidden chamber of my heart and kept hoping he would return, but he never did.

These people's arrival and occupation of the land had brought only pain, sorrow and anger. To clear the land of trees and vegetation was so easy. All they did was light fires under each and every tree and then let them burn. Once the tree collapsed, they came with two skinny oxen and pulled the trees along to form a makeshift fence around the land they were clearing. The actual physical work on their part was minimal; the fire, and then their animals, did the hard work.

Our road out of the Conservancy was now a trip from hell. Where once hundreds of wild animals had crossed our path or grazed the grass on either side of the dirt road, now all one saw were burning trees, cleared land for crops that would never ever grow because of the low rainfall, and not an animal in sight.

The people were killing the animals in their thousands, but all we could do was concentrate on the immediate area around us, to try to stop total annihilation. Often we found poachers' camps where they had set up a meat rack made from cut branches and then made a fire under it to smoke the meat. The meat taken out of the conservancy was normally smoked, so it would last longer for resale. We would find the remains in the camps of whatever they had managed to kill. In our area it was normally two or three kudu, or a couple of waterbuck and a warthog, sometimes a few impala. The camps were never full of carcasses, as the poachers had realised we were walking the area and clearly did not know we were unarmed.

They killed as many animals as they could using a snare line and took the meat out of the area. Roger had told us that none of them kept meat at the huts they had built. Perhaps they were aware of the possibility of law and order one day being restored and their crime no longer being given the protection of politics.

So far we had removed all the snares near the hippos, but I knew the hippos sometimes walked as far inland as six to eight kilometres in one night. We could not go too deep into the interior – the men could ambush us and our own lives would be in jeopardy. Roger's game scouts had been attacked so many times since the initial invasions, and they were armed with shotguns and .303 rifles. We would be too easy to dispatch. I just had to pray that the hippos would be aware of the danger the wires held and avoid them.

On a few occasions I bumped into Job while walking on my own. Initially he was quite polite and asked me how my husband and I were, and I would return the greeting. Then he would push his luck, saying things like, 'I see you have two vehicles. Give me one.' Or, 'I know you go to Chiredzi once every three to four weeks; take me with you.'

I tried not to show the hatred I felt towards him and his kind, instead telling him that we only had one vehicle, as the Land Rover belonged to the Trust. That we could never take anybody with us to Chiredzi as we always brought back a full load of game pellets, food for the animals and our own supplies, so there was never any room. I tried to remain polite, but I was sure he was aware of my true feelings.

Then one day I lost it again. Jean and I found a poached kudu bull cut up and smoked in a tiny riverbed close to the house that Job had stolen. Later that day we bumped into him. Jean asked what the hell was going on, but in a polite way, making out that it could not possibly have anything to do with Job.

In the meantime both of us knew he was the man in charge, which meant he organised all the poaching in this area. Silas had even told us this, Job being his uncle. Job told Jean that the government had given him permission to kill any wild animals, that the only ones he could not kill were rhinos. Well, that was like putting a red flag in front of me. I spat back that that was total bullshit. Killing wildlife in a wildlife conservancy was still classified as poaching, and if it was now legal, why did his people smuggle the meat out of the area at night in their ox carts?

Whoops, now he was mad!

These guys hated confrontation when they were alone, without backup, and in the wrong. Once they lied, they continued to lie and could get very verbal while doing so.

I walked off before I totally lost it and Jean once more pacified the prick. From that day on I could never bring myself to be polite again. The man was not only a liar but was also responsible for killing thousands of animals. He probably had his men kill my wonderful Arthur, and for that I would never forgive him.

I went back to the hippos' pool on my own that day, sitting with them for many hours trying to rationalize how I felt.

I had come to Africa to try and help animals, to do something positive.

Here I was trying to protect hippos, and around me all these animals were dying. I asked myself over and over again if I was right to try to fight these people. Could we win? Or would I eventually find they killed even the hippos, and that I would be helpless to stop it?

Over the years the hippos and I had developed amazing bonds. Bob seemed to read my mind, because on that particular day he got closer to me than I had ever allowed before. I suppose it was a little foolhardy on my part. After all, he was still a nearly three-ton wild hippo bull, but I was so upset that I did not back away.

I found him directly in front of me. Not more than a foot, if that, separated us. His magnificent face, with that huge hippo smile and the dark brown eyes, stared at me. He then opened his mouth and showed me the full expanse of a hippo gape. I could count every individual tooth, even his back molars, he was that close. He crashed his huge head back into the water, so that I got covered in a cascade of spray. Calling his almighty hippo bellow, to my astonishment he proceeded to roll in the water. For a few seconds all four of his feet were in the air, as if he were trying to amuse me.

I didn't care what any academic would tell you about studying animals, and never to attribute human motivations to their deeds. This day was very special. Bob was, I believed, really trying to brighten up my mood and he managed to do so admirably.

So we continued, and the days merged into weeks, then months.

One day we were walking past a new cemented pan that I had built for the hippos in case of another drought, when, to my joy, I found Tembia, Bob's son. He was now ten years old and had been away from the family for a couple of years.

Initially he had lived in the weir pool close to where Job and his men had moved. They had obviously harassed him and driven him away. He was clearly trying to establish a territory, but there were not many in our area that had not been taken over by Bob. The pan was neutral ground, so at least he could spend the daylight hours in it without fighting Bob, who was less than a kilometre away in his own weir pool next to our house. The hippos no longer used the pools in the area that the invaders had taken over.

As we approached the pan to have a closer look at Tembia, I saw to my horror a young guy with a catapult in his hands, aiming stones at Tembia. Every time Tembia surfaced to breathe the guy shot a stone at him, but as he fired Tembia submerged and so far none of the stones had hit him. I knew that if he did hit Tembia he could damage his eyes, but there was also a strong chance that if he did it once too often, Tembia would leave the pan, charge and more than likely kill him.

The ignorance of the fellow was hard to believe and we rushed towards him. Without thought, Jean grabbed the offending catapult and broke it across his knee. I then went into a long monologue of how dangerous his stupid game was and that by harassing Tembia he could either be killed or make Tembia very angry, so that the next person who came along would be charged and perhaps killed.

He was so blank that we could have been speaking to a rock; his eyes registered hardly a thing. Then I realised he was stoned.

Many of the invaders smoked marijuana. When their leaders wanted a mob to be obedient they often gave it to them to smoke before going off on a raid. He was so stoned he could hardly stand up, which explained why he had missed Tembia. Normally these guys are excellent shots as they eat anything they kill, from rodents to snakes.

It was pointless trying to hold a conversation with him, but he obviously had got the message as he was keen to get away. We waited quite a while to be sure he had gone, and then I spent some time with Tembia, calming him down. Fortunately he was none the worse for wear, but it took a while to soothe him. The boy had made him angry and he had just reached the age where a bull does not normally back down.

What this incident brought to my attention was that none of the animals could expect to survive this invasion of lawlessness and poaching. Sooner or later somebody would be killed by a hippo and it would not be the animal's fault. Present circumstances all pointed towards such an outcome. If you harass an animal that has the ability to kill but is not normally dangerous, it will at some stage reach a point of no return. These people had been interfering in the hippos' lives for too long; an accident was just waiting to happen.

It was but three days after the incident with the two poachers and the bow and arrows and our narrow escape, that I heard the sound of a rifle shot somewhere close to the river. I knew that there were no white hunters in the safari camp across the Turgwe. It could mean only one thing: a poacher, but this time with a rifle, something that had not happened in our area.

As I was working this out another shot was fired, practically stopping my heart from beating. It came from close to the house and the hippos' pool. Without any thought of the consequences I started running towards the weir pool. I was praying that nobody had shot one of the hippos and that I would find them all unharmed. Jean was not far behind me, but he had used his head and grabbed the

Conservancy radio. He was calling Roger, asking him for a group of scouts as somebody was shooting right next to our home.

At the weir all the hippos were behaving quite normally. I realised that the sound of the shot had carried on the wind and was not as close as I had first thought. Jean caught up with me, saying that I had to stay put in case the poacher was nearby. He had radioed for backup and we would wait for the scouts to arrive.

Miles, one of Roger's hunters, arrived along with a group of 12 scouts. Quickly, they all trooped after Jean towards the area from where the shots had been fired. They were not too keen to go after the poacher as this was not Roger's land. The shooting had come from the Angus side, a property that no longer had a manager. He and his wife had left when the problems had started.

Jean returned after an hour or so. The scouts had found one of the bullet casings but no sign of an animal killed. They believed he had shot at some kudu and missed, as there were tracks of running kudu but no blood spoor. They had found the tracks of one person.

Even though he was armed, as well as very cocky to be shooting right near our home, the poacher had run off. Jean decided that we could no longer afford to be unarmed and that he would go over to see Roger about borrowing a rifle, so that we could do our patrols with a little more safety.

I was not happy about this.

For years I had lived in the bush with only my wits to protect me. Rifles made it too easy to kill. I felt they were dangerous in a person's hands as they built a false confidence. Jean knew how to use a rifle, having done his military service in France, but he was no hunter and I wondered what he would do if we were faced with armed poachers and had the ability to fight back. There was no way I could persuade him differently. He told me we were crazy to continue going out without a weapon. He would go and see Roger in the next couple of days to make a plan.

The poacher came back the very next day, just as we finished a cup of afternoon tea and coffee. This time we heard not one but three shots, one after the other, coming from the koppie behind our home. We jumped into the Land Rover and headed in that direction, but at the top of the driveway Jean gathered his thoughts and decided to call Roger first.

Roger was out and Rae, who did Humani Safaris' books, answered the call. Jean told her we had heard shots and were going to investigate, but could she ask Roger or someone at Humani to send out scouts. Rae told him that it was not possible, as Roger was driving his scouts to a snare line they had found. We were on our own.

Jean believed we might be ambushed if we continued to drive into the koppie, and it would be better to go on foot to locate the man's position. He said there was no way we could arrest the guy as we did not even have a pair of handcuffs and were unarmed. At least we could try to identify him and then give the scouts his description. Maybe we could even frighten him off, but whatever the case, we couldn't just sit at home and listen to him shooting the animals we were trying to protect.

We quietly left the vehicle, being careful not to slam a door, and began walking through the bush in the direction of the rock koppie.

My mouth was dry. I thought I could hear the blood pounding in my ears. As usual, we walked in single file, but this time we were not looking just for snares; we had an armed man to watch out for and we were definitely in danger. I kept telling myself that these people were normally cowards. If you stood up to them and showed no fear you could come out on top. But a man with a weapon, facing a man and a woman without even a catapult between them, may not follow this kind of logic.

The walk to the base of the koppie proved uneventful and the pounding in my ears stilled as I allowed myself to take some welcome deep breaths. I realised I had been holding my breath during that short walk.

Jean and I were walking using the trees as camouflage. Just as we reached the corner of the koppie, coming around the bend, we saw four men.

In that instant our eyes met.

One man was holding a rifle, one other, I think, had a shotgun. What happened next was so quick I did not have time to think or to study what was in the man's hands. The guy with the rifle raised it and Jean screamed at me to hit the ground.

Well, I know that in the Westerns on TV that looks easy, but when done in reality it really hurts. I fell flat on the ground and the African soil is hard. There was no rifle report, and when I dared to raise my

144

head I realised that all four men had disappeared. They must have gone back the way they had come.

Jean and I were alive and they had gone. Four men against two unarmed people. Unbelievable. Maybe somewhere there was still a tiny bit of sanity left in these poachers' minds and they had not reached the point of shooting to kill.

My entire body was shaking. I knew we had been exceedingly lucky that they had decided to run. Jean assumed that they thought we had backup – why else would two people approach poachers, unless they had armed scouts nearby?

Our own stupidity could have been the reason we had not been harmed.

Later that day Jean went to see Roger and borrowed a small calibre rifle. He duly came home carrying a .22 with a letter from Roger giving us permission to use the rifle as protection against rabid dogs and in order to protect Roger's property. Most of the land we were walking on belonged to Roger, so he could cover us in this way. It was only a light weapon, but it should hopefully act as a deterrent once word got around that we were now armed.

From that day on we only left the house on patrol if Jean-Roger had the rifle with him. He was even reluctant to let me go to the hippos on my own, but I managed to persuade him that I could not study them properly if he was there. It was not something for which he had much patience. After a maximum of half an hour with the hippos I could see him becoming restless.

If the hippos were to relax in my presence, they did not need somebody fidgeting and drawing attention to himself. I knew that Jean-Roger did not feel for the bush and the animals as I did, and it was best if we kept some things separate from our relationship. I saw his point and knew that if I did bump into poachers it could be dangerous, but I had to have some time alone with the hippos.

Fortunately, the hippos were spending more and more time in the weir pool right next to our house, and the chance of my falling foul of a poacher there was pretty remote. With all the patrolling we were doing I could only spend about two hours a day now with the hippos, so I had to make the most of what time I did have.

FOURTEEN

Bob

Bob continued to impress me with his trust in me. I had never in my life had such a reaction from a wild animal. Arthur Warthog had been wonderful, allowing me to touch and scratch him, but Bob appeared to really listen to my words and react to them.

These days, the hundreds of people who had visited Bob and his family over the last decade were a thing of the past. If Bob saw a handful of strangers in one year it was a lot. Yet he would still open his mouth in a huge gape when I asked him to show how wonderfully impressive he was. He would come to within a few feet of where I stood or sat by the pool and, if far upstream in the river, would come downstream when I called his name. He was an amazing animal and I knew that all I had learnt about the hippos was mainly due to this territorial bull and his acceptance of me.

When the day had been particularly awful and we had found a lot of snares or a dead animal in a snare, I would go and talk to Bob to restore my energy, to help me realise why I was there. His wonderful bellow, a kind of happy hippo roar, restored my jaded thoughts so they could blow away on the breeze. I could then once more focus on the hippos.

Bob was busily interested in mating two of the females, Abe and her daughter Odile. Odile had just reached seven years of age and was fully capable of having a calf. Most of the Turgwe hippos became pregnant at a very early age, as early as five years, which, according to all the reference material I had about hippos, was not correct. The funny thing was that over the years of study I had witnessed many things that did not check out with the reference books. I did not know if it was because my hippos were different, or if, because I knew them all individually, I could see things more clearly.

Having spent so many years studying them, I had noticed patterns. I found many of their behaviour traits repetitive rather than just a fluke. The books stated that at around ten months they were weaned, but all my calves kept on suckling up to 18 months to two years of age and, in the odd case, two and a half years. The udder was full and they were drinking. It was not just a suck or two; it lasted for up to ten minutes in one session.

Bob, I knew, was an old hippo, and perhaps his age had saved him on many a day when hunters had seen him displaying in the river. His lower canine teeth were broken; one had broken off completely in a fight with Happy. It now sat on my bookshelf. The other was short and worn down with age.

The canine teeth never stop growing as they have open roots, but because of Bob's advanced age the teeth were brittle and broke off more than they grew. He depended on his back teeth for eating, grinding the grass with these. Hippos graze with their lips and then eat the grass using their back molars. Those I could see only occasionally when he gave a huge gape. I believed Bob was well into his forties, as people who had visited this area a long time ago talked about him and I had seen old photographs that clearly showed it was Bob.

On 31 January 2003, Bob followed Abe and Odile up to another weir called the Majekwe. This weir had been Happy's home at first. Abe had been one of his females. Happy had not reappeared since 2002 and I feared that he might be the dead hippo bull that the game scouts had found. I kept hoping that he had just gone away, as one bull had been seen at a dam before he followed the tracks of a female hippo. The cow had been living at the dam and both sets of tracks were seen heading off towards the Mkwasine River.

Over the next two days I saw Bob with Abe and Odile and Abe's younger calf, Tacha. They had been joined by Wish and her son, Pavodok. Bob seemed content, having left the rest of his females near our home. He showed off for me there as well. Obviously, he did not mind my being close to him in this new territory.

Then, without any warning, my world fell apart. The fourth of February began like any other day, but by evening I knew I had lost the most important hippo of all of the Turgwe hippos.

My beautiful Bob had died.

Bob had been the largest hippo bull in the entire Turgwe River. He was also the oldest. In the years that I had lived here he had always been the most dominant of the hippo bulls. Bob had been the 'boss' and the most special of all the Turgwe hippos to me.

It was through knowing Bob and learning from him about hippos that all of the projects that this Trust had achieved and everything that had happened here with the hippos had occurred. Bob had taught me and allowed me into his space. A wild African hippo bull had let a human female be part of his daily life.

In 1990, when we moved here and I found 15 hippos living in two small groups below our camp, Bob was the first hippo I met. In fact, Bob wanted to kill me when I came into contact with him. Being a sport hunting area, the safari clients had shot hippos. Some of Bob's family had died at the hands of man. He was not overly impressed with humans.

As the most dominant bull, his stance was one of assertiveness, which he showed by large gaping yawns with his eyes narrowed and an expression of anger. If I came too close to the riverbank he would gape and often charge, a huge cascade of water thrown into the air.

He hated the sound of rifle shots. He would panic, gape aggressively, and attack even his own family members if they were too close to him after a shot was fired. Bob was not a passive hippo; he was muscle and anger. Yet over the years this wild, savage fellow had turned into my very special friend.

Bob took three years to make his peace with me, perhaps to view me as one of the river's inhabitants. He learnt to recognise my voice. I, in turn, discovered that the sight or scent of me got him mad. Then I was just another dangerous human.

However, if I talked and called him by his name, chatting to him as I would to any other animal, he would calm down. It took three years, but at the end of that time I could sit just a few feet from Bob on the river's edge. He would go about his business as if I was not there.

Bob's acknowledgement even stretched as far as mating his females while I stood six metres away. Twice he had fights with other hippos and I stood watching, taking photos, and he was not the slightest bit bothered by my presence.

Bob would come when I called him. He could be 450 metres up-stream in the Turgwe River. He could be hidden from my sight under reeds, he could be on land opposite me, and I would call and he would come. He would move towards wherever I stood. Often he would be moving under water and just a slight ripple on the surface or the light catching his bulk under water would tell me he was on his way. Then a loud roar of expelled water would announce his arrival, his head shooting out of the river, his mouth in a huge, open-mouthed gape.

Bob had come to see me.

Bob did this to such an extent that during the happy years from 1995 to 1999 safari clients accompanying me were given the most magnificent show. Bob performed for these people.

If his family were sleeping on land and began to panic and start their rush back into the river when I approached, either alone or with safari clients, all I had to do was talk to Bob. He would stop them by lifting up his head, his alert, intelligent eyes not missing a thing, and he would listen. After a little while of my constant greeting monotone he would lie down on the sand again and his family would follow his example.

During our life together Bob became a media star. He was photographed and the chief hippo in practically every article written about these hippos. He was seen on American, Australian and British TV, as well as the Discovery Channel. Bob had always been the king, and the star among these amazingly wonderful animals.

Bob also probably saved me on two occasions from being killed. I had been too blasé, too enamoured of the beautiful parts of Africa to look too much at its uglier aspects. Crocodiles fascinate me, but twice Bob woke me up and made me aware that I was becoming a little bit too familiar with these prehistoric predators. Both times the crocodile could have easily grabbed and eaten me if it had not been for Bob.

In those days, the main problems we had here were natural, and sometimes I could spend six hours each day just studying the Turgwe hippos. Watching them often watching me, but also getting on with their lives. It became so easy that I was not even noticed, as long as I announced my presence and talked to them on my arrival.

The honour of being in the space of wild animals, of watching them mate, play, fight, groom each other, roll in the water and generally get on with being hippos, was all thanks to Bob.

I would speak and on more than one occasion he would answer me, so it could not have been a coincidence. His loud roar of greeting sounded more like a laugh than the scientific term of wheeze honking! Bob would greet me with his most recognizable call. Of all of the hippos, his voice was the loudest and deepest.

When I left the hippos I would always say goodbye. One does not sit with wild animals for six hours and then just get up and walk off. In my eyes, one thanks them and pays them the respect they are due. Bob always, always, called out as I left the group. Several journalists even mentioned this in their articles.

Bob was so very special.

When I nearly became a meal for the crocodile it was Bob who let me know that the wily predator was about to lunge out of the water and end my days of hippo observation. Some people may ridicule this, but over the years I have watched several of the Turgwe hippos let other animals know about danger. Nobody knows why hippos do this.

Sometimes Bob left his family, which he would do each year. In the old days, before the land invasions and the takeover of the hippos' grazing lands by these so-called war veterans and their minions, Bob had two permanent territories. It was to those areas I took the safari clients. For an hour or so they met a bunch of hippos that were very different to your average group, all thanks to Bob.

It always felt different when I visited his family and Bob was off on one of his jaunts. The space was obviously empty of big Bob, and although all these hippos had their own characters and ways, it was Bob's presence that I missed. I would be so overjoyed when he came back to the family.

I would fear for Bob, but not from another hippo. For Bob, I feared man.

Opposite our home was a sport hunting area. There used to be a bow-hunting and photographic area downstream. Now that part just had the invaders, war vets and no animals, as they had killed so many and the other animals had fled.

At first I feared the safari hunters. A wealthy hunter will pay up to US$6 000 to kill a hippo in his prime. Bob, being a bull, was a likely candidate. The owners would constantly tell me they were going to kill him. It was their idea of humour.

When you spend hours with an animal, learning things you never knew. When you see that animal for what it is. When you watch it being a father, a fighter, a protector, a clown, and you think of some person killing him so that they can mount his ancient head on their wall, far away from Africa, well, it cuts a large hole into your heart.

Funnily enough, those were the so-called good days.

I had always feared man with regard to my Bobby. Yet I am thankful. I am thankful and humbled by his ending. Bob left us as Bob lived. He died fighting for what was his, a hippo cow on heat, Abe. Another bull ended my old hippo's life.

The game scouts who came to our home that day reported finding a dead hippo. They did not know it was Bob, but the minute they described him my stomach knotted and pain gripped my heart.

Bob lay in a tiny pool of water. He was not lying on his side but sitting propped up against a granite rock. His head was resting on another rock. This was a position Bob often took, as his head was very large and so very heavy. Any convenient leaning object, inanimate or living, was used. Often one of his family members became his leaning post.

His legs were folded quite naturally under the bulk of his body. He had been dead for a couple of days, but nature's dustmen had hardly touched him. The worms had begun their clean-up job and one of Bob's back legs had been slightly eaten by a small crocodile, but in general he looked amazingly untouched.

In fact, the most incredible thing was his face and his facial expression. I had always been able to gauge Bob's behaviour by his face, the way he held his head, how he gaped, how he opened his eyes.

Now Bob had his mouth slightly agape, but it rested on the rock facing the pool where his two females, Abe and Wish, and their calves, Tacha and Pavodok, were living.

There was no sign of pain, struggle, fear or panic. He looked as if he had just given a huge sigh and left us. I even photographed and videoed my Bob for the final time. This may sound macabre, but he looked so beautiful, even in death.

There was another bull with the females. I only saw his nostrils and twice he put his head out of the water to breathe, but on both occasions his movements were so quick that I could not clearly identify him.

It was getting late and the riverbed we crossed to find my Bob was still soft from the rains. We needed to leave them and drive back to our home.

Bob had died the way he had lived. As a bull, defending his right to a family, as the king of the hippos.

This time he had been a little bit too old, too slow to win the battle, but he would always be the champion to me.

There would be disorder now. At home by Hippo Haven were 16 of the hippos. One male, Storm, was Bob's son. Storm had just turned six.

If the other bull that had killed Bob came down to this pool, he might chase Storm away. Hippo bulls mature at the age of about 11 or 12. Storm was big for his age as he had his father's genes, but he was still a baby in hippo bull terms. At this moment he was looking after the other hippos, but he was too young to become the territorial bull for the family.

Then there was Tembia, Bob's other son. Tembia was conceived when I fed the hippos during the horrendous drought of 1992. He was born in June 1993. Tembia looked so much like his dad. He had been living around these hippos for the past year, spending up until Christmas living in the cemented pan that we built for them. Now, with the rains having flooded the Turgwe and creating more channels and deeper areas for a single bull to live, he had moved away again.

He was old enough to try to look after the family, but he would not remain the territorial bull for this area if he were challenged by the bull I had seen the previous day.

It would be necessary for me to identify this bigger bull. It could be Happy or it could be a stranger. It could stay up at the Majekwe weir where it killed my Bob or it could move down here, taking over the main hippo group. The hippos needed a dominant bull to live with them. I could only wait to see what was going to happen.

I held no anger or any resentment towards the bull that had killed my Bob. Bob died as a hippo bull should. Living free in the wild, not in captivity. Not dying from starvation due to old age, when his lips would not have been able to tear up the grass and his teeth became too worn to eat it. He did not, thank God, die at the hands of man. A poacher or a sport hunter did not kill him. His head would not adorn anyone's wall.

Bob would still be alive in my heart; he would always remain that very special hippo. He was the star in my first video, *For the Love of*

Hippos. He had given so many people wonderful photographs over the years, and my photos of his face are all over my home. He was also the Trust logo; the sketch of his face is on the Land Rover. Bob could never die, but there was, as with any death, a terrible emptiness and heaviness in my body. A large, sinking feeling in my tummy, and such aloneness.

I sat with his family the next morning. Abe and Tacha had returned to the group. Only Wish and Pavodok were still up at that weir with the new bull. The hippos were their same lovely selves. Storm was playing open-mouthed pushing games with his little sister, Hope. Blackface, Bob's favourite female hippo, slept quietly with her calf, Inonde, leaning against the riverbank. Blackface had mellowed over the years, but was still unpredictable and would charge out of the water on two to three occasions each year.

The rest of the hippos behaved like hippos. None of them appeared to miss my lovely Bob. Missing somebody or something is perhaps just a human emotion. Maybe these hippos were far cleverer than us. I knew elephants mourned their dead and a monkey or a baboon would carry a baby who had died until its body mummified. I was sure that Blackface was in mourning, as she was quieter than she had ever been in the past.

I would have to learn to stop listening for Bob's voice. Several times that day I had heard the hippos calling as they normally did. I had to check myself as I found myself listening for Bob. I would learn to get over the pain of his not being around. In a way my selfishness of wanting him still here was wrong. He was free and probably being a great bull hippo wherever he was right now.

I felt terribly sorry for his supporters, as many people had adopted Bob. He was the most popular of all of the Turgwe hippos. A couple of his parents had actually been here and met him. All I could do was write and tell them that Bob had had a good life. For a wild hippo bull, he had lived a long life. He became a very famous and important hippo, not just for other hippos but for humans as well.

Thanks to big Bob, there is a Turgwe Hippo Trust, and thanks to Bob I had spent those last years having a privileged relationship with a very special animal. Somehow I had to find the strength to move on and continue to help the hippos, but I would never forget my Bob.

FIFTEEN

An accident waiting to happen

Three days after Bob's death Tembia joined the hippos near our home. The very next day, much to my astonishment, Robin appeared in the weir with Tembia. Robin had fed with the hippos during the drought and I always thought he was Blackface's son since he is also a black-skinned hippo. I thought he was perhaps Bob's offspring, having been allowed to eat alongside Bob and the others during the drought.

Ten years previously he had left this area, moving 22 kilometres downstream into a natural pool. Later, one of Bob's females, Lace, and their son Tembia, joined him. Robin accepted Tembia and the three of them spent the following years living together. Once Lace had conceived by Robin, he chased Tembia away from the pool. Tembia eventually found his way back here. Robin stayed with Lace and his new calf, Enfin, and had never once returned to this area. Now, only a few days after Bob's death, he was back, as was Tembia. How did they know about Bob's death? Did hippos have the same telepathic ability as elephants?

This time Robin would not accept Tembia and started chasing him, since Tembia was then much smaller. He was no match for Robin, even though Robin had a gammy leg. His right front leg was misshapen, bent at an angle, as if at some stage in his early life he had twisted it badly and it had not set properly. He walked well but had a slight limp, so I doubted whether he could run as fast as another hippo.

Wish had not rejoined the family and Abe had also left, taking Tacha and moving up to the Majekwe weir, where Tembia joined her and Wish. Tembia was very young, just under 11 years old, but the two females appeared to prefer his company to Robin's, as they did not return to the pool near our home.

Robin took the family away from Bob's weir pool, moving just under a kilometre upstream into a natural pool. This pool I had named the Owl Tree Pool, as a pair of Pel's fishing owls often perched in the canopy of a large Jackalberry tree adjacent to the pool.

Perhaps the weir pool still held too much of Bob's scent, as Robin would not live in it. Now that he had a family he had become docile and somewhat shy in comparison with his behaviour during the drought, when he and Bob had harassed Happy. He also seemed to have forgiven me for throwing oranges at him, since he was not in the slightest bit aggressive.

Jean-Roger, as I had predicted, ended up having to use the rifle in a manner that was incredibly upsetting, but sadly all part of the new Zimbabwe in which we now lived.

Occasionally on our patrols we heard dogs barking and knew that they were with poachers but, not having any means to stop them, we had little choice but to ignore them.

Now when Jean heard dogs close to us he investigated. So far he had ended up having to shoot four dogs. The poachers had been trying to dig a warthog out from its burrow. Directed to it by the barking dogs, Jean had arrived at the warthog's hole to find two poachers with about seven dogs. They immediately ran off, but Jean shot four of their dogs. He had found two skinned baby warthogs, with no sign of the mother or any other members of her family.

I found this dog killing horrendous and had to take myself into a quiet place to try to adjust to this new turn of events. It wasn't the dogs' fault that they had been brought into the area by these men to be used as hunting tools. Rationally, I knew the dogs were probably better off dead, but even so it was still very difficult to condone. In Holland I had volunteered at an animal shelter where dogs and cats were given refuge, and now my own husband was shooting dogs. It was all because of these land invasions that these terrible things were happening.

Then the poachers started hunting kudu and bushbuck with their dogs right by our home.

On two occasions, first with five dogs and then with three, they were directly in front of the house. The five dogs surrounded a large kudu bull, obviously having chased it a long distance, for it was completely

156

exhausted. Its sides heaved with the exertion and its tongue lolled, yet it still held its ground while the dogs leapt about trying to bring it down.

Jean shot three of the dogs before the others were suddenly whistled off from afar. The dogs took off in that direction and Jean could just make out the poachers as far upstream as the riverine bush. Every shot that Jean had fired when shooting those dogs wracked my body and I felt as if I, too, was dying, flinching and feeling quite sick. Yet when I looked at the kudu standing there without even the strength to run away from the sound of rifle shots, I realised we had to make a choice. If we didn't stand our ground the poachers would swamp our area and every hippo and all the other animals around us would die. Sometimes you have to fight fire with fire but, my God, it was soul-destroying.

Fortunately, after about half an hour the kudu recovered. Jean and I watched it from the house as it shook itself as though coming out of some kind of trance and slowly walked towards the river. There it took a long, slow drink and I realised it would make it, thanks to Jean's intervention.

The stress of this new life, with death right next to my own home, was taking its toll and Jean and I had begun arguing. Stress created anger, which we took out on each other. I knew if we did not have the rifle and if Jean was not prepared to use it more animals would die, but it was so morally destructive. I wondered for how long our nerves could handle it. Violence creates a violent backlash and killing is an evil pursuit that can only give its perpetrators bad karma.

One Sunday morning as I prepared our breakfast, I again heard at least three dogs barking. They sounded very close, almost at the bottom of our camp. I shouted to Jean in the bathroom, telling him there were dogs nearby, realizing as I did so that I was sealing their fate. He rushed through, grabbed the weapon and dashed out.

Then I heard shots and the yelps of dogs and, in a totally cowardly manner, stuck my fingers in my ears to block out the sound of the dogs yelping in pain. Clearly, Jean had wounded one.

After a few minutes he returned, his face deathly pale. He said, 'I have just shot a poacher.'

He told me what had happened. Apparently, he had arrived at the bottom of our camp and, opening the rickety gate, had run down to the hippo path. He had realised that the dogs were near our pan, the one we built in the '92 drought. Next to the pan was a warthog hole where NafNaf, the son of Arthur, often lived. NafNaf, like his father, would often visit our home at night for food, but never a tummy rub. Only Arthur had allowed that intimacy.

Jean had seen a man kneeling down next to the hole holding a long piece of wood, which he appeared to be poking into the hole. Around him four dogs were running around, barking like crazy. Jean shouted at the man, who leapt up and rushed off. Jean then turned to shoot at one of the dogs. He missed with his first shot and wounded it with the second. As he took aim again and was about to pull the trigger, he saw the man's back in the rifle's sight.

Unseen by Jean, a bow and arrows lay on the ground exactly where the dog was standing and the man had come back for them. Jean was already pulling the trigger, so all he could do was push the rifle up, hoping he did not hit the guy.

The guy fell down, but Jean assumed this was just a reflex action, more or less as we had done that time we met men with rifles in the bush. So Jean told him to stay where he was and then shot the other dogs. When this was over he told the man to get up. The guy pointed at his shoulder where, to Jean's utter horror, he saw some blood seeping through his shirt. The guy said he couldn't move or stand up. Jean told him he would get help and ran all the way back to me.

To say Jean was in a mess was an understatement. I called Silas, telling him to grab a wheelbarrow and follow Jean to the pan. It turned out that Silas knew the man. He was actually his blood cousin, the nephew of Job Mangula and, according to Silas, one of Job's main poachers.

From the moment they returned with the man in the wheelbarrow I had to take over, as Jean was in such a state. I suggested they go straight over to Roger and Anne to check on his injury. Anne, before marrying Roger, had qualified as a nurse. I told Jean he had to report to the police at the nearest station, which was over two hours away. I would stay home alone so Silas could help the man into the vehicle and, as he knew him, keep him calm. His name was Tatenda Mangula.

I asked Jean to radio me once he knew what was going to happen. I was trying to be practical and to keep Jean calm, but I was extremely frightened. Tatenda did not seem to be badly hurt, but it would mean more trouble for a white man to shoot an African, even though he was poaching, than if a war vet shot one of us. Jean could be locked up immediately.

I spent the next hours waiting at home, worried stiff. I used up all my prayers asking for Jean to be able to return home and all to be OK for the man and for Jean. As our home had no security fence and was not really lockable, somebody had to stay at home, but waiting for news was in many ways worse than being with Jean.

A little later, I received a radio call from Anne telling me that Jean had gone on to the police and not to worry.

Anne told me that Jean had picked up Graham, the Conservancy man in charge of security, and they had taken the poacher to the police. She thought that Tatenda was not badly hurt, just in shock. She suggested I try to organise a lawyer for Jean-Roger and gave me the name and phone number of Roger's lawyer, who lived in Chiredzi.

I asked her to contact him by phone and she came back to me saying he would work with Jean, but on no account should Jean-Roger make a statement until he, the lawyer, was present. The police would probably want to come out here, but Jean should not say anything officially until the lawyer was with him. Jean should go back to Chiredzi the next day and pick him up – that is, if Jean was not immediately arrested.

I managed to get hold of Jean on the radio, for, as it turned out, Jean was at that moment driving back into the Conservancy, accompanied by two policemen.

They arrived an hour later and Jean filled me in quickly. The police had been relatively all right about the incident and, in fact, seemed totally unconcerned about the health of the poacher, just telling him to sign a paper. It took time to sort out the official records, and when they asked Tatenda what he had been doing he admitted that he had been 'hunting'.

After half an hour or so they had told Jean to take Tatenda into Chiredzi, drop him off at the hospital and then return to them. There he was to pick up two details, a sergeant and a corporal. After that they came home to take notes and go to the spot where the incident had happened. Initially, they thought they would get a statement, but when Jean explained what the lawyer had said to me, they were fine. Everything was extremely relaxed, considering the seriousness of what had occurred.

Jean said that they were never anything other than pleasant. They said in their opinion it was obviously an accident and that Tatenda was a fool for poaching right on our small property. Jean had given them the bow and arrows, and had taken one of the shot dogs with him as evidence.

As they were chatting in the gazebo, who should come stomping into our home but Job, accompanied by another man. He gave us his ugliest scowl and then, in front of the police, loudly declared, 'Mr Paolillo, I have just been told by my men about Tatenda, my son, that you have shot him, while he was out looking for my cattle. What do you think you are doing?'

Jean replied, 'How can your nephew have been looking for cattle when he had his head stuck down a warthog's hole, with dogs and a bow and arrows? Plus he had a stick and was trying to dig the pig out of its hole.'

He bit back further words as the policemen were listening to everything, but Job, in full hearing of both policemen, raised his voice. 'Mr Paolillo, if you tell these policemen that my son was poaching animals, you and your wife are going to have many, many big problems.'

Well, that did it. Jean lost it.

'Fuck you, Job! Are you now threatening me in front of these policemen? Well, you can just shove it. I am only saying what happened and the police have got the evidence. Now it is up to the courts of Zimbabwe to decide what has happened here today, so you had better keep away from my wife and my home, or else.'

The police kept silent during this entire exchange. It was only when things looked as though they might get out of hand that they stepped in. Ignoring Job, they suggested that they go over to where the incident had happened. They walked off, with Job and the other man following them.

After about half an hour they all returned. Jean then had to drive them the nearly two-hour journey one way back to the station. Job had apparently made more threats at the warthog hole, but Jean had wisely ignored him. He finally got home at well past ten that night, totally exhausted, but at least he had not been put in jail.

The hospital doctor decided to keep Tatenda for further examination. The lawyer told us that we should not go anywhere near Tatenda while he was in hospital, as it would look as if we were trying to interfere with the course of justice.

A part of me hated Tatenda and I felt it would be justice if he were to drop dead, as he must have been responsible for ending countless animals' lives. Yet I knew that if he died Jean would be booked for murder, even though the shooting had been an accident and Tatenda was openly poaching.

The next day Jean once more returned to Chiredzi, where he picked up the lawyer and the police. On the way back the lawyer asked Jean to drop him off near the house in which Job was squatting. The lawyer said he wanted to have a word with him. It turned out that the lawyer used to be the chief prosecutor in Chiredzi until he quit to work independently, and he knew Job Mangula, whom he had twice prosecuted in court.

After meeting Job, he said Job would not bother us again. He had told him that if he interfered with us, he would be the one in jail. His nephew's case would be tried by the law and not by politics. Somehow his words had sunk in, for Job never came near us again, keeping away from our home. He even stopped using the dirt road that led past our house to the communal lands.

The lawyer reassured me that Jean would be coming home and, sure enough, five hours later, in drove Jean. He had been booked for attempted murder, but without any arrest. The case would now go the legal route, starting at the magistrate's court. As matters stood at the moment, he was free to go about his normal life and would be told when to appear in court.

In the meantime, we phoned the hospital and were told that Tatenda was in a satisfactory condition, but that the bullet was stuck in the front of his chest. The doctors had decided not to remove it as this would be more dangerous than leaving it there. They said he was young and could easily live with a bullet in his chest.

We arranged for a second doctor to check on Tatenda privately, as the last thing we needed was negligence on the part of the doctors. This doctor was a local man who was on good terms with the doctors at the hospital. He confirmed that their diagnosis was correct. Because of the small calibre of the weapon the bullet was tiny, but the X-ray showed it was lodged in the front of one lung. It would be unwise to take him all the way to Harare to be operated on.

At the end of the month Jean got a call from the police telling him to report to the magistrate's court in Chiredzi the next day. Tatenda was out of hospital and the court would now decide on the procedure. Jean was very nervous and I knew I would be more of a hindrance than a help if I went along with him, so once more I remained at home.

All that happened was that the case was remanded for another month. The lawyer would inform Jean when he had to go there again. As it involved a two-hour drive one way in to Chiredzi, we were very lucky. Roger told us that some of his game scouts were being remanded on a weekly basis and he had to provide transport and send them in each week.

So we continued our lives. Roger suggested we see Barry across the river and borrow a shotgun from him, since the police had confiscated Roger's .22. Barry agreed, so we were back to having a weapon at the house.

I was very unhappy about this, but Jean would not listen. We had quite a number of arguments about it, but he still got his own way. He refused to patrol in the bush without a weapon. He reckoned that he still had to kill any dogs if they came near our home. All around us was death and devastation, and now my husband could end up in jail. I wondered where the end was to all this. Was this kind of life all we would know from now on?

Helping the hippos was one thing, but having Jean charged with attempted murder, quite another. And the situation in Zimbabwe was not improving. Every day new atrocities occurred. More and more white people were removed from their farms, often with only 24 hours' notice, and that was if they were lucky. Many people were leaving the country and there did not seem to be anything positive at all to hang on to.

Hippo Haven was our home. We had built it with our own hands and had put most of our savings into it. The hippos were the most important part of my life and our home and surroundings were as special to Jean-Roger. We spent many a night discussing our lives, and decided that we had to remain looking after the hippos and pray that somehow these problems would lessen and things would revert to something approaching normal.

For the rest of the year and into the next half Jean had to go to court every month and then every two months. Each time, after waiting a few hours, his case would be adjourned. Amazingly, the poaching in our area had slowed down dramatically. The poachers were now scared of

Jean, we found out! Two people could only do so much when it came to patrolling the bush and removing snares, and so any slackening of the poaching pressure was welcomed. We still found snares, but about a third of the number we used to find previously.

Finally, in May 2004, nearly one year after the incident, Jean went to the court as normal, but when his name was called the magistrate informed him that the case against him had been dropped due to lack of evidence. He was free to go and would not need to continue reporting to the court. She added in a low voice that he should keep the outcome quiet and not advertise it too much, just in case some people disagreed with it.

Jean came home that afternoon with a smile that lit up his entire face. After nearly a year of living with the fear of a prison sentence, the relief that it was all over was immense. Maybe the tension and strain that had etched his face for so long could at last fall away.

Most people in our area were amazed at our good fortune. Other whites who had been in similar positions years before the political unrest started had been sent to jail and had faced awful problems. Some had been in and out of court for years; or worse, in and out of jail, booked and then released, only to be rearrested. Jean had always had a lucky streak.

Amazingly, Tatenda got caught poaching just two months after this outcome, this time by Roger's scouts. He was cutting up an impala ram and had several snares in his possession. When taken to the police station, he was given a paltry fine and released into Job's custody. Once again, politics took precedence over justice.

Poaching once more escalated in our area and we began spending more and more time on our patrols, trying to cover larger areas. With the dry season, the hippos had to go further into the bush to find grass. We were now finding small mammal traps set for squirrels and birds, or tiny rope snares attached to branches in the koppies that had been set for the dassies (the rock hyrax). It was as if the poachers didn't intend to let anything survive.

On one day we removed over 65 small mammal traps and 205 dassie snares. If the traps and dassie snares had been successful the poachers would have been able to sell even that meat, for they would have made money with the amount of animals killed. It was obvious that these people would not stop killing until every living thing was gone. How we had managed to keep all the hippos alive until then was miraculous.

We could not afford to go away from home for more than a couple of days at a time since the road passed right by the invaders, who knew of any movements we made. We were trapped and, if we had to go away for more than a day or two, had to leave singly.

We would perform the stupidest antics to leave without the poachers knowing we were both away from home. Often one of us would drive the pickup and the other lie down on the passenger seat, head in the driver's lap. As we passed the huts, the people saw only one of us leaving, and we would do the same when we returned. It was a ridiculous way to behave, but we knew that if they knew neither of us was at home they would have more confidence to come and poach in our area.

The stress of our lifestyle meant that we snapped at each other regularly and our tempers were short. The drive over to Humani depressed me badly. Once a month we drove to Chiredzi, going through the area they had taken over. My spirits sank on every occasion we had to use the road.

All you saw were mud huts, cut and burning trees, cattle, goats and people. Only two short years previously there had been wild bush and wild animals. My hatred towards these people consumed me and I spent every single day plotting revenge. This mental attitude was very unhealthy and very bad for us both.

For years I had argued with and at times verbally attacked the white hunters who killed the occasional animal in our area. Now, in a short time, these invaders had systematically wiped out not one or two animals, but entire families. Where once hundreds of animals had crossed the road and gone about their natural lives, now you were lucky if you saw one kudu or eland on that same road.

That particular drive had been one of the prettiest in the conservancy. Roger had stopped all hunting around that area years before and had built his Turgwe Safari camp, a beautiful open-plan camp for photographic safaris. The animals had been very tame compared with those in other areas. In that 20-minute drive to Humani you would come across wildebeest, zebra, impala, kudu, bush pig and warthog. Often cheetah would be seen in the daylight hours and at night, if you drove along that road, you could guarantee one or two leopard sightings. One black rhino used that area as part of his territory and every year an elephant herd moved around there for a month or two.

My hippos had lost half of their grazing lands when the people took over the Chlabata area. They had also lost the pools downstream, which had been part of Bob's territory every year during the rains. In the initial stage of the invasions they had tried to keep on living in those areas, but the war veterans as well as the people they had encouraged to settle on the land had thrown and catapulted rocks at the hippos and generally harassed them. Jean and I on a few occasions witnessed this. Once we tried to reason with them and the three men became so abusive that we backed off. On another occasion I saw four men throwing huge rocks at the hippos and I lost it, shouting at them from the bank above. The men came charging at me. The only thing that saved me was that I was above them and could get back to camp before they made it to the top of the bank.

The hippos learnt to avoid those areas and, to compensate for their loss, Jean excavated two new pools in the river by using the Trust's sand pump. The constant poaching and Jean's having to kill dogs was seriously affecting my mental health. Saving a warthog but killing a dog seemed so counter-productive, and yet it was an evil necessity. The dogs were so starved of food and affection that in a way, perhaps, it was kinder, but it still went against all my beliefs. The girl born in England had had to harden her heart so much to live in Africa. I was now a woman who could act as tough as most of the men without showing a spot of emotion, but inside it was totally different. Death and the killings were eating into my soul.

I tried my best to alleviate my unhappiness by monitoring the hippos' progress. That year five new babies had been born and I was fortunate to see two of the calves, Zen and Chubby, on their birthday. No hippo had replaced Bob in my affections, although a young male, Kuchek, named after my pony, was the cutest of them all.

Tembia was rapidly becoming more and more like his father in his behaviour and his looks. On occasion he opened his mouth in a wide-mouthed gape for my camera without any malice, just like his dad used to do. Perhaps having been so close to Bob in his younger years, he was now copying his father. As he grew he looked more and more like Bob, even having the same colour disfigurement on his lower inside jaw, a large black mark.

I was lucky in having my passion for the hippos to give me a break from the daily patrolling, plus I had the letters that I received from some of my hippo supporters, which always gave me a wonderful morale boost. Jean-Roger had nothing, and our financial situation was perilous. We had been living off our savings and the odd bit of money I made from writing articles about the hippos, or from my photography.

The video I made of the hippos was a Trust project. We were not employed by the Trust, as the Trust's earnings were far too small to give either of us a decent salary. It did now pay for the animals and for Silas, but we lived off of our own resources and these were rapidly shrinking. Jean knew he couldn't go back to geology and leave me alone at home, and if I went away all the animals we had fought for would be dead within a week of my leaving. And we were sure the invaders would take over our home. We were trapped.

The tension also affected our health and stamina. At times I had to really push Jean to make him come along on a patrol. The daily picking up of snares and the occasional dead animal found was so soul destroying that he was becoming sick of it all.

He did not want to give up our home and our environment, but, not being an animal person, he would have been content to stay at the house and just protect our immediate surroundings. I told him that if we were to stick it out I was only prepared to do so if it meant putting all of our energy into saving what little wildlife we could. Otherwise my years of helping the hippos and all I believed in were pointless, and I might as well have left this stressful existence to start again somewhere else.

During all of this tension, young Zen was attacked by another hippo.

It is not uncommon for a male hippo to attack a younger male. If the younger male is not careful it can be killed. The older bull knows that at some stage they will compete for territory and if he can remove the youngster before he becomes too much of an opponent, he will. In Zen's case it could even have been another female who attacked him, if her own calf was a male.

I found him living away from the family. He had several wounds, of which two severe cuts stood out – one near an old wound low on his stomach and the other in his neck. In my opinion neither was life threatening as he was still grazing on the day I came upon him. He was on land and, although he looked awful, I believed he would survive.

166

Two days later I heard shots in the exact area where Zen was hiding, a channel of the Turgwe River less than a kilometre downstream from his mother and the main family group. As his mother had given birth again, she had not been in a position to protect him from the attack, so he had cleverly removed himself and gone to hide up in this new area.

As it meant crossing the river to investigate the shots and because I have such a volatile temper, Jean-Roger told me to stay at home. He would see what had happened. My instincts told me that Zen had been hurt or killed.

Jean was gone for a few hours. On his return I took one look at his face and knew that my worst fears were right. Zen was dead. Jean had found tractor tracks at the channel pool where something large had been dragged and loaded, probably Zen.

He had continued walking towards the hunting camp, his anger mounting as he walked. He turned a bend on reaching the Gwezi River and came across Frikkie with a client standing by a baobab tree, at the foot of which lay a dead leopard. Hound dogs surrounded them and it was obvious they had shot the leopard after the dogs had forced the animal to take refuge up a tree. Leopard hunting with dogs is allowed in Zimbabwe and yet poachers with dogs have their own dogs killed. Is this not hypocrisy?

When Jean confronted Frikkie, he did not deny anything. He told Jean that he had seen Zen and his wounds, videoed him and then told Barry (the owner of Makore Ranch) that Zen was on his last legs. Barry had checked the video and as the client, Geoff from the United States, was keen to add a hippo to his trophy list, they decided to shoot my Zen. Zen was still a baby, a juvenile. He had only recently been ousted from the family group. Six months previously he had still been suckling, and yet this hunter was taking his head back to the United States to stick on a wall as a trophy. In human years Zen was a seven-year-old boy. What next would they hunt? A baby? A hippo calf?

There was nothing either of us could do, as it was too late for Zen, but I made a point of mentioning it at the next Conservancy meeting. I knew that the majority of stakeholders looked upon it as nothing. I was banging my head against a brick wall. If you hunt animals and kill them for money, you cannot possibly see them as deserving a natural life. They are just commodities.

Between the security situation and people like Frikkie and his totally unethical ways, the months blurred into each other and still the poaching continued. It was not often that laughter could be heard at home or that any break in this daily routine could be enjoyed. For over three years we had been removing snares. We had found over 2 000, but we knew these were just a drop in the ocean. For how long could we continue without a break? Intimacy and romance had gone out of the window with all this stress and it was only our close bond that kept us together. We had not even had time to recover from Jean's affair when all hell had broken out in Zimbabwe.

Then things got far worse than we could ever have imagined.

SIXTEEN

Poachers and police

The poachers started harassing us at our home. They began by walking in the riverbed below the house carrying fishing rods. This was pure subterfuge, as by following their tracks we found set snares along the river's edge, the tracks clearly showing us that they were responsible.

When Jean noticed a group of men he would leave the house, going down to the river and trying to talk to them, telling them that fishing was not allowed. They were walking on our property and that the fish had been so reduced in number downstream that these pools were not to be fished. He pointed out that they had taken over 14 000 hectares of land with 16 kilometres of river frontage, while our land was a total of three-and-a-half hectares with a tiny part in the river. So these fish should be left alone. They just laughed at him, and then they would become belligerent.

Jean stood his ground, telling them we knew they were setting snares. If they did not want us to bring in game scouts to arrest them, it would be best if they went away. This always ended up with a lot of noise and shouting on their part until they realised Jean was not going to budge and they returned to the area they had taken over.

On occasion I would be alone at home while Jean went into Chiredzi for the day, and they would see his car leave. They would wait a while, then arrive below the house and begin calling and shouting and making a hell of a racket. I would send Silas to tell them to go away. He always returned with the same words. They had told him that they owned the river and I should shut up, or else I would not be happy. So one day I made a show of fighting back. I told Silas to go down and tell them I was going to get the game scouts. I drove off to Humani, revving the vehicle loudly as I left. I knew full well that there

169

would be no scouts available during the day, but my ruse paid off. Silas said the minute I drove off they left.

We would constantly find roadblocks of trees and rocks across our only access road. We would just stop and put the wood into the pickup to use later for firewood, thus saving Silas the job of cutting new wood for the boiler. Then we would remove the rocks. This became a weekly event as they began to push us, hoping we would back down. The pressure of having them in our face so regularly, with Jean continually having to tell them to get lost, became even more taxing.

One day we found them sitting at the hippos' pool, but on the island-side of the river. To get there they must have crossed the bush island, as the place where they sat fishing could only be reached through the island or by crossing the river full of crocodiles.

Jean was so angry when we saw them that he completely dismissed the presence of probably over 17 crocodiles. He ploughed through the shallowest part of the river towards them. At one point in the crossing he suddenly found himself chest-deep in the Turgwe. It was incredible that no crocodile took him at that moment. He carried on towards the men, who had started screaming at him, realizing they now had an advantage. He was but one man trapped across the river with six of them on the opposite side. I heard him saying, 'Be careful if you hurt me. My wife is filming you.'

This really made them mad and they shouted even louder, especially when they saw I really was filming them. Two of them ignored Jean and headed downstream, an easier route that would lead them to me. Jean, in turn, decided he had better return to me as they were becoming too abusive. He walked away, heading towards the weir wall.

To cross that weir wall was foolhardy, as the river was at its deepest there and the crocs always hid there to catch fish. I tried to look unconcerned as I slowly turned my back on the two approaching poachers and headed in the direction of our house.

I was hoping like mad that Jean would manage to cross over and catch up with me before they did. Fortunately, his luck held and he crossed the wall, meeting me, and we headed towards our home, with the two men, who had now been joined by their colleagues, continuing a furious shouting match behind us.

At the front of the house Jean told me to keep videoing while he turned back to confront them. There they lost their momentum, taking the route to the side of our home and shouting hysterically as they walked along. One man pulled himself up onto a tree's branch, hanging there imitating a monkey. If it had not been so unsettling it would have been funny. He thought it made him look aggressive, I suppose, like a large baboon would look, but he was a skinny man and only looked foolish.

I had caught it all on video, but the experience of being confronted by these six men full of such hatred left a bad taste in our mouths for the rest of the day. I wondered what they would do next. In the meantime, the hippos were getting twitchy and were not as calm as they used to be with me.

A few days later, Jean left the house accompanied by Silas to do some road repairs. Trees had fallen across one of the dirt roads on Angus. I was washing clothes in the bath when I heard the hippos calling more than normal. I left the washing, grabbed my binoculars and peered down to the river to see what had disturbed them.

As I came back in the house I heard Jean calling me.

He told me that as they left the house Silas noticed two men walking in the riverbed. Jean told Silas to wait for him and went down to tell the guys to move off. On his arriving in the riverbed the men had disappeared, but he could clearly see their two sets of tracks. He followed the tracks, which arrived at the bush island and went inside it. Then he saw they had left two homemade fishing rods at the entrance to a hippo pathway that went onto this island.

Jean knew that my 19 hippos, including six calves, were all on the island, probably sleeping. He couldn't believe that the men were so foolish as to go into that thickly bushed place. As he picked up the fishing rods, he heard the hippos snort and begin to make a lot of noise. Being too close to the bushes for comfort, he backed away and came home, telling me that he thought the two men were on the island with the hippos.

I replied that if they were, they deserved anything that might happen to them. Eventually I would really regret that remark.

Jean then went off with Silas to repair the roads.

Coming home, on the upstream part of the river, Silas suddenly called to Jean, pointing. Coming out of the bush island were two sets of human footprints. Jean realised that the guys had somehow crossed the island, exiting at that place. He was amazed that they had gone along the entire island without being hurt and felt that it was pretty unjust how the devil tended to look after his own. Then he forgot all about it.

We carried on with our normal day, unaware that this incident would have such serious repercussions. Soon our very lives and our pets' lives would be jeopardized.

It was early morning. Jean had gone up the koppie behind our home to make some phone calls as with the introduction of a cell phone setup we now could send emails on our laptop and make calls by climbing this rocky hill. I walked out of the kitchen into the backyard and could not believe what greeted my eyes.

Walking purposefully towards the house was a mob of 25 men. Among them were two wearing the uniform of the Zimbabwean police. Another man I immediately recognised as one of the poachers who had harassed us that day by the river. He strode up to me and demanded to know where Jean-Roger was.

When I told him I was ordered to go and fetch him, and the man instructed one of the others in the group to accompany me, with one policeman coming along as well. My heart was hammering and I felt breathless, trying to cope with whatever was about to happen. I knew that the mobs did what they wanted to do, but I was surprised they had two uniformed policemen with them.

As we climbed the 60-metre koppie we met Jean on his way down and, before I could say much, the war vet/poacher told him to follow them. It was about a missing person.

Jean was relatively calm, but then he had not seen the mob of people back at our home. Once there, the entire mob demanded that Jean go with them. They all started walking out of the property, heading down towards the river. All I could do was wait at home and pray. I knew that whatever was going to happen, I had to stay put. Jean had given me a reassuring smile as he walked off. I managed to count at least 25 men and realised another bunch was sitting over by the baobab near Silas's home.

The next 15 minutes or so dragged by with my imagination working overtime. I kept telling myself Jean had two policemen with him; surely they would keep the mob at bay? The clock ticked far too slowly.

I went to fetch the hand-held Conservancy radio, thinking that maybe I should call the Whittalls, when suddenly I heard lots of shouting and noise. The mob was coming back up the riverbank. To my horror I saw that Jean's hands were behind his back and clamped in metal handcuffs. I rushed towards the mob, demanding to know what was going on.

Once more my man told me to keep calm. He tried to tell me what the situation was, but the mob was angry and making a hell of a racket. I ignored them all and asked the policeman to tell me what was going on.

'Madam, your husband is under arrest. The evidence I have just seen makes it necessary for me to handcuff him and take him to the police station at Chiremwaremwa in Matsai.' Chiremwaremwa police station was probably about an eight-hour walk from our home.

While I was trying to take in what the policeman said, the other policeman told me to contact my neighbours and get a four-by-four drive vehicle to them. He told me what route they would be walking.

Before I could argue the mob started getting twitchy, demanding of the police that they get going. Jean managed to tell me that it looked as though someone might have been killed. They had all gone to the hippos' island and found bits of clothing and a spattering of blood on a tree. If somebody had been killed, they seemed to be blaming Jean-Roger.

He managed to smile, even under such tremendous pressure, and then they were leading him away, his hands cuffed behind his back. One policeman and the man who had harassed us at the river stayed at the house and told me to contact someone in the Conservancy on the radio while they listened.

Still clutching the radio, I called everyone I could think of. Of course, no one answered, as by now it was lunchtime. Eventually I called 'Emergency! Emergency!', which had the desired effect. Graham, the Conservancy security officer, replied. I told him in a few short words that Jean-Roger had been arrested by a mob and two uniformed policemen. I added that he was being walked back to Matsai, and could he please get hold of Roger for me and ask him to come over straight away.

When I finished speaking, I turned to say something to the two men to find them gone. I had not seen them leave.

Twenty minutes slowly passed, then in drove Roger. He was furious, but not with me. I knew he was worried and I explained quickly what had happened. He ordered me to get in the Land Cruiser with him and Peter, a hunter who worked for him. In the back of the vehicle were three trackers. I said I could not leave the house and animals. Silas was away on his week off, so there was no one to keep an eye on everything. I gave him two bottles of water and some sandwiches that I had hurriedly made for Jean. Jean suffered from a form of hypoglycaemia if he did not eat regularly. It was incredibly hot, and he had no water and had not had his breakfast.

Roger was not happy to leave me alone but the priority was to find Jean, so he drove off, engine revving as he tore along the dirt track. By now the radio was too flat to send messages, but I could still receive. For the next five hours my life became a nightmare.

I heard Roger call to others in the Conservancy, as everybody had by now been alerted. It seemed that they had not used the route the policeman had told me they would. All traces of the mob and my man had disappeared.

At one stage I heard Roger saying to another Conservancy member that he seriously believed this was a kidnapping and that those had not been genuine policemen with the mob. On hearing this, I nearly cracked up. If it was true, Jean might be being beaten or, worse, killed. It had happened before to farmers in Zimbabwe, in the last bad years. Nearly 90 per cent of the time kidnappings ended up with a body.

My own fears were at peak level, but I kept telling myself to be positive, to think good thoughts, not to let the negative get a hold. My animals sensed my fear and were loving, but I was terrified for Jean-Roger. I had to keep reminding myself that he had always been lucky and that somehow his luck would hold out. Only a few months previously a white man on one of the properties on the other side of Roger's had been badly beaten, but I tried to drive such thoughts from my mind.

Jean-Roger had been marched off at around nine in the morning. Finally, at four in the afternoon, Jane and Arthur arrived. As they arrived, sneaking up from the riverine area, there were Neil and Gary Duckworth from the hunting camp, accompanied by two armed game scouts. The boys had their hunting rifles with them.

After so many hours of tension and worry, suddenly seeing their faces did it for me: I burst into tears. All of them were kind and Jane in her no-nonsense way and Arthur in his dry-humoured manner told me to stop blathering and go and make some tea, as they were all thirsty. Tea was the universal answer to problems in Zimbabwe. It was the first time any of them had seen me cry.

Once we were all seated with our tea I told them what had happened. Neil suggested I go back with Jane to her home, but I was adamant. We had been fighting poachers for years. If I now left home because they had taken away my husband, the people down the road would probably come to loot and burn. Everything we had been trying to achieve would have been for nothing. I knew Jean would expect me to stay at home, and, anyway, the animals needed me.

Eventually, we compromised. Neil left me the two armed game scouts and then the others left. I still had no idea what was happening to my husband. While people had been present it had been easier to alleviate any fears, but now I was alone again I had to really take a grip of myself.

Finally, at eight that night, Rae contacted me by radio.

'Hotel, Hotel.' (This was our call sign, on account of the name Hippo Haven.)

'Hotel, Hotel, don't know if you can hear me. Karen, please press your buzzer once if you can.' This I duly did, so Rae would realise that the battery was not strong enough for me to respond.

'OK, Karen, Roger's got Jean-Roger. They picked him up five hours after leaving you. He is OK. I repeat, he is OK. Roger says to come to his house early tomorrow morning and he will let you know what is going on. OK, Karen, over and out.'

So, I thought, was Jean with Roger now, or what? But at least Rae had said Jean was OK. I did not sleep that night, spending most of it tossing and turning and analysing her words. Was Jean in prison or at Roger's? Surely if he had been there, they would have brought him home? My mind jumped from one scenario to the other. Eventually, in sheer exhaustion, I fell asleep, but not for long.

Just before first light I woke up. The game scouts were in the small house we had built for Silas years ago. I told them to keep an eye on our home and my animals and that I would not be too long, and drove off in a rush.

That drive to Humani seemed to last for ever, but on walking into

Roger's house I found Anne, who immediately gave me a cup of tea. She told me to sit down and listen to what had happened.

'Karen, it is all right, Jean is OK now. Roger found him at just near three in the afternoon. He looked really dreadful, like a little wizened old man. He was so dehydrated, all shrivelled up, but they had not hurt him.

'Apparently they walked in the opposite direction to where they told you they were going. They went through the bush, passing by all the squatters on Angus. Jean was handcuffed the entire time.

'One man pushed him to walk fast, the rest of the crowd walking at a normal pace. The one little policeman was incredibly brave, as he stuck to Jean like glue. The mob did not touch Jean, but along the route they kept shouting, "We have the murderer!" It seems that a meeting had already been organised with the chief war veteran for that area, a Mr Goni, and they were taking Jean there.

'It was John Mabasa who found Jean. They saw tracks going off and figured out the direction and by tracking finally met a young boy. He told them the people had just gone past with the *murungu* (white man). Roger found Jean just as they entered the Matsai. A bunch of women had joined the men and the crowd was getting terribly dangerous.

'Jean-Roger told us they were a minute or two away from explosion. The women were ululating and starting to shove him. Roger managed to get Jean onto the back of the vehicle alongside the policemen. Eight or so of the crowd of men jumped on as well and then Roger drove off in the nick of time.

'Roger went straight to the police station, but dropped off one of his trackers to try and get information. Later, Roger learnt that this meeting had been set up and all the people that poached around you and all of the squatters were there waiting for the arrival of Jean-Roger. If Roger had not come along then, Karen, I don't know what would have happened, but it would have been ugly.'

Anne did not need to say more.

She went on to tell me that the Matsai police station was a tiny prefab building and the policemen there did not want to hold Jean in the event of a mob coming for him. They told Roger to take Jean all the way to the Mkwasine police station. This was closer to Humani and Hippo Haven and on a drivable route; it just meant that Roger had to return via the Humani homesteads.

I had put a cooler bag with the sandwiches and water in Roger's vehicle and Jean had drunk most of it before getting to the police station. Once at Roger's, Anne forced him to eat a heavily salted ham sandwich. Hand-feeding him, as he was still cuffed, she filled him up with salt tablets and lemon juice.

Jean sweats really badly and I could just imagine how much liquid he had lost that day, with no water to replenish it. He told Anne that they had stopped at one village and the crowd had drunk and then offered Jean some really dirty-looking water. He had decided he would rather dehydrate than give them the pleasure of an upset stomach on the walk. Also, he was trying to look on top of the situation, as if he was not fazed by walking so many kilometres with his hands cuffed on the hottest day of the year.

Anne said Roger had sent Jean on to the police with one of their drivers and got hold of Graham, telling him to be ready to be picked up. On arrival at the police station they made Jean sit on the concrete floor like any common criminal, removing his shoes and leaving him handcuffed. The police did, though, put his hands in front of him before putting the handcuffs back on.

Finally, at ten that night they removed the handcuffs: he had worn them for over 12 hours. They then told Graham that Jean could go home to Graham's house but must report the next morning to go back to the scene of the crime with the police.

At eight in the morning I heard my husband's deep voice on the radio. Roger grabbed it before I could and was told by Jean that they were all on the way back – Jean, the police, and Amos, the brother of the supposedly missing man. The police wanted trackers from Roger, and he had to be ready to go with them to the hippos' island.

At last, for a couple of seconds, I could speak to Jean. The entire Conservancy, as well as the police, could hear the radio but I did not give a damn. I told him I loved him and was waiting at Roger's, and to keep being the strong guy I knew he was. I also managed to do this without tears, as I knew he needed me to be strong as well.

Only after the set was off did I feel the emotion taking over and disappeared into the bathroom to take control of myself.

At ten they drove in. I had barely a second or two to hug him and then everyone was off again. Roger told me to come along with him. Jean was with the police and Graham.

When we reached our home they all went off to the island, but Jean suggested I stay at the house. The thought of the hippos down there with all those people was worrying enough, but he said if I was there it might make matters worse. Roger and Peter had brought rifles and my heart was in my mouth. What if the hippos charged them? Who would die?

The noise that the men made on arriving at the island could be heard clearly up at the house. Roger explained to the policeman that I had told him that 19 hippos with six calves, two of them under one month of age, were in there. It was insanity just to crawl in. It was best to frighten them off with noise. As the island was more than a kilometre long, he hoped they would move further into it.

I dreaded hearing a shot but, thank God, there was none. Finally, they all reappeared. Then the questions began.

The policemen were carrying the clothes found the previous day. Yet they were strange. There was a shirt, in one piece. Then a pair of trousers with a belt and a pair of underpants ripped identically: on both the one trouser leg was neatly ripped off at the crotch. Two *manyatelas* (handmade tyre sandals), but with no marks. The clothes did not have any blood on them.

Roger's trackers had found evidence that a hippo had attacked. There was plenty of scat and the tracks of more than one hippo, as it was one of their sleeping areas. The imprint of their bodies could be seen clearly in the sand. There was quite a lot of blood against the one spindly tree within the clearing, and his trackers had found drag marks.

They had also found the tracks of a large crocodile and drag marks over a distance of about 12 metres from the blood to the river. In the eyes of the trackers, a hippo had killed someone and the croc had taken the body back to the river.

The policeman told us that Jean would now have to go back to the station. I timidly asked him if my husband would be coming home. He smiled at me and told me not to worry, that he would be back home that night. He was a sergeant and a very good man, which we discovered over the next few days as we dealt a lot with him.

Later that night Jean came home. He had borrowed a vehicle from Roger and we fell into each other's arms even before he was out of the vehicle's door. Jean was exhausted. His eyes were sunken and ringed in black from lack of sleep, but he was home. That night we slept the sleep of the dead.

He had to go back two days later to the police station, where he was to be questioned by the Criminal Investigation Department (CID). Once more I remained at home. The waiting was worse than being with Jean-Roger, but he knew I would not be an asset.

Once more he returned well after dark and this time he looked far worse than on the previous occasion. He told me that he had been grilled for four hours that morning and a further two hours in the afternoon, just like you see in the movies.

His interrogators, five of them in the morning and an extra three in the afternoon, had shouted at him on and off for all that time, telling him that they knew he had murdered the man.

Apparently Amos, the brother of the missing man and supposedly one of the two men that Jean-Roger and Silas had seen walking, had told eight different versions of what Jean had done to the man. Each story was more ridiculous with the telling, from Jean having held the man upside down over the river, and then calling his pet crocodiles, which had eaten the man, head first; to Jean cutting up the man with his panga, then feeding him to the crocodiles piece by piece; to Jean calling his tame hippos and having them murder the man while Jean watched, and so on and so on.

We only found out about these stories later. While Jean was being interrogated these were some of the allegations that were thrown at him.

Jean had contacted the same lawyer we had used before, but they told him he was not allowed to be present during the interrogation. After an entire day of questioning, Jean was told that he would be contacted to come back to the station again.

He came home to me completely washed out. Jean had a problem with being questioned. Having been raised a Catholic, as a little boy making confessions had always upset him. If I ever questioned him he always lost his temper and could be most unpleasant.

During that entire day with the police he could not afford to lose his temper. He had to take it, and I think in many ways that was the worst part of all for him. He knew he was innocent, but the constant questioning really got to him.

At the end of six gruelling hours, the police told him that he was being charged with murder. However, they said he could go home and would be contacted, if and when they needed to see him. This was against all normal police procedure, as murder meant an immediate jail term until bail was set or the case was heard. If you were a foreigner, your passport would be confiscated and only then was there a chance that you would be allowed bail. Jean was just told to go home!

For the next few days we were in limbo.

We went shopping in Chiredzi and while we were away the police came back and once more went to the island, this time accompanied by the CID. Silas had to make a statement and they took away some bones they had found on the way to the island. The crazy thing was that these bones were part of a kudu or large antelope's vertebrae; they had lain by a rock for the last six months, having been washed there in a previous flood. All these men ate meat and all of them would certainly know what they were, but they took them anyway, telling Silas it was for forensic purposes.

This all happened two weeks before a very important political event – an election. Our lawyer had already told Jean-Roger that this was only to do with politics and absolutely nothing with truths and hippos. Jean decided to contact the French embassy and the consul asked Jean if he wanted them to intervene. Jean said not for now, but maybe later.

SEVENTEEN

Mobs and madness

A few days later Roger came around. His first words sent fear like a sharp pain coursing through my body.

'Karen,' he began, 'I'm afraid it's bad news ...'

My thoughts instinctively turned to our hippos. I imagined another dead, maybe a hippo caught in a snare. I imagined that Tembia, perhaps, had grown enraged at being taunted and had finally charged at one of the war vets.

'They're coming for you, Karen,' Roger said. 'I heard it through one of my informers. They may even be here tonight.'

He paused, considering slowly.

'It's time to go.'

We had heard the rumours among the workers on Humani Ranch, who now shared their world with the war vets who occupied so much of Roger's lands, that the war vets, incensed at the way Jean-Roger seemed to have been exonerated of killing one of their own, were coming to drive us out, once and for all. We knew all too vividly what this might mean: our house put to the torch, Jean-Roger and I dragged outside, beatings, and much worse. If we stayed, Roger seemed to be saying, we were gambling with our lives.

It felt like defeat to run now but Roger was adamant: we need only leave for a couple of weeks, until the dust settled. Hopefully, in time, this particular peak of the war vets' fury would subside and we could safely return to our home. He himself had been forced into beating the same kind of temporary retreat the first time the war vets appeared on his land and began to threaten his family. The entire Whittall clan had evacuated on five occasions.

I hated the thought of leaving. I hated the thought of the animals we would have to leave behind, the precious animals that still came to our home – Steyl the kudu, Biscuit the vervet, and even NafNaf, whom we had sworn not to let down. Then, of course, there were the hippos. Even more so, I hated the thought of the snares the war vets might set in our absence, snares we might have removed, and how many bush pigs, kudu, warthogs and other animals would find themselves slaughtered and sold into the bushmeat trade because we were forced to flee.

As Roger insisted, though, there was little time for second thoughts. He knew the people far better than we would ever do and we had to listen to him. I was deeply indebted to him for saving Jean's life and had to trust his judgment.

I made a final trip down to the pools, there to spend a peaceful hour watching the hippos half-submerged in the water, while the new calves, Chubby and Tsakus, leaped porpoise-style around each other. It was a moment of pure peace, but I knew we were in the eye of a storm.

Before dusk, we were gone.

Silas told us he would be better off staying at the house and guarding it, since the war vets would make his life impossible if he sided with his employers and joined them. This way, he believed he could keep the house safe for our return. Their anger was direct at us, not him.

We made plans, but I refused to leave Kitsy, my 20-year-old blind and nearly deaf cat, or my tortoise. Africans eat tortoises as a delicacy. My goats were all pets, all hand-reared, all orphans from Humani. Yet Roger wouldn't budge. He told me I had to leave them behind.

Two weeks are not long, but it seemed an age.

People were kind. Initially, we stayed on Hammond Ranch. Hammond was in the Conservancy, so I felt a bit better being still in the bush, but then we went up to Harare to stay with friends, Pam and Alex van Leenhoff. Alex was one of the trustees of the Turgwe Hippo Trust. As they had already had their farm stolen and most of their own animals killed by the land invaders, they knew exactly what I was feeling.

In the middle of all this, my health gave me a huge scare. I am sure it was stress-related, but a lump grew literally overnight on my right breast. It was hard and sore and quite big. I had to rush off for a mammogram and they found something they wanted to investigate. Next step: surgeon and a biopsy.

I could not have a full anaesthetic as I am allergic, so had to go for a local. Lying down on the bed in the tiny clinic in Harare, I was so scared that I was shaking from head to toe. The old nurse was so gentle with me. The surgeon kept his counsel, but seemed a good sort. Two other nurses stayed close by.

As I lay there practically hyperventilating, a picture of my Bob and the others became clear in my mind. Then suddenly the nurse said – which, come to think of it, was pretty naughty of her, but typical of Africa's laid-back attitude – 'Oh, my dear, it looks like your hippos have been good to you. It looks very much like a cyst.'

Too scared to look at what was going on, I was staring at an un-painted, chipped wall in the clinic. But when the surgeon had stitched the cut he had made, he, too, told Jean that he could not be 100 per cent sure until he got the results in a week, but it did look very much like a cyst and nothing malignant.

We still had to wait ten days to have this confirmed but, boy, what a relief when I was given the all-clear.

On the last day of the two weeks we came home to find most things OK. The animals at home and all of the hippos were fine. Some of the wildlife in our area, though, had disappeared. We'd always had three klipspringers living on the 'phone' koppie; they had gone, as had some of the kudu. I just told myself that they were OK, having moved somewhere else. As with so many animals over the last few awful years, I needed to believe they were alive and had left the danger zone.

The very next day we drove to Masvingo to sort out my Zimbabwean passport. I had been offered a free flight to visit the United Kingdom later in the year. A small animal charity, the Hwange Conservation Society, had kindly invited me to talk at various places about the Trust and the hippos, mainly to veterinary students at universities and at a few zoos and village halls.

It would be a three-week trip and my first time back to the country of my birth in 16 years. Jean-Roger would remain at home to look after everything and daily record the hippos' behaviour for me. It would also allow me to meet some of the hippo supporters.

So it was all go. But the night had more in store for us.

We drove home exhausted, having dealt with passport officials who had done their utmost to stop me from renewing my Zimbabwean passport. We had heard from other white people that certain civil servants had it in for the whites. We had unfortunately met two such officials.

Somehow, after eight hours of queuing and hassling, they had accepted my application for a new passport. We paid the extortionate price and were on our way home. If only we had known what we were coming home to!

The hippos bellowed as I left the vehicle and then I saw Silas rushing towards me. He shouted, 'Madam, get back in the car and go now, now! Do not stay!'

He was overwrought. His normal cheerful smile had gone and there was a grey cast to his ebony skin. Joining him, arriving at a run, were Zivai and Taurai, the two game scouts. In louder voices, they shouted, 'The people have been here. They may come back! They are so angry, you must go.'

Jean-Roger was walking around to us and then I saw them: a large gang of young men marching into our home, their expressions dour. Several were carrying beating sticks.

They said nothing and, as they came closer, a much older man stepped in front. This grey head had authority. The mob as one crowded us, and the fear I had lived with for the last two weeks was a sudden reality.

They were confronting us in our home. If it had not been so frightening it would have been surreal. These people were trained to hate and we were facing at least 30 youth brigade fanatics. Many appeared stoned on *mbanje* (marijuana) and they were obviously worked up.

In those split seconds I wondered, Am I going to die? Will I be raped first? Will Jean-Roger be made to watch? Is this the end of a hippo lady's dreams? Are my husband's hopes that our home, the house we built with our own hands, will remain ours until we die of old age, now about to be destroyed? Is this what happens to a person's passion, to the dream that I have held since a child?

I stood there, held like a startled buck trapped by a car's headlights at night. Most of my wildlife heroes had been murdered in other African countries. Was I now, along with Jean-Roger, about to join them?

These people had entered our sanctuary and I knew I must do something, and very quickly.

I noticed their attention was focussed on Jean-Roger, so I started

184

to walk slowly towards the kitchen and to Taurai, who was near the door. Nobody stopped me. I turned the corner and grabbed his arm, dragging him into the house, and we bolted through the living room and out of the main front door. I reached our small gazebo, pointing down into the Turgwe River below the house. I told him, 'Taurai, go now! Cross the river, then run fast, as fast as you can to the Mokore safari camp. Tell the Duckworths what is happening here and ask them to come quick and to bring help!'

Taurai seized my arm.

'You must come, too! Come now! You must leave and we cross together.'

I told him to go, for I could not desert my husband and our home and animals.

Without a backward glance I returned to the mob. They seemed totally uninterested in where I had been. Jean-Roger had just lost it. I heard him shout, 'Like fuck you will!'

I realised I had to intervene or Jean would be lucky to get out of this with only a beating.

He had really lost it. Fists clenched at his side, eyes wild, he took a stride toward Grey Hair. In a circle around him, the young men of the mob scented blood. If I did not intervene this would be over before help came. My husband had already been through so much, accused of murder, kidnapped and marched for countless kilometres through the bush. It had been a form of torture. I could not let this be his end.

I stepped forward. Afraid, dry-mouthed, shaking inside, I knew that subservience was required. If I had the audacity to speak out and try to talk to the grey-haired man, I had to come across as a meek woman. In their eyes, I had to be lower than their own cattle.

I begged for Grey Hair's attention. Slowly, I dared to put my hand upon his arm. 'Sir,' I began. 'If I may, can I speak to you of these matters that have brought you to our home?'

Out of the corner of my mouth, I spoke in French, so that only Jean-Roger might understand: please, I implored him, go to the house.

I began to talk. I had spent many years learning to calm a rampaging hippo with only my voice. I knew the soft intonations that would bring me close to one of the most dangerous animals in Africa. Perhaps a mob was something like a wild animal. Perhaps, for once, these men would listen to reason. Could I talk us out of danger, save not only our lives, but also those of the animals that I loved so much?

For the next 45 minutes I spoke about all that had happened in our area, telling him how I lived my life in order to protect the hippos. I spoke of the great drought, for surely he remembered it, and how all of the animals I had helped to survive it were now being butchered, wanton destruction for profit's sake. I told him how I had always known this land did not belong to me, that Jean-Roger and I were visitors to this part of the world, but that we were here to protect it, not to take it away or destroy it.

My husband was always telling me I was a brave woman. One man, a Conservancy landowner, having visited us recently with his safari people to meet the hippos, later that day told Jean-Roger that I had the courage of a lion.

The mob stood motionless as Grey Hair allowed me to talk. Jean-Roger had removed himself and was inside our home, hopefully using the radio to call for back-up. It was up to me now to talk and somehow keep both of us and all of our animals from harm.

Africa and its cultural heritage are all about words. In all traditional homes the old stories are the people's history. They pass on their great-great-grandfathers' tales and never forget anything of their past, keeping a verbal record of the old ways with their narrations. I knew that to talk now was right, and it worked.

Eventually Grey Hair interrupted me and told me that now he and his men would spend the night with us. I was to provide them with food and shelter and in return the next morning a meeting would take place. I had to call the main owners in the Conservancy. They would be told to come to our home and after the meeting we would be evicted, so that the others would realise that they had to listen to him.

Silas had already managed to warn me that while the people had been around our home earlier that day they had collected a huge pile of old wood to make a large fire. They had told him they were going to kill and eat a couple of my pet goats. Shadow, my largest male, would be the first to be eaten.

I knew it was imperative to divert them from such thoughts. Now, in the pitch dark, I found myself walking around with 31 men, many of them still stoned. I showed them to the tiny house we used for the game scouts and Silas's small house. Grey Hair told me they would all squeeze inside.

Grey Hair also demanded food, but all we had was our normal diet of baked beans and rice and a tiny bit of maize meal for Silas and the animals. I had to give it to them, otherwise their attention might move to my goats. In the meantime, I managed a quick word with Jean, asking him to radio Roger and tell him to come to our rescue. Could he ask him to please bring some meat and more maize and come and help us?

Finally, I rejoined Jean in the house. Then my nerves took over. My entire body shook, my knees, even my bottom, everything. I had remained completely calm and in control for over an hour, but now I let go.

I told Jean that I did not know if we truly were safe, but at least we were in the house and they were outside, not in here with us. We had never designed the house with security in mind.

I suggested that we move our mattress upstairs to our open-plan attic, taking the shotgun, and then barricade the top of the staircase. If the people did come in and attack, then at least we would be above them and might be able to keep them at bay.

Other whites had been killed in Zimbabwe in similar cases, so it was not a totally far-fetched thought on my part, especially as so many of those guys were not in control, being stoned and obviously having been promised a bit of fun.

After about an hour I heard the sound of an approaching vehicle, and then realised there were more than one. I suggested to Jean that he remain in the house, as I was afraid seeing him would antagonize the mob, and I moved out into the dark. Two Land Cruisers were approaching. One stayed just outside the perimeter. Roger got out of the first one with Peter Wood, one of his hunters, and Roger Davies, Jane's son, accompanying him. In the back of the Cruiser I could make out John Mabasa and Gilbert, Roger's head game scout, as well as two other scouts. As I walked towards them, Grey Hair and a group of his men came forward. All were very visible, as they had put on white T-shirts with election slogans. They were carrying their beating sticks.

Roger gave me a quick look over, realised I was relatively calm, and turned to Grey Hair, introducing himself and holding out his hand.

For the next ten minutes the two men discussed our fate. Grey Hair told Roger they were staying with us and that he expected Roger to come back with the other Conservancy members the next morning.

Roger looked at me, and then said with a raised voice, 'Mr Goni, we now are introduced and I know that Mr and Mrs Paolillo will be perfectly OK in your company. Tomorrow morning we will continue to have talks about your grievances. In the meantime, my men here have meat for you and your people, so if you can just pick it up from the back of the vehicle I will come back tomorrow with the other Conservancy members. I just want to accompany Mrs Paolillo into her house as I want to speak to Mr Paolillo, then we will go home.'

I couldn't believe what I had just heard. Was Roger really going to go and leave us here with this mob? Did he really think we would be OK?

The two of us walked towards the house and it was only once inside that I raised my fears. Roger believed that to move us would be risky, as the mob then could do whatever they wanted to our home. He did not think they would touch us, and added that he would be back the following morning with the police. We should not worry.

Easier to say than do, but we had no option. As Roger drove away I really felt as I imagine that small orchestra must have felt as they played their last notes on the sinking Titanic.

As it was, nothing happened. We spent one of the worst nights of our lives, hardly sleeping. Before sunrise we had put our mattress back on the bed and drunk about our eighth cup of tea and coffee. Silas arrived at 5 am, telling me that the previous day people had stolen a few items from around the house: a large battery for the Land Rover, some tools and a raincoat. He said they had kept him and the game scouts sitting on the floor most of the previous day and had even taken the game scouts' rifle away from them, but gave it back just before we arrived.

At 5.30 am the mob made a point of walking around the house carrying a fishing net as well as several home-made rods, and headed down to the hippo pools. Roger radioed us at 6am, telling Jean that nobody would be coming to the house. They had contacted the police and been told that on no account were any whites to have a meeting with the mob. The police said that they were going to handle it all. Roger and the others should not become involved.

This meant we were on our own, with no other back-up. Would

the police really come and, if they did, whose side would they be on? Also, how long would it take them to get here? The police station was a good hour and a half's drive from our home.

Three hours later, we heard the sound of an approaching vehicle and in drove a ZRP Land Rover, from which stepped two uniformed policemen. The mob stayed away while we explained briefly what had happened.

The sergeant informed us that they couldn't arrest anyone for threatening us, as we had not been injured. They couldn't arrest them for trespassing, as there was no fence around our property, so they had not broken in. But they had stolen items, which was a criminal offence. We needed to make a statement, after which they could be booked for theft and arrested.

For the next hour we wrote statements, never a fast process in Africa. In the meantime, one policeman visited Grey Hair. As we were putting the final dots to the statements, I saw passing by our window mesh three of the mob. Astonishingly, they were carrying the stolen goods on their heads: the battery and a bag of tools. The third one had our raincoat over his arm.

The sergeant went out. When he came back he said, 'Mr Paolillo, it appears that your goods have been returned, so I would suggest you drop all charges. Forget about everything and we will have a word with them. I am sure they will all be happy to go back home again.'

Again, the logic of Africa baffled me. These people had come to evict us and burn our home down. Now the police were telling us to forget about it!

Silas had also mentioned that they had cut the rope attached to our borehole engine and it was quite likely that they had caused the engine to drop to the bottom of the borehole. This meant we would no longer be able to pump water, and it would be impossible to recover the pump from the 45-metre drop. The borehole had been a gift to the hippos from a company in Bulawayo.

Fortunately, way back Jean in his careful manner had put clips under the pump just in case the rope ever snapped, so the pump was still where it should be. I felt we should charge them for malicious damage, but the police said no, and to let the matter go. They would talk to the mob and sort out any problems.

Four long, slow hours later, the police returned.

Apparently Grey Hair had decided that they would all leave, but the new plan was that we were going to pay for a big spiritual meeting. It would be held here next month. He wanted a minimum of 100 people to come and appease the spirit of the man who had supposedly been killed.

We had to provide food and drink for this meeting and they intended to spend an entire day at our home. The police suggested once more that we agree, so reluctantly we did.

Then, amazingly, they left while the police remained with us, only departing an hour or two later once they were sure the people had all walked off.

I could not believe it was over and that no harm had come to us – but then my prayers had obviously been heard.

Once we were alone, the tears fell. I was a pretty pathetic mess. I rushed down to the hippos' pool, as I was so afraid that the hippos might have left the river, probably having been harassed by this mob the previous day.

Much to my relief they were all in their pool, but definitely very nervous, as they all snorted when I arrived until they heard my voice. None of them looked as if rocks or other objects had been thrown at them; there were no new cuts to their heads. They had been so quiet the previous evening, with not one hippo calling that entire night. I wondered if they had realised the danger we all had been in.

Later that day Jean and I sat looking at our magical river view. Holding hands, we wondered aloud if our life here was ever going to be safe again. Could a mob at any time just walk into our home and take it over? The next time, would the police still be on our side, or would some political statement turn the tide and one or both of us be hurt?

We counted our options on one hand.

My biggest problem was the hippos. Jean's was our home, which he had built mainly with his own hands and of which he was incredibly proud.

I knew if we walked away now and gave up, the hippos would die, as would all of the animals we had kept alive for so many years. Within a very short time the people would kill some if not all of them. They would definitely finish off the antelope, zebra, warthogs and smaller mammals that were still alive only through our constant vigilance and surveillance.

Jean's main difficulty was the home and our way of life. Before the people invaded, he had appreciated that we had a very special lifestyle. The house that we built with our own hands was still his pride and joy. He had sunk all of his savings, even cashed in his life pension, putting everything, including his hopes and dreams, into the prospect of remaining here for the rest of our lives.

Jean was still French, but his old life in Europe was far behind him now. His once-manicured hands were these days more often than not cut and covered in grease. He had become accustomed to the privacy we had here. He enjoyed his long-drop toilet with its amazing bush view. He had even become used to our unbelievably restricted diet – no small thing for a Frenchman! He had made friends with the 30-odd vervet monkeys who daily visited our home and had his favourites, like Biscuit. She had honoured him by bringing her newborn baby and sitting on his lap the day after it was born, still with its umbilical cord attached.

Jean was not too bothered by the silence now, or nearly so. He believed he would find it very difficult to go back to how he had lived before he met me.

For me, the animals were my main focus for living, and the hippos and their welfare were of paramount importance. The people overseas who had adopted a hippo or sent donations had become more to me than just foster hippo parents. Many told me that I was an inspiration to them. So many of them lived in suburbia, but they knew that their small contributions went into the ground here in Africa and physically helped these animals. When we used the sand pump to remove the silt that often formed in the hippos' pools, it was their adoption money that paid for the fuel and the equipment. These people believed in me; they trusted me to continue to help these magnificent animals.

Apart from the hippos there were the other wild animals, the whole African scene. I knew that the wildness that had lived in me since I was a child was actually Africa. How could I walk away from it all?

The future of Zimbabwe was one great big question mark. We all could lose: the people, the animals, the land. It had happened to so many others in African countries. Yet those who had remained in other places now benefited from a new Africa. Would Zimbabwe be the same? Would we, by remaining here, be able to help Africa and its inhabitants, and live out our lives in this very special and so very different land?

EIGHTEEN

Hippo happenings and change

Life did indeed carry on, if with a somewhat macabre twist now we lived with a murder charge hanging over our heads. Like everybody who lived on the land in Zimbabwe, either the odd farmer still left with a small portion of his original farm or people like us in a bush environment, we lived with the ever-present packed suitcases jammed full of treasured possessions and important documents just in case of the worst scenario: total eviction.

On one ugly morning I again questioned my belief in remaining here to fight for the animals' future. One of the animals that was part of our lives, Sid, the huge male Chacma baboon, fell victim to the poachers. As always, with my acute hearing I picked up dogs barking in the distance, the yelping calls that signified they had cornered a wild animal.

Jean had no weapon at that time apart from the pepper spray, but he dashed off towards our hippo pan, in the direction of the noise. Thirty or so minutes later he returned, carrying a blooded sack. He told me he had come across two poachers with four dogs and as he arrived he saw them cutting up an animal. He realised it was a baboon and, on later inspection, believed it was my lovely Sid.

Sid was one of the elderly male baboons, the gentleman of the family. He had lost his canine teeth, either in a fight with another baboon or owing to his advancing years, but his character was the gentlest out of the entire troop and he had been the protector of the very young baboons. Though big and powerful looking, he could do little harm without his teeth and was always getting beaten up by the other baboons. His nose and mouth had been ripped many times in fights, but these wounds always healed, leaving only tiny scars. Sid could always be found cuddling a tiny baby while its mother foraged or went about other business; he was the eternal father. Jean-Roger had recognised him by the broken teeth and the scars.

Jean had got to within six metres of the poachers without their knowing, but then a dog barked. He rushed forward, intending to use the pepper spray, but the poachers just took off at speed. They left behind their axes and machetes, the sack and Sid. Jean brought home what he could carry of my Sid: his head, arms and legs, which the bastards had already cut off and put in a tree. They had started skinning him and were cutting into his body, preparing to smoke the meat to sell. As hardly any people in Zimbabwe eat baboon or monkey meat, the poachers would tell them it was something else. It was only afterwards that people realised they had been cheated.

Within 20 minutes of Jean coming home the games scouts arrived, Jean having radioed them. The three of them and Jean went after the poachers, tracking them for two hours for about eight kilometres until they finally lost their spoor. The men were moving on the run towards one of the invaders' villages on Angus ranch; the same village where the people who had come as a mob lived.

When Jean and the scouts left, I stood by the sack that contained Sid's remains, but I couldn't bear to see him in pieces. Instead I walked towards the river and gently lowered what was left of him into the murky depths. In a very short time I spotted the bubbles rising to the surface that meant a crocodile was on its way. Giving dead animals to the crocodiles, I felt, was in tune with nature's code.

Sid's death, following the many before him, tore a new chunk out of my heart, but what frightened me most was that even without any onlookers, the tears would not come. His image continued to haunt me, but the tears remained trapped inside my aching heart. I knew that if I ever let down my barriers I probably would have difficulty closing the floodgates. So many emotions had been stored in me over those harsh years living in a land of such savage extremes. There is no softness in Africa; it is black or white, and not just culturally. Many of the women are not like the women I knew in England. There is an abrasiveness and lack of sensitivity; and most of the men still imagine a world where they are the dominant force.

But then there is the other side of the coin. Last night, the rising moon was orange and near to full. I stood looking out at the land I loved with all my being. Suddenly I heard the crashing of branches and there, close to the house, were the elephants.

In the moonlight their bodies looked even larger than in reality. They seemed to glide and float like moon-walkers as they passed me by. One large form strolled by the entrance to our home. She must have heard me calling to Jean to come and see, but she did not seem upset by my voice.

I watched them moving single file to another area further away from the house. It was a truly magical sight. Then the hippos called. For that moment, life was perfect.

I thought about how, over the years, the bond I had formed with Bob had grown to encompass his entire family. How seeing them thrive, thanks in great part to the people overseas helping me to help them, had brought me such joy and made up for so much of what we had endured.

The relationships built up between me and the hippos, baboons, monkeys and all the animals that surround our lives make me believe that this is where we belong. Jean loves the monkeys and puts up with the baboons. He has named many of the baboons, so even under his gruff attitude I believe he secretly likes them more than he admits. The trouble with baboons is that they can be very destructive, as they have no notion of acting carefully with people's possessions. They constantly break our mesh windows or pull out the thatch from the roof. Since it is usually Jean who has to fix this, understandably this annoys him. Yet as I keep telling him, the animals belong here – we are the intruders.

Only the other day we had an amazing experience with Robin, who is now the dominant bull of the home hippo group.

For once, Jean-Roger had come with me to see the hippos, something he only did on a few occasions every year. We arrived at the pool and found that Robin and one of the younger calves, Kiboko, were missing. I was apprehensive. With people poaching and many living so close to our own home, when an animal went missing, I automatically feared the worst until they came home again.

Suddenly something made me turn around and there, a few feet from where we stood – which, foolishly, was directly in front of a hippo trail into the river – came Robin, followed by little Kiboko.

Now, I knew my hippos well, but to confront Robin by being in his territory and stopping him from entering his own pool, well, that was insanity. My first thought was to run, but there was not a tree or anything else nearby to climb. In that instance there was only one thing to do, which we did. I shouted at Jean to get into the water and at the same time hurled myself into the pool, with Jean following directly behind me.

There were huge submerged rocks and one of them connected with my shin, but the pain only came later, as the adrenalin had taken over. I was certain Robin's anger would be unleashed at any second. I had forgotten that hippos are gentlemen and only attack if you really provoke them. We had left his space and that was what counted.

Robin calmly entered the pool not more than half a metre from where we were, and ignored us totally. Here all three of us were in the river, two of us definitely not belonging, and he just turned a blind eye! If I had not been so nervous, I could have taken a really good photo. Even after all those years I always remembered that the hippos were wild and I should not underestimate them. Robin, though, was proving that my fears were uncalled for. Then, as if to throw egg on my face, Blackface was suddenly right next to him and she also chose to ignore us completely. The most aggressive of all the Turgwe hippos had two people not only in her face, as such, but also in her space in the river and she chose not to see us. Amazing!

I made a mental note to listen to the hippos more often, for they had far less aggression in them than my fellow man.

During my daily vigils with the hippos, I observed quite a lot of behaviour that I had never found in any research material. It is known that hippos secrete a kind of red sweat at times. Supposedly, its main purpose is to act as a sunscreen of sorts, but I had found that more often than not it would be secreted at times of severe stress.

Every year when the river flooded you would find one or more of the females with red faces and necks. When the mob suggested that the hippos had killed that man they could have been right, but not in the way they claimed – that Jean had called his 'pets' and they had murdered the man on his instructions. However, the behaviour of one hippo in particular after that so-called incident made me think that perhaps she had killed him.

Cheeky had been completely covered in the red gel at that time, which I had assumed was to do with a flood that had occurred just before the incident. I had not known then about the supposed dead man. Cheeky's face, neck and the soft parts of her body had almost changed colour and the reddish tint had been very prominent. Her character also underwent a remarkable change.

Blackface was her mother and as a youngster Cheeky had been full of herself, but she had never been aggressive towards me. Suddenly this had changed and, very much like her mother, she would make an occasional snort of warning that would grab my full attention to find not a charging Blackface, but instead, Cheeky. Twice she followed it up by actually leaving the water, and this was only a month after the drama with the war veterans and the police.

It made sense, as out of all the new mothers, her calf, Relief, was the youngest, born in early January. The incident with the poacher and the mob took place in late February. She would have been highly protective of her new baby, as they had only rejoined the family a few weeks previously. I tried to calm her down by talking as always, and slowly over the months she did regain her confidence, but she was very assertive and often angry with any visitors, who these days were few and far between.

With the land invasions, tourism had practically dried up in Zimbabwe. The hunters still came to shoot the animals, as they were boosted by the fact that they all carried guns. Yet any tourist who did brave Zimbabwe during those years never had a single problem. The war veterans had been instructed not to bother the foreigners; it was the locals and the Zimbabwean whites who were their targets.

What this meant for fundraising for the Trust was that the 1 000-odd people who used to come along on safaris and whom I had stopped coming when Jean and I had our personal problems would no longer visit Zimbabwe anyway. The Conservancy was now run 90 per cent as a hunting safari set-up. All the owners still needed incomes to run their properties and sport hunting paid the way.

I still had the adoption programme and I was forever racking my brain for ways to bring in funding. Jean and I had no personal income as Jean had not been able to go back to work because of the ever-present security situation, but we lived frugal lives anyway. We never took a break or a holiday, and lived on a very inadequate diet of mainly beans, rice and a bit of cheese. I think that our pets probably ate better than the two of us combined.

By 2006 our finances had become so limited that Jean knew he had to go back to work. It would be a risk to leave me alone, but if I joined him or stayed elsewhere, everything we had achieved so far for the animals would be lost, as one of us had to be at home at all times. So, to cut the apple in half, we put word out that we needed someone who could stay with me and perhaps keep the bad guys at bay. Although I have one heck of a bad temper and can out-swear an oil-rig worker, I am still petite and a woman. Jean knew only a man and preferably an older guy, or at least a solid-looking one, would keep the war veterans and their lackeys at arm's length.

We have a talented friend up in a Harare, Patrick Mavros, a silver-smith extraordinaire. His animal creations are world famous. Even royalty in the UK and Spain and probably elsewhere have bought some of his spectacular, one-of-a-kind silver pieces. Hippos are one of the most beautiful of all of his designs and are animals of which he is exceedingly fond.

Patrick's manager knew a man who might fit the part. We met the man together and he seemed OK. Solidly built, muscular and stocky, with a bushy beard and a past as an ex-service man. He agreed to work for nothing, as he loved the bush.

Jean had been approached to work on a contract basis for five weeks in Kyrgyzstan, which meant he would be nearly halfway across the world in central Asia. It would, though, give us enough money to last for a year or so. It would be tough going for Jean, up in the mountains on a horse for all those weeks while he searched for gold.

The man said he would look after me and, as I am not in the least mechanically orientated, it would be great to have someone to turn to for help. We now ran a generator that produced electricity for our pump into the river and filled up both hippo pans. At the same time we could run the house lights and the satellite setup, which gave us the luxury of broadband and emailing from our house, enabling me to reach the outside world for the hippo adoptions and communications. The man was also supposed to accompany me each day on snare patrols. I knew we could not afford to stop our anti-poaching work while Jean-Roger was away.

He arrived as Jean-Roger left and, from the minute we were alone,

I realised we had made a mistake. He preferred to eat and laze around, often spending most of the day in our guest cottage. There he fiddled around making candles and all kinds of hobby-type pursuits rather than walk in the bush with me or help me with menial tasks. When I did manage to get him to come on patrol with me I did not feel safe.

We would often hear the voices of illegal settlers, so I would suggest we discreetly move out of their way and keep hidden until they passed. As he had never lived here during the harsh years or had these same people threaten his life, he could not understand my behaviour. Before the invasions I, too, had believed that all Zimbabweans were happy, intrinsically good people, but after being subjected to some of the things we had seen, and realizing that some of the people were totally influenced by evil mentors, my perceptions had changed.

I had seen them go ballistic, and when you are confronted with man at his worst, you really see how humans can very easily return to our primeval past and become very primitive indeed.

I kept telling him that when we heard people in the bush we had to be especially cautious, but he looked at me as if I were mad. I realised that to patrol deep into the bush with him would be too risky as he was bound to try to talk to any poachers. I knew exactly what the outcome would be. That had been our own approach years ago and too many awful situations had resulted from such an attitude.

These guys meant business and, unless you had been living in the bush or on land where invasions had taken place, you had no idea of the trauma and fears that they could create in one's mind.

The six weeks of Jean's absence crawled along. I was sure that some animals were being snared, but I was just too afraid to go deep into the bush with the man. The relief of seeing my husband on his return was tremendous. We both decided that in the future, if Jean went off again, we would have to think of a new way for me to remain safe. I had a lot more faith in Silas than in any stranger to this kind of life.

Unbelievably, two years after the horrendous experience of Jean-Roger being arrested as a supposed murderer, Zimbabwe and its contradictions surprised us yet again. The previous year had been quiet on a security level, with just the daily poaching and snare patrols that were now part and parcel of our lives.

I heard voices and walking into our camp came 15 men. I recognised the leader as Mr Goni, the war veteran – the leader of the mob that came to evict us. This time he was smiling and his men did not appear stoned, with their usual gruff expressions gone.

Remembering Zimbabwe's cultural ways, I shot into the house and grabbed a small bag, filling it with groceries taken from my store cupboard. I approached Mr Goni with deference, offering the gifts. What happened next really took the wind out of my sails. If I hadn't seen it with my own eyes, I would never have believed it.

Mr Goni squatted down on the ground and clapped his hands in the way of someone showing respect to another within the Shona culture. Normally this is reserved for women towards their men, or for youngsters towards their elders. He was a man in his late sixties, possibly even early seventies, and he was clapping me! I had no idea what to do, but tried to look as though this kind of thing happened daily. He then stood up and thanked me and asked if my husband was around. Jean-Roger was returning as we spoke, since Silas and he had been out doing road repairs thanks to the elephants. I believe elephants have a great sense of humour and are forever knocking down trees that then conveniently close off roads. They are far better at creating a roadblock than any of the invaders in our area.

Mr Goni was just as polite to Jean-Roger. It was as if that awful period when he had threatened our lives and the lives of my animals and wanted to burn our home had never existed. He had come along about our neighbours, who, as far as he was concerned, were illegally hunting on the land that he and his men had taken over. As both of us are totally against sport hunting we couldn't make any comments. We suggested he go over to their safari camp and speak to them himself. After a little while each of his men shook our hands and then they left, leaving us flummoxed at this new turn of events.

Since that day we have not had another mob at home. We have continued to catch poachers, but now employ four game scouts. So at least Jean-Roger and I are not spending every single day searching the bush for snares. We do still patrol, though, either with the scouts or on our own. To make sure that the game scouts do the work we ask them to carry out, we cannot just rest on our laurels. Jean has managed to work some more in geology, bolstering our savings a little. Each time I have remained alone at home, but I have had the backup of the game scouts and Silas. The six of us have managed quite admirably.

NINETEEN

Blackface and Five

Jean believed I needed another well-earned break, but we still could not leave together. Patrick Mavros had offered to pay for my flight to the UK so I could give some presentations about my work with the hippos at his shop in Fulham, London. The only problem was Blackface.

As an elderly female, she had not conceived after having had her last male calf, Five, so he had been fortunate enough to life with his mother for the last nearly five years. Robin, the dominant bull, and even Kuchek, as a young male, were beginning to assert their male stance, so he was constantly being harassed, but his mother took the brunt of these attacks.

She had left the family, moving into a smaller pool adjacent to their weir pool. Blackface had many cuts on her hide, but none of them was life threatening. With her contrary character I had such a special love for Blackface and, after what had happened to Zen, I was terribly afraid she might move further away. If Frikkie the hunter saw her, he could react in the same way as he had done with Zen.

Jean would have to drive me up to Harare and be away from Hippo Haven for a day, but he insisted that all would be fine and it was time I did something other than worry about the animals.

The English trip was very rewarding, especially encountering such enthusiasm from the people who attended my presentation. Patrick had even invited little schoolgirls to another presentation. This was a real joy as they were very keen to ask questions and learn more about the hippos. However, during the last week there I received an email from Jean-Roger telling me that Blackface had disappeared just after I had left. He had been searching for her and her son, hoping he would find them, so as not to have to tell me upsetting news.

I was in England, but my instincts and intuition told me she was dead. I was not sure about Five, her son, but I knew I had to get home as quickly as possible.

All of the excitement of the UK was lost in my fears for both of the hippos, but once home I could not find either of them – no carcasses, nothing. I had been gone for three weeks and, while nature's scavengers can make short work of most animal remains, normally something is left to tell the story. I questioned Jean-Roger over and over again on which areas he had searched until we were once more snapping at each other.

My feelings for Blackface were on a par with what I had felt for Bob. She had always been the one hippo to keep me on my toes and remind me never to take advantage of the special bond that had formed between these incredible animals and me. She was the best mother, she had mourned Bob when he died, and she was the dominant hippo in the family group when the bull was away. She knew the best places for the younger members to graze and during the rains guided them to safe havens in the adjacent small tributaries. She was a hippo that stood out from the others.

There is nothing worse when you work with wild animals than to have them disappear and not know what had happened. Over the years there had been deaths, but I always found the bodies. The missing hippos were either young males that had been kicked out of the family and found a place to hide up in, or young females aged between five and six years. I had discovered that some of them moved to other river systems in the Conservancy and joined unrelated families. Occasionally one of these females would return to our area accompanied by a calf. I believe that they knew exactly what they were doing, not breeding with their own relatives and instead bringing an unrelated offspring to join the group. I never saw a female mated by a member of her own family.

Yet Blackface was too old to move away. Five was dependent on her, as he always had had her protection.

Silas told me that while Jean-Roger was up in Harare dropping me at the airport, he had heard three shots before dawn close to where Blackface had moved. When Jean queried these shots with one of the workers over at Mokore, they mentioned that Frikkie, my nemesis, had been hunting in that area. At night the only animals that they normally shot were lions or leopards, using bait to bring the cat close and microphones placed near the meat to hear the sound. With a spotlight shining on the cat, only a bad shot could fail to kill the unfortunate animal.

On asking other workers, some mumbled that Frikkie had been after leopard, but others kept quiet. My instincts told me he was responsible, but I had no proof. Laura Simpson in the States, who had run a huge animal charity there for many years, suggested I use a psychic, but one that dealt specifically with animals. I was not sure if I wished to follow such a route.

As a troubled teen, I had visited a clairvoyant who had been not only amazingly accurate in much of what she told me, but who was also instrumental in my finding out that the man my mother had been married to was not my biological father. My natural father was a vet and a man with whom she had fallen in love, leaving her husband. Unfortunately for my mother, she then fell pregnant with yours truly. In her era, people of my mother's breeding did not have affairs and the vet in question lost most of his clientele once they discovered he had left his wife and son to live with my mother. Then, horror upon horror, she discovered she was pregnant with his child. This caused further scandal.

My mother tried everything to get rid of the unwanted foetus. Even drinking a bottle of gin while sitting in the bath, a supposed natural inducer of a miscarriage, but I obviously was quite obstinate even then. Jack, my natural father, gave her quite a few medicaments from his animal dispensary, but none worked and I stayed firmly lodged. To this day, though, I have an aversion to the smell of gin!

The clairvoyant knew a lot of this and, as I had no knowledge of it at all, it was remarkable. My mother admitted it once I confronted her. It made me realise that there was so much more to our world than we could ever know.

Jean-Roger, as a scientist, should have dismissed such psychic experiments as ridiculous, and yet he had more belief in the energies and out-of-body experiences than I did. Perhaps his Latin blood, as well as his sister Anne-Véronique with the ability to feel sickness in a person by just standing nearby, gave him an added awareness. Whatever the case, he believed that there was a lot of truth to psychic abilities.

So I ended up contacting a woman, French-born but living in the UK, who is a psychic as well as a very proficient animal healer. Oephebia told me that Blackface had been shot and killed, and her description of the hunter fitted Frikkie to a tee. The timing, the situation, all of what she told us, could not have been imagined.

Later, a year or so on, a man who had worked at the safari camp told me that it was true that Blackface had been shot. Her head had been removed and sent to the United States as a trophy for the American client to gloat upon. At the time of Oephebia's statements Jean had gone over to the safari camp and spoken to the owner. His opening words had been, 'Have you got proof? Have you found a bullet casing?' He was on the defensive from the moment Jean set foot in the camp. So although we had no physical proof, I believed with all my being that once more Frikkie had killed one of my hippos.

This killing had not been from necessity, such as over-stocking or any of the bullshit that hunters use to justify their sport. It was out of pure vindictiveness. He is the head hunter responsible for killing elephants when they cull in the Conservancy and, like everyone in this area, is fully aware of my anger and disgust at this most evil means of killing animals. Whole families of elephants are wiped out in a couple of minutes by three or four men shooting at them continuously, while their trainee hunter passes them another loaded gun. Elephant families, when threatened, naturally gather into a tight bunch to protect their young, and so to shoot and kill up to 17 animals instantly is like shooting plastic ducks in a fairground gallery. It is bloodlust pure and simple for any man to take part in such a barbaric event.

Frikkie did not work again at the safari camp. Soon after this he was used only for culling purposes and no longer hunted opposite us. This in itself pointed another finger at him. I will never know for sure, but as we found absolutely none of Blackface's remains, I believed Oephebia that she had been hunted.

In the meantime, I knew I had to find Five, as he was now at risk. Without his mother to protect him from the other bulls he could easily be attacked and killed. I eventually located him living on the bush island in the middle of the river. On two occasions he came out in the daytime so I could clearly identify him. He had lost condition, but was alive.

Then one morning, while on my own daily snare patrol around

the hippos' main grazing areas, I came to the tiny river called the Chichindwi and noticed a rock with a terrapin sitting on it. The only thing was that the rock had not been there two days previously. On closer inspection, I realised it was a dead hippo. I knew before even getting close enough that it would be Five. His head was under the water, but his recognizable dark skin as well as two prominent scars hit my stomach with an instant pain. The death of any animal is incredibly harsh, but when it is one of the hippos it etches a new scar that never heals. I tried to examine him, but could not enter the water owing to the presence of a couple of crocodiles. I ran home to get help.

Later that day all of us, Jean, the scouts and I, returned to Five's body. We waded in with tow ropes from the vehicles, confident that so many people in the water would hold the crocodiles at bay. We tied a rope to two of Five's legs and began to pull him back to land. We could only pull him while the water was deep enough to float his body, since once the water became too shallow his weight was impossible to shift and no vehicle could be brought down to the river's mouth. I managed, with the help of the others, to turn his body over to look for the cause of his death. It was obvious that he had been attacked by another hippo, and I found the fatal wound under his jaw. He had bled to death from a huge gash that had severed one of his major arteries. A blood trail led into the bush island, where he had been hiding when I last came across him.

Jean and I cautiously followed the trail, as elephant, rhino and buffalo often use that island as a refuge. We found the exact spot where a fight had taken place. It was more of an attack than a fight, as Five had been far too young to take on an older bull. He had started bleeding profusely by a clump of bushes, and had run back to the pool for safety. There he had died. My only consolation was that by bleeding to death it would in some ways have been a peaceful end, as he would have finally gone to sleep, just like my darling Bob had done so many years before.

At that moment I was more angry than emotional, as I realised that Frikkie's killing of Blackface had resulted in two deaths. Without his mother, Five had not stood a chance against another bull.

We decided to pull Five back into the pool to allow the crocodiles to feed on him, rather than any lions. We did not want the lions to get a taste for hippo meat, as they are the chief natural predators of hippos.

It was at times like these that I found it hard to stay positive and look to the future. It would be my job to notify the adoptive parents of Five. One woman in particular, Hilary, living in the UK, had become a good friend. I had stayed with her and her lovely husband John when over there. She had loved Five like one of her own children and dogs, and it really hurt me to tell her this dreadful news. I felt responsible for these hippos, not just on a conservation and protection basis, but also in terms of all of the parents that had adopted them over the years. Many of them had become good friends of mine, either virtually or in person.

Yet, as I have said before, Africa is a land of extremes. If you live in Africa, you end up acting like a tortoise. You develop a hard shell that covers your body and when troubled, you tuck your head deep inside. But you still have to eat and survive, so sooner or later the head pops back out again and on your way you go.

We had kept going through all of the land invasions and insecurities. We had faced poachers, mobs and more. There had been the death of loved animals, too, and now there would be two hippos' deaths that I would have to come to terms with and overcome my sorrow.

Forty-nine hippo calves have been born from the initial 13 animals that I saved during that horrendous drought. I am now known as a hippo expert and am being used by BBC Wildlife Magazine in the UK and the National Geographic channel in the United States as such. I have given presentations about the hippos at the Royal Geographic Society's Ondaatje Theatre in London as well as at universities and at the Edinburgh Zoo.

I have to think positively. The Trust continues to prosper, for I am always trying to find new ways to raise funds to help these amazing animals. We have joined all the networking channels.

Only recently, a video I had filmed had over 27000 hits on our Turg-wehippomark channel on YouTube. I had been in the right place at the right time. As I watched a young hippo calf that had just been born I witnessed the most incredible crocodile-hippo behaviour.

A young crocodile of about two metres in length came in close to Tacha the mother's hindquarters, close to where the calf was milling around. For a few heart-stopping moments I feared for the calf's life, thinking that the crocodile was going to attack. I should have known better.

Tacha began to push out the afterbirth sac. Then something astonishing occurred – right in front of my eyes. The crocodile started feeding on the afterbirth. He would pull at the sac, breaking parts off from Tacha's body, and then throw huge chunks of the sac back into his throat.

This continued for the next five minutes. For once I had the video camera and could catch it all on film. The calf – a little female, who was later named BonBon by my dearest English friend, a famous animal sculptor called Suzie Marsh – had returned closer to her mother's head.

The crocodile went on feeding as more and more afterbirth was released. The whole time Tacha was aware but seemed uninterested in what was happening at the rear end of her body. It was only when BonBon moved again towards her mother's bottom that her attention was caught. As the crocodile took another huge lump of afterbirth Tacha suddenly spun around. I believe she was protecting the calf, for she grabbed the crocodile in her mouth and then threw it. The crocodile landed in the river about four and a half metres away, the lump of afterbirth still firmly clamped in its jaws. To my utter amazement the crocodile calmly continued to eat the sac, as if nothing untoward had happened. Tacha had had enough and moved herself and BonBon to a shallower part of the river pool.

These kinds of experiences make all the problems of living in Zimbabwe fall away. Then I enter the magical world of nature and her inhabitants. I believe that this kind of interaction between crocodiles and hippos probably happens a lot more often; we just are never lucky enough to witness it.

Alongside the hippos, the baboon troop of which darling Sid had been a member is now firmly ensconced in our lives. The troop leader Joe, his second-in-command Spazzy, and, if Spazzy is away, a huge male called Bella, share our lives from dawn to dusk. They stop off at our home, using it as their playground with their large family of over 40 baboons, and they roost in the trees by the house every evening. One in particular – Vixen – has adopted me, and to my utter disbelief will actually groom my hair. She painstakingly sifts through each strand. The worrying thing, though, is when suddenly she appears to find something nutritious and eats it, as she would do with a fellow baboon!

Vixen is completely wild, but for some unknown reason she has moulded her life into mine. The umbilical cord was still attached when she came over to introduce me to her firstborn, whom we named Terry. Since then she has had Zorrette and is now pregnant again. We are, I believe, the only people in Zimbabwe and possibly Africa who live with a wild troop of baboons. Every day we witness amazing interactions, and they also protect me as if one of their own.

Late one afternoon painted wild dogs killed an impala just below our home. I rushed down to the riverbed with my camera, hoping to catch some interesting video. As I arrived the one wild dog ran past me and Spazzy lunged at it. He must have thought the dog was going to attack me. As soon as the dog was away he returned to my side as if nothing untoward had happened. Thanks to the baboons I can walk right up to other animals in the bush as long as I am accompanying the troop. The animals do not fear me, as they are not alerted of any kind of danger by the baboons. It is amusing at times to see the look on a kudu or impala's face when they realise there is a human among the group.

As the Trust now has game scouts this means salaries, accommodation and all the things that come with expanding. I now have regular volunteers, usually two at a time. They donate to the Trust and then stay here for a couple of weeks to share the work we do in the bush. We feel the security situation is now stable enough to have people come and stay. For the last few years many foreigners have experienced the beauty of this land. Some of them are my hippo supporters and others are people who have heard about the Trust. They assist us in our daily work, be it by doing daily snare patrols, digging in the river to divert channels towards the hippos' pools, or hard graft like road repairs and such like.

Then there is the nice side of studying the hippos, going on game drives with me, and seeing other wild animals. They feed the family of baboons and monkeys their treats. The volunteers soon learn to sit comfortably in the gazebo with up to ten baboons sitting beside them on the chairs.

Jean-Roger and I have been through many trials and tribulations, but we have survived and, most importantly, we still love each other. Even after 20 years we still hold hands and do not like to be too far away from each other for too long. In a way, we prefer each other's company to any other.

Zimbabwe is by no means the country it used to be, but, like everything in life, change happens, and some of the changes are not so bad. The poaching continues and we can never let down our guard, but our game scouts have taken some of the load off our shoulders.

I have had the privilege of having had thousands of people who over the years have touched my life. Their own dedication to the hippos keeps me going. A few I have actually met, but many are faceless strangers, yet the words they write to me have always kept me going, especially during the very bad years.

Jean's love and his support have been my backbone, but, most importantly, these hippos have taught me that respect is the key to understanding a wild animal, especially one whose fearsome reputation is undeserved.

The future of these wonderful animals is still very much in our hands. We know that if we had not stuck it out here during the harsh years, not one hippo would be alive in the Turgwe today. So we will move on and not let the deaths of Blackface and Five, those two beautiful hippos, make us falter and consider giving up.

Blackface's demise must act as a spur for me to build more resilience, to fight adversity and to look for solutions. I will continue to protect the hippos from any natural or unnatural event for as long as I shall live.

Hippo Family Tree

Family tree 1

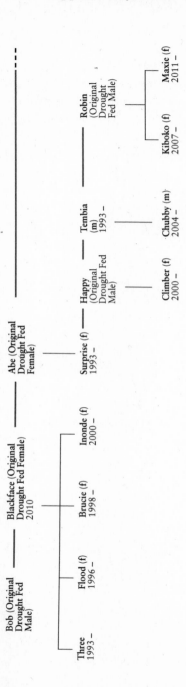

Bob (Original Drought Fed Male) ——— Blackface (Original Drought Fed Female) 2010

Three 1993 –

Flood (f) 1996 –

Brucie (f) 1998 –

Inonde (f) 2000 –

Abe (Original Drought Fed Female)

Surprise (f) 1993 –

Happy (Original Drought Fed Male) ——— Tembia (m) 1993 – ——— Robin (Original Drought Fed Male)

Climber (f) 2000 –

Chubby (m) 2004 –

Kiboko (f) 2007 –

Maxie (f) 2011 –

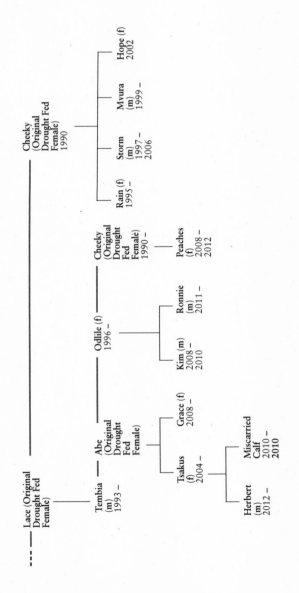

Family tree 2

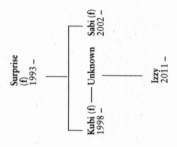

Surprise
(f)
1993 –

Kubi (f)
1998 – —— Unknown

Sabi (f)
2002 –

Izzy
2011 –

Family tree 3

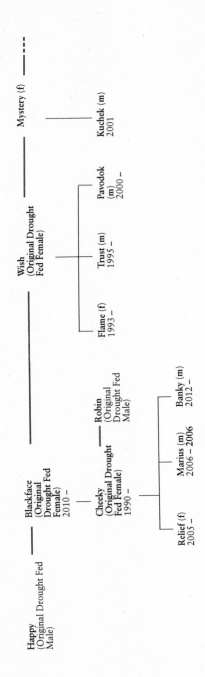

Happy
(Original Drought Fed
Male)

Blackface
(Original
Drought Fed
Female)
2010 –

Wish
(Original Drought
Fed Female)

Mystery (f)

Cheeky
(Original Drought
Fed Female)
1990 –

Robin
(Original
Drought Fed
Male)

Relief (f)
2005 –

Marius (m)
2006 – 2006

Banky (m)
2012 –

Flame (f)
1993 –

Trust (m)
1995 –

Pavodok
(m)
2000 –

Kuchek (m)
2001

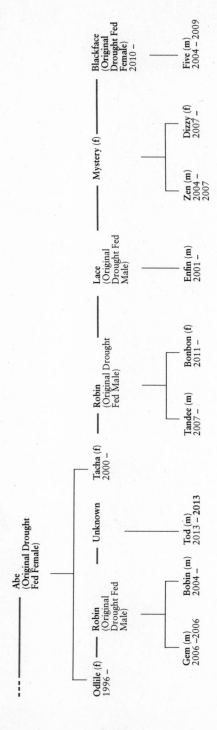

Family tree 4

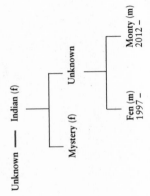

Family tree 5

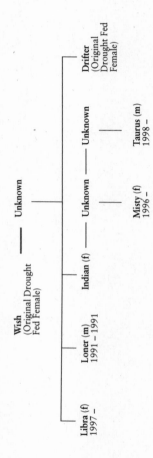

Wish
(Original Drought
Fed Female)
———— Unknown

Libra (f)
1997 –

Loner (m)
1991 – 1991

Indian (f) ———— Unknown ———— Unknown

Misty (f)
1996 –

Taurus (m)
1998 –

Drifter
(Original
Drought Fed
Female)

Prepared by Jan Rees
Created with Family Tree
Maker

Thank you from Karen

Firstly, and most importantly, I would like to thank Roger Whittall of Humani, Zimbabwe. Without your assistance during one of the incidents mentioned in this book my husband might not be with me today.

George and Madelon Hulme, and the Schenck family: my thanks for your kindness in accommodating us when we had to evacuate from our home for a while. Not many people would give a temporary base to eleven goats, five cats, one tortoise and two people.

To my friends Alex and Pam van Leenhoff, who also provided us with a place to stay. Having lost their own farm, they managed to forget their personal traumas and gave us and our animals sanctuary, while retaining their humour and hospitality.

Thank you to Silas Matyarutsa, who is more than just an employee assisting me with the hippos. He loyally stuck by us through harsh times, even having the courage to remain behind and guard our property when we had to leave with all the animals. He refused to accompany us or return to his own family, choosing to look after our home and keep an eye on the hippos.

To all the Turgwe Hippo Trust supporters: a massive thank you, not only for funding our work, but for giving me the moral support to keep going through the tough times.

A special thank you to Laura Simpson, former chairperson of the World Society for the Protection of Animals in the USA, and who is now running her own registered charity, The Harmony Fund. Thank you, Laura, for continuing over the years to believe in what I do.

To Ruedi Ammann of Switzerland: thanks for always being there for the hippos when they need you.

To Maya Donelan: what would I do without you and the boys?

Michael Spurling and Michael Whittall: thank you all for your friendship and help beyond the bounds of friendship.

My dear friend, Suzie Marsh, an animal sculptor whose talent brings tears to my eyes with her wonderful hippo sculptures. Thanks, Suzie and Doug, for opening your home to me in Cornwall when my spirit needs a sea break.

To Jenny Bowen, who first came here with Operation Raleigh as the youngsters' expedition leader: thank you for your support and friendship over the years.

To Sarah Chilvers in the UK who kindly helps the hippos alongside her other animal charity work.

To Venise Grossman, who created the Trust's website, followed by Alice Egoyan, both lovely Americans. To Mark Powell of the UK, who took over the site from them and has helped me tremendously every time I return to the UK. A big thank you also to Patrick Jandard of France for presenting a website with a new look, which will firmly propel the Turgwe Hippo Trust into the twenty-first century.

Thank you also to Steve Gordon of Canada and Cinda Lautenschlegar of the USA for all you both do for the hippos.

To Patrick Mavros and his family for your support of the Turgwe Hippo Trust, and the gold hippos made by your talented hands and purchased by my husband for me.

To my trustees, Alex van Leenhoff, Oscar Rotham and his lovely wife, Linda: thank you all for guiding this woman's sometimes stubborn and unconventional ways. To retired trustees, Rolf Chenaux-Repond, the late John Shaw, Sybille Doppelfeld, the late Otto Babovic and to Liz Dobbs.

A big thank you to authors Tammie Matson, Sally Henderson, Caroline Carver, Sharon Pincott and Bookey Peek for telling me to write the book and not lose heart.

A special thank you to Caroline for introducing me to Hilary Johnson of the UK, the person who I believe is really responsible for my book getting out there. I am the author, but, Hilary, you shaped my long-winded sentences and sorted out the punctuation, forgotten while the thoughts tumbled on to the pages. Without you, perhaps I would not have had the faith to continue. You always believed in me, the hippos and their story.

To my agent, Euan Thorneycroft at A.M. Heath Ltd, London, UK. Euan, you are not only a great agent, but also a very lovely man.

To my editors, Iolandi Pool and Genevieve Adams, thank you for your help with *A Hippo Love Story*. To Frederik de Jager and all at Penguin South Africa: thank you for publishing my story.

A special thank you to the animals that have made me the person I am today. My heart is forever grateful for their trust in me. Kuchek, the best-ever Welsh Mountain pony; Gemini, a very special goat; Smudge, a long-haired black and white pussycat who has travelled far, and stayed long with me. To Tony, a special tortoise who taught me that reptiles can show love. To the wonderful Arthur Warthog and his kin. To Boon, the vervet monkey, and his troop. To all the baboons, but especially the remarkable Sid, whose life was lost at the hands of poachers, but whose family still lives with us today. To the baboon boys, Spazzy, Bela and Joe. To a very different baboon, Miss Vixen, who took it upon herself to groom a human being and allow me into her life. To every animal I have had the privilege to live with and get to know over the last decades; most recently the tiny baby mongoose, Squiggle, who has taken over our hearts, making our animal family complete.

This book would never have been possible without one very special animal that changed my life for ever: Bob, the dominant bull hippo. His trust in me allowed the Turgwe Hippo Trust to be born and for this story to be told. Thank you to his extended family of Turgwe hippos, old and young – especially Blackface, whose demise has made me stronger in the fight to protect her kind.

To my late mother, Joan Kirtley, for introducing me to the honour of living with animals, and for instilling a love of all animals in me during my childhood. Mum, you allowed me to spread my wings and fly. Your own independence and courage has definitely rubbed off on me.

Lastly, but without doubt the most important person in my life: Jean-Roger, my gorgeous Frenchman. Jean-Roger, your humour and quirky ways still hold me captivated. Twenty- five years down the line and, as promised in our marriage vows, we are still holding each others' hands. Your immense strength is the primary reason we are still here. I may have the determination, but you have the faith and the luck.

By loving me your life changed forever, taking you away from a high-flying career and into an uncertain world – a bush life with dangers, and an extreme lifestyle which was surely not envisioned when you obtained your doctorate. We have been tested more than anyone should be, but at least we can say our life is never boring. Your sunbird salutes you and loves you.

To contribute to the Turgwe Hippo Trust, please go to www.savethe hippos.info, or visit our Facebook page at www.savethehippos.info.

Karen Paolillo